BLACK HISTORY

in the Philadelphia Landscape

BLACK HISTORY

in the Philadelphia Landscape

DEEP ROOTS, CONTINUING LEGACY

AMY JANE COHEN

With a foreword by Wendell E. Pritchett

TEMPLE UNIVERSITY PRESS

Philadelphia | *Rome* | *Tokyo*

TEMPLE UNIVERSITY PRESS
Philadelphia, Pennsylvania 19122
tupress.temple.edu

Library of Congress Cataloging-in-Publication Data

Names: Cohen, Amy Jane, 1964– author. | Pritchett, Wendell E., writer of
foreword.
Title: Black history in the Philadelphia landscape : deep roots, continuing
legacy / Amy Jane Cohen ; with a foreword by Wendell E. Pritchett.
Description: Philadelphia : Temple University Press, 2024. | Includes
bibliographical references and index. | Summary: "Recounts events in
Philadelphia African American history. Each brief chapter addresses a
different topic, exploring the event itself and how it is marked in the
landscape, whether through a historical marker, a monument, a mural, or
some other means. Chapters conclude with suggested ways to learn more
about the topic"— Provided by publisher.
Identifiers: LCCN 2023034592 (print) | LCCN 2023034593 (ebook) | ISBN
9781439923658 (paperback) | ISBN 9781439923665 (pdf)
Subjects: LCSH: African Americans—Pennsylvania—Philadelphia—History |
Monuments—Pennsylvania—Philadelphia. | Historic
sites—Pennsylvania—Philadelphia. | Philadelphia (Pa.)—History. |
BISAC: HISTORY / United States / State & Local / Middle Atlantic (DC,
DE, MD, NJ, NY, PA) | SOCIAL SCIENCE / Ethnic Studies / American /
African American & Black Studies
Classification: LCC F158.9.B53 C644 2024 (print) | LCC F158.9.B53 (ebook)
| DDC 974.8/1100496073—dc23/eng/20231018
LC record available at https://lccn.loc.gov/2023034592
LC ebook record available at https://lccn.loc.gov/2023034593

Printed in the United States of America

9 8 7 6 5 4 3 2 1

To the Philadelphia Cecil B. Moore Freedom Fighters,

Karen Asper Jordan, Kenneth "Freedom Smitty" Salaam,

Bernyce Mills DeVaughn, and Richard Watson,

and in memory of Mel Dorn.

As Diane Nash said,

"I'd like you to know that before we met you,

we loved you."

Responsible citizenship . . .

is not principally about noticing what's bad;

it's about constructing what's good.

You need to defeat the things you do not love

by building the things you do.

—EBOO PATEL

CONTENTS

PART III: TWENTIETH CENTURY

CITY OF PHILADELPHIA

1. **Stenton and Dinah memorial** 4601 N. 18th Street
2. **Dinah** Stenton Park Recreation Center, 4601 N. 16th Street
3. **Women of Germantown** 5722 Greene Street
4. **Richard Allen Lane Station** 200 West Allens Lane
5. **Fair Hill Burial Ground** 2901 Germantown Avenue
6. **Philadelphia Female Anti-Slavery Society and Underground Railroad** 2900 Germantown Avenue
7. **Byberry Hall** 3003 Byberry Road
8. **Robert Purvis house** 1601 Mt. Vernon Street
9. **Belmont Mansion Underground Railroad Museum** 2000 Belmont Mansion Drive
10. **Johnson House** 6306 Germantown Avenue
11. **John S. Trower** 5706 Germantown Avenue
12. **FAB Church** 6700 Lansdowne Avenue
13. **Julian Abele Philadelphia Museum of Art** 26th and the Parkway
14. **Sadie T. M. Alexander house** 700 Westview Street
15. **ACES Veterans Museum** 5801 Germantown Avenue
16. **Greenbelt Knoll** SW Corner of Holme Avenue and Longford Street
17. **Zion Baptist Church site and Rev. Leon Sullivan** 3600 N. Broad Street
18. **Tribute to Rev. Leon Sullivan** 1445 W. Venango Street
19. **David Richardson** 5650 Sprague Street

KEY
- ● SITE
- 🛡 HISTORICAL MARKER
- ○ MARKER/SITE
- ■ MURAL

(Map design by Nikki Hagedorn.)

CENTER CITY & SOUTH PHILADELPHIA

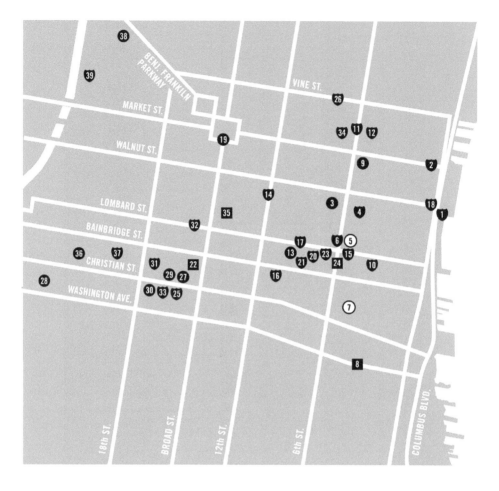

KEY

● SITE

⬣ HISTORICAL MARKER

○ MARKER/SITE

■ MURAL

(Map design by Nikki Hagedorn.)

1. **The Pennsylvania Slave Trade**
211 S. Columbus Boulevard

2. **London Coffee House**
SW Corner of Front and Market Streets

3. **Washington Square**

4. **St. Thomas's African Episcopal Church**
SW Corner of S. 5th Street and St. James Court

5. **Mother Bethel Church**
419 S. 6th Street

6. **Free African Society** 419 S. 6th Street

7. **Bethel Burial Ground**
Between 4th and 5th between Catharine and Queen Streets

8. **The Colored Conventions Movement and Beyond**
Courtyard Apartments,
315 and 351 Washington Avenue

9. **Presidents House memorial**
SE Corner of 6th and Market Streets

10. **James Forten house**
336 Lombard Street

11. **Pennsylvania Hall**
150 N. 6th Street

12. **Philadelphia Female Anti-Slavery Society**
151 N. 5th Street

13. **William Still house**
625 S. Delhi Street

14. **William Still**
244 S. 12th Street

15. **Lombard Street Riot**
SE Corner of 6th and Lombard Streets

16. **Frances E. W. Harper house**
1006 Bainbridge Street

17. **William Whipper house**
919 Lombard Street

18. **The Liberation of Jane Johnson**
211 S. Columbus Boulevard

19. **Catto memorial (A Quest for Parity)**
South Apron of City Hall,
west side of the block site

20. **Octavius V. Catto**
812 South Street

21. **Institute for Colored Youth**
915 Bainbridge Street

22. **Remembering a Forgotten Hero
(Octavius Catto)** 1427 Catharine Street

23. **W. E. B. Du Bois**
NW Corner of 6th and Rodman Streets

24. **Mapping Courage (W. E. B. Du Bois)**
601 South Street

25. **First African Baptist Church (former site)**
1600 Christian Street

26. **First African Baptist Church Cemetery**
SW Corner of North 8th and Vine Streets

27. **Julian Abele house**
1515 Christian Street

28. **Julian Abele Park**
22nd Street from Montrose to Carpenter

29. **Jack and Jill of America**
1605 Christian Street

30. **Christian Street YMCA**
1724 Christian Street

31. **Mercy Hospital**
NW corner of S. 17th and Fitzwater Streets

32. **Frederick Douglass Memorial Hospital**
1522 Lombard Street

33. **John C. Asbury**
1710 Christian Street

34. **Alain Leroy Locke**
701 Arch Street

35. **Alain Leroy Locke**
Juniper and Cypress Streets

36. **National Marian Anderson Museum**
762 S. Martin Street

37. **Marian Anderson**
1910 Fitzwater Street

38. **All Wars Memorial
to Colored Soldiers and Sailors**
20th and the Parkway

39. **1967 Black Student Walkouts**
2100 Winter Street

WEST PHILADELPHIA

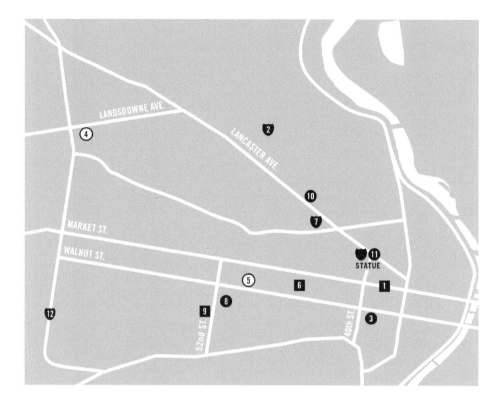

1 The Legacy of Bishop Richard Allen
and the AME Church
3801 Market Street

2 Stephen Smith
1050 Belmont Avenue

3 W. E. B. Du Bois College House
3900 Walnut Street

4 FAB Church
6700 Lansdowne Avenue

KEY

● SITE

♥ HISTORICAL MARKER

○ MARKER/SITE

■ MURAL

5 Paul Robeson House
4951 Walnut Street

6 Paul Robeson
4502 Chestnut Street

7 Muhammad's Temple of Islam #12
4218 Lancaster Avenue

8 Malcolm X Park
5100 Pine Street

9 Breaking Chains
500 S. 52nd Street

10 New Africa Center
4243 Lancaster Avenue

♥**11** Martin Luther King 1965
STATUE 40th and Lancaster Avenue

12 MOVE Bombing
S. 63rd and Osage Avenue

(Map design by Nikki Hagedorn.)

NORTH PHILADELPHIA

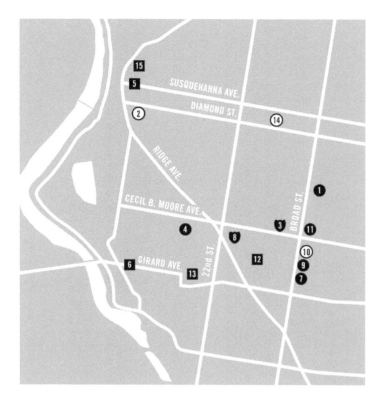

1 Charles L. Blockson Afro-American Collection
1330 Polett Walk

2 Henry Ossawa Tanner House
2908 W. Diamond Street

3 Universal Negro Improvement Association
1609 Cecil B. Moore Avenue

4 Fruit of Islam House
2503 Oxford Street

5 Malcolm X
Ridge and W. Susquehanna Avenues

6 Malcolm X
3032 Girard Avenue

KEY

● SITE

♥ HISTORICAL MARKER

○ MARKER/SITE

■ MURAL

7 OIC Philadelphia
1231 N. Broad Street

8 OIC original site
N. 19th Street between Turner
and Oxford Streets

9 Leon H. Sullivan Human Services Center
1415 N. Broad Street

10 Sullivan Progress Plaza Shopping Center
1501 N. Broad Street

11 Cecil B. Moore Subway Station
NE side of Broad Street
and Cecil B. Moore Avenue

12 Cecil B. Moore
1416 N. Bouvier Street

13 Cecil B. Moore
Philadelphia Freedom Fighters
2219 N. College Avenue

14 Church of the Advocate
1801 W. Diamond Street

15 Father Paul Washington
3300 Ridge Avenue

(Map design by Nikki Hagedorn.)

FOREWORD

Wendell E. Pritchett

My grandparents arrived in Philadelphia at the turn of the twentieth century, migrating from different parts of the American South. They were drawn to the city by the vibrant African American community and the (relatively) strong economic opportunities the city presented for Blacks. They settled in the western parts of Philadelphia, created their families, and laid the foundation for my parents.

My parents were the first in their families to attend college, and they became leaders in the fields of education and the arts. The foundations they built on made it possible for my sister and me to attend, and to work at, some of the most prestigious institutions of higher education in the world.

Amy (Rosenberg) Cohen's ancestors had arrived in Philadelphia from Europe in an earlier era. They, too, found opportunity in the city, and Amy is proud of her deep Philadelphia roots. Amy's and my family's journeys intertwined when she and I met in second grade, at Friends Select School (one of city's oldest). We have been friends ever since, and I have learned much from her, as you will in reading this book.

History, James Baldwin wrote, "does not refer merely, or even principally, to the past. On the contrary, the great force of history comes from the fact that we carry it within us, are unconsciously controlled by it in many ways, and history is literally present in all that we do." History is how we understand ourselves, as individuals and as communities. History is how we make sense of the past, present, and future.

But some histories have been given more weight than others. The stories of people of color, of women, of LGBTQ communities and others, have often been ignored in larger narratives told about the United States (and elsewhere). Amy Cohen, through her work in the Philadelphia schools creating a first-of-its-kind African American history curriculum, is someone who has labored to rectify that exclusion.

The history of African Americans, in Philadelphia and elsewhere, is crucial to the broader understanding of our communal history. African Americans played a fundamental role in building this country, its institutions and culture. In this book you will read many of those histories, of the people who were brought directly from Africa (Philadelphia's slave history is sadly robust) and the many more who migrated here from southern states in search of opportunity.

Much of this book is about the places where African American history happened. Philadelphia has a rich history of institutions, many of which greatly influenced our nation. All of these institutions, from the colonial period to today, were shaped by Black Philadelphians. Thousands of people travel through or past Washington Square in the Olde City on a daily basis, but few of them know, as Cohen tells us, that park's importance for enslaved people and freed Blacks in the 1700s. It was there, feet from where the Founding Fathers declared independence (for some), that Blacks connected with family and friends on their (infrequent) days off.

Whether you know the details or not, it's impossible to pass the Mother Bethel African Methodist Episcopal Church, the nation's first Black church, on Sixth Street and not feel the history. But many of the most important sites of Philadelphia Black history have been erased. Few erasures were more poignant than the destruction of Pennsylvania Hall, a vibrant center of the abolitionist movement that was burned down for being so. The histories of these places and others, present in this book, help us understand how complex, and often painful, our history is.

Other historic places, such as Cecil B. Moore Avenue and Progress Plaza, both legacies of the Civil Rights Movement, continue to serve as focal points for African Americans in the twenty-first century and as places where the fight for social and economic justice for African Americans continues. Their histories remind us how far the city has traveled and how much farther it still has to go.

Since its founding, Philadelphia has played a central role in the development of this country. As elsewhere, African Americans played a fundamental role in that journey. A greater understanding of the history of African Americans in Philadelphia, which everyone will get from reading this book, helps us all better understand ourselves.

BLACK HISTORY

in the Philadelphia Landscape

INTRODUCTION

In 2005, the School District of Philadelphia mandated a year-long course in African American history as a requirement for high school graduation. I volunteered to teach the new course and continued to do so for eight years. That experience transformed my understanding of American history, Philadelphia history, and our country and city in the present day.

Before I taught African American history, I confess that I had what is probably a typical Yankee perspective: slavery, lynching, Jim Crow, and voter suppression were part of southern history. The North, by contrast, was the home of abolitionism, the Underground Railroad, and the Harlem Renaissance; it was also the destination of Black Americans during the Great Migration. In my African American history class, I chose to emphasize local history, and I was quickly disabused of the myth of stark regional difference.

Slavery was common in seventeenth- and eighteenth-century Philadelphia. The nineteenth century was a time of anti-Black riots, limited economic opportunities for African Americans, and violent voter suppression in the City of Brotherly Love. Though Black people fleeing the South flocked to Philadelphia in the early twentieth century, the city was nicknamed "Up South" because of the racism encountered by migrants.

Teaching the course changed how I viewed my hometown, and I came to understand that institutional racism and white supremacy are deep-rooted and persistent features of our national story—North and South alike.

In recent years, increased national attention has been paid to Black history. I remember meeting a couple from Tulsa in 2017 who were surprised that I had heard of the Tulsa race massacre of 1921. On the one-hundredth anniversary of that terrible series of events, commemorations were broadcast on television; front-page articles were printed in the mainstream press; and a terrifying reenactment was depicted in *Watchmen*, a popular HBO series. Similarly, Juneteenth has gone from a celebration known only within segments of the Black community to becoming a federal holiday.

Greater attention to Black history has led to increased interest in Black representation, and lack of representation, in the landscape. Some of the reactions to this increased attention have been positive; some have been negative and even violent. Cities including Richmond, Virginia, and New Orleans have removed Confederate statues; others have refused to do so. The infamous 2017 "Unite the Right" rally in Charlottesville, Virginia, was organized after the City Council voted to remove statues of Robert E. Lee and Stonewall Jackson from a public park. Arguments over the names of buildings, schools, and streets have roiled communities across the country. The emergence of the Black Lives Matter movement and the massive response to the police murder of George Floyd have intensified demands for change.

Furthermore, in the era of *The 1619 Project* and political conflict about critical race theory and the teaching of Black history in schools, evolving interpretations of American history have become central to political discourse. The "anti-woke" backlash against a more inclusive, less romanticized view of the past underscores the power of history in shaping individual and national identity. History is crucial to debates over gentrification, affirmative action, structural racism, reparations, voting rights, mass incarceration, and other timely topics.

In this book I explore the ongoing process of altering our landscape to acknowledge the deep roots and continuing legacy of Black Philadelphians. My understanding of how these changes take place is based on the following generalizations:

- History is not the past; it is an ongoing process of interpreting the past.
- The past does not change, but our understanding of it does.
- Historical interpretations often reveal more about the times in which they are written than they do about past events.
- As our historical interpretations evolve, our monuments reflect new understanding.

Not all monuments are monumental in scale. The website of Monument Lab (https://monumentlab.com/about), a Philadelphia-based organization that encourages discussion and activism around the intersections of history and public art, defines a monument as "a statement of power and presence in public." I like this broad definition because it includes much more than traditional statues or large installations. Thus, Pennsylvania's ubiquitous blue-and-yellow historical markers are monuments. Plaques, street names, names of public buildings, and so forth are monuments, as well.

In recent years, the number seems to have increased of honorary street names in which the person or group honored is listed on a strip of red below the existing street name on the traditional green Philadelphia street sign. While driving around, I notice that many, perhaps most, of these mini-monuments celebrate African Americans. Not surprisingly, however, the City of Philadelphia does not maintain a centralized list of these sign alterations. I can only speculate based on my own observation that Black Philadelphians are frequently acknowledged in this way.

Murals are also monuments. In Philadelphia, we have a plethora of wonderful ones thanks to Jane Golden and her team at Mural Arts. Unfortunately, murals are vulnerable to developers to a greater degree than other monument formats, and during Philadelphia's recent building boom, many beloved murals have been knocked down or covered over. Nonetheless, murals are an important way that Philadelphia's Black history is conveyed in public space.

All kinds of monuments, from the naming of a building to the erection of a statue, are conceived of and put in place by human beings. Monuments collectively reflect the values of a society, but one by one they are the product of the political views, pride in heritage, or peculiar passions of an individual or small group of people. The types of people and events memorialized in the landscape are subjective and, as such, perpetually up for debate. As you will discover in the chapters ahead, the ongoing process of making Black history visible is fraught with power struggles, racial tensions, and competing visions of appropriate representation. I view these arguments as further evidence that we care deeply about our history and value the importance of our public spaces.

I hope that by reading this book you learn more about Philadelphia's rich and complicated Black history and that you gain a new appreciation for where to find visual echoes of this heritage as you traverse the city. I also hope that this book helps you to understand the importance of preserving historically significant structures. Recent years have seen the demolition and paving over of too much of our history, and Black historical sites tend to be particularly vulnerable.

Most important, I want readers to embrace the idea that Black history is integral to American history. Africans, unlike most immigrant groups, were brought here against their will and suffered generations of brutal chattel slavery as enslaved people who literally built our nation's wealth. The ongoing implications of the white supremacy on which the United States was founded have set up an entrenched system of structural racism that is reflected in ongoing economic and social inequality.

Nonetheless, it has been Black Americans who have consistently pushed the United States to live up to its highest ideals of liberty, justice, and equality. Black resistance, persistence, organizing, and advocacy have expanded rights for all Americans. I believe that an honest, inclusive understanding of history is the best path toward reckoning with our past and achieving a better American future.

I have organized the book chronologically, so if you read it from start to finish, you can get a solid overview of Philadelphia's Black history. Each chapter, however, can stand alone and be read in whatever order you choose. Some chapters include "Reflection" sections contributed by people who have direct knowledge of the relevant history or the alterations to the landscape.

All chapters conclude with ideas for continuing your exploration of Black history and the Philadelphia landscape. Most small museums and house museums struggle to make ends meet. I invite you to support these places by visiting them and meeting the docents, staff members, and volunteers who are dedicated to sharing the city's African American past.

I also encourage you to get involved in shaping the landscape. In this book are numerous examples of street name designations, markers, murals, and monuments that were created at the behest of ordinary people with an extraordinary commitment to make the past visible in the present.

Now, a few disclaimers.

I have done my best to present accurate information based on extensive research using primary and secondary sources. Some of these sources, however, include contradictory information, even about basic facts. Furthermore, the material in the book covers a wide expanse of time, and I am not an expert on each period included in the book. Almost every chapter has been reviewed by someone who has either academic expertise or personal knowledge of the topic. I apologize for any errors and assure you that they are unintentional. In addition, all URLs included in the "To Do" sections of the book were operating at the time of publication.

I chose the chapter topics based on a combination of my knowledge, my interests, and my sense of which topics convey important information about major historical trends. I obviously could not cover every aspect of local Black history. There are significant events that receive no mention (e.g., the Philadelphia Transit Company strike of 1944, which, unfortunately, is not yet visible in the landscape; someone out there should at least apply for a historical marker). Others get only scant coverage (e.g., the MOVE bombing, which is chronologically beyond the scope of this work, and I recall the event so vividly that it is difficult for me to think of it as "history"). I admit that I have given short shrift to athletes, artists, and musicians. Perhaps there will be a second volume of this book with such figures as the focal point. Or maybe you or someone else will be inspired to write such a book. As Toni Morrison said to the Ohio Arts Council in 1981, "If there's a book that you want to read, but it hasn't been written yet, then you must write it."

Finally, I am a white person who has inserted myself into the Black history space. Not everyone is comfortable having me here. I have tried to be respectful and sensitive, and I have sought the wisdom and knowledge of African American historians (both experts and amateurs), librarians, tour guides, museum personnel, and people who lived through events described in the book. I know that I write from a place of privilege. I hope that I have made the most of that privilege by writing a book that helps to bring people together in our common humanity and shared affection for our city and its diverse residents.

PART I

Seventeenth and Eighteenth
Centuries

1

CHARLES L. BLOCKSON

Collecting and Marking Black History

Charles Blockson is considered by many the father of local Black history. His eponymous collection at Temple University has provided untold numbers of students and scholars with resources, and his books have brought African American history to general readers and academics. Blockson is also a pioneer in making the Black experience, including slavery in the city's early history, visible in the Philadelphia landscape.

A Brief Blockson Biography

Charles Blockson was born in 1933 and raised in Norristown, a small city a few miles from Philadelphia. He became intrigued by Black history while listening to his grandfather sing about the Underground Railroad, the means through which Blockson's great-grandfather had escaped enslavement in Delaware. When a white teacher told Blockson that "Negroes have no history," he became determined to prove otherwise and began amassing historical Black sources. Blockson started collecting at age nine and gathered materials that reflected the local, national, and international Black experience.

An exceptional high school athlete, Blockson was sought after by many colleges. He chose to study at Penn State, where Roosevelt Grier was a football teammate. Unlike "Rosey," Blockson turned down the opportunity to play with the New York Giants and instead joined the U.S. Army for two years.[1]

In 1972, Blockson was hired by Norristown Area High School to teach African American history and advise on racial and cultural issues. He continued to collect works related to the Black experience, traveling widely to accumulate books and other sources. Blockson also worked on tracing his family history, and his first book, *Black Genealogy*, was published in 1977. He eventually published thirteen books and has lectured all over the world.

Blockson donated his collection of about twenty thousand items to Temple University Libraries in 1984. Today, the Charles L. Blockson Afro-American Collection is housed in a well-appointed suite of rooms in Sullivan Hall on Temple's campus. More than half a million items are included in the collection, which is considered one of the world's foremost repositories of information related to Black history and culture. Visitors to the collection can see a stunning variety of materials that includes books (e.g., first editions by Phillis Wheatley and W. E. B. Du Bois), artifacts (Civil War–era recruitment posters for United States Colored Troops), sheet music (belonging to Paul Robeson and Josephine Baker), photographs (works by the chronicler of mid-twentieth-century Black life in Philadelphia John Moseley), letters, and more. Blockson was among the first people I spoke to when I began writing this book. He died at the age of eighty-nine in April 2023.

The Historical Marker Project

In 1990, only two historical markers in Philadelphia were connected to the African American experience.[2] One commemorates the first written

---

1. As a person born on the cusp between the Baby Boom and Generation X, I most closely associate Rosey Grier with the song "It's Alright to Cry," from *Free to Be . . . You and Me*, the gender equality-themed album and television show of the early 1970s. Grier was also a bodyguard for Robert Kennedy and is credited with wrestling Sirhan Sirhan to the ground after he assassinated Kennedy.

2. Pennsylvania's historical marker program was launched in 1913. Until the 1980s, staff members of the Pennsylvania Historical and Museum Commission (PHMC) decided where markers should be erected and worked with local historical societies and community organizations to raise funds and plan dedication ceremonies. That changed when budget cuts decimated the PHMC and it began accepting nominations from members of the public. The criteria for historical markers are strict, and the application process is straightforward but rigorous. A panel of historians and other history professionals reviews the applications and makes recommendations to the PHMC.

protest against slavery, a 1688 document written by Germantown Quakers. Nominated by a group of Quakers, the marker was installed in 1983 and is situated on Germantown Avenue near Haines Street in front of a strip mall dubbed Freedom Square. The other, erected the following year, was at the original site of St. Thomas's African Episcopal Church, near Fifth and Walnut streets. It had been nominated by members of the church, which is now located at the intersection of Lancaster and Overbrook avenues.

Along with Charles Blockson, Dr. Bernard C. Watson spearheaded an effort to dramatically increase the number of historical markers in Philadelphia related to Black history. While Watson is five years Blockson's senior, his life followed a similar trajectory. Like Blockson, Watson was enamored of learning history at a young age. He served in the U.S. Air Force during the Korean War and later worked as an administrator for the School District of Philadelphia. Watson was hired as a professor at Temple University and became the chair of the Department of Urban Education and, eventually, the school's first Black vice president. Both men have received the prestigious Philadelphia Award for service to the community.

Watson was appointed president of the William Penn Foundation in 1981. Recognizing the dearth of Black historical markers, he conceived of the African American State Historical Marker Project. In 1991, a grant of $92,000 was awarded to the Blockson Collection to put together applications for markers related to Black history. Thanks to this effort, seventy-four marker applications were approved by the PHMC. In his introduction to *Philadelphia's Guide: African-American State Historical Markers*, a booklet published by the Blockson Collection and William Penn Foundation in 1992, Blockson refers to the joint project as "the largest of its kind in any city within the United States."

Blockson's initial group of markers represents diverse time periods and varied fields of endeavor. The thirty individuals honored include musicians, artists, and business leaders. Churches, theaters, and hospitals are among the twenty places Blockson successfully nominated, and the twelve organizations on the list range from the Free African Society, founded in 1787, to the Opportunities Industrialization Centers, launched in 1964.

Of the 332 state-authorized markers in Philadelphia in 2022, 107 were on African American topics. In other words, nearly one-third of Philadelphia's historical markers are about Black history. More than half of them are from Blockson's first group of applications.

Charles Blockson (*center*) at a book signing in 1997 for his friend and colleague Bernard C. Watson (*seated*). At left is James S. White (1932–2020), a managing director of Philadelphia under Mayor Wilson Goode and later a high-level administrator and trustee at Temple University. The James S. White Residence Hall on North Broad Street is named in his honor. (Special Collections Research Center, Temple University Libraries, Philadelphia)

A Most Meaningful Marker

Although this large group of successful nominations in 1991 was unprecedented, Blockson has stated that he is most proud of a marker that was dedicated in 2016. Located on the shores of the Delaware River at Penn's Landing, the marker reads:

THE PENNSYLVANIA SLAVE TRADE

African people, first enslaved by the Dutch and Swedes, survived the brutal voyage from Africa to the Caribbean islands and the Americas, debarking on the Delaware River waterfront as early as 1639. William Penn, other Quakers, and Philadelphia merchants purchased and enslaved Africans. As the institution of slavery increased, these courageous people persevered and performed integral roles in building Pennsylvania and the nation.

Blockson worked on this application in collaboration with the Philadelphia Middle Passage Ceremony and Port Marker Project (MPCPMP), a national effort to educate Americans about the horrors of the Middle Passage, to underscore the role of enslaved Africans in building this country, and to place markers at ports of entry. The unveiling of the Pennsylvania slave trade marker took place on the Philadelphia branch of the MPCPMP's Ancestral Remembrance Day, a time to commemorate the many lives lost during the Middle Passage.

As the birthplace of freedom, the cradle of liberty, and the place where both the Declaration of Independence and the Constitution were written, Philadelphia has not been closely associated with slavery in the public imagination. As the first few chapters of this book make clear, however, slavery was an integral part of the city's early history. Enslaved people toiled on the shores of the Delaware River decades before the arrival of William Penn in 1681, and their presence persisted into the nineteenth century. As early as 1639, enslaved Africans had been brought here by force to labor for the Dutch and Swedish settlers who lived near present-day Wilmington, Delaware.

The slave ship *Isabella* arrived in Philadelphia in 1684. The 150 captured Africans on board were sold quickly to the approximately one thousand European settlers living in the brand-new city. Slave labor was used to clear early Philadelphia streets of trees and to construct some of the first houses in the city. Until about 1730, most enslaved people were brought to Philadelphia from the Caribbean in small groups. From about 1730 until 1760, demand for enslaved labor increased, and some Philadelphia merchants sent ships directly to West Africa that returned with cargoes of hundreds of people in chains. A substantial portion, likely about 15 percent, of those forced aboard in Africa perished en route. Demand peaked when the Seven Years' War (1756–1763) in Europe depleted the supply of indentured servants from the Continent, another integral component of the early Philadelphia workforce.

Isaac Norris, a Quaker merchant and one-time mayor of Philadelphia, was among Philadelphia's busiest slave traders. Ironically, the city of Norristown, Blockson's hometown, was named for this man who profited from commerce in human beings. Numerous prominent Philadelphians were also involved, either directly or indirectly, in the slave trade. The London Coffee House at Front and Market streets had a platform on which prospective buyers could examine enslaved Africans

An 1830 lithograph depicting an auction of enslaved people at the London Coffee House during the colonial era. A historical marker at the site (the southwestern corner of Front and Market streets) was nominated by Charles Blockson in 1991.
(Library Company of Philadelphia)

at close range. A historical marker there was among those successfully nominated by Blockson in 1991.

Philadelphia was a port city. Enslaved people built ships; worked as stevedores; and labored in shops that produced rope, barrels, sails, and other shipping materials. Enslaved people helped build the homes purchased with the wealth produced by trade at the city's bustling wharf and toiled inside those homes as domestic workers. Disturbingly, enslaved people also worked on converting standard cargo ships from throughout the colonies into slavers by installing shackles, ventilation holes, and crude toileting facilities. On the eve of the American Revolution, one of every six Philadelphia households owned enslaved people.

No wonder Blockson singles out the erection of the Pennsylvania slave trade marker as one of his proudest accomplishments. The facts stated in yellow print on blue background indicate that Black people inhabited and built the wealth of our city from the very beginning. Although Blockson's teacher tried to tell him that his people had no history, his life's work of collecting, researching, writing, lecturing, and institution building have certainly proved otherwise. Blockson's dozens of markers took the history contained in his collection out of the archives and into the streets of Philadelphia.

To Do

► See the Pennsylvania slave trade marker and then view the exhibition "Tides of Freedom: African Presence on the Delaware River" at the nearby Independence Seaport Museum.

► Visit the Blockson Collection at Sullivan Hall (1330 Pollett Walk) on the Temple University campus. Hours and other information can be found at https://library.temple.edu/blockson.

► Go to the Pennsylvania Historical and Museum Commission's website (https://share.phmc.pa.gov/markers) to find the many listings for African American markers.

► Watch the video *Marking History in Philadelphia*, an interview with Charles Blockson about historical markers, available at the Voices of the Civil Rights movement website (http://voicesof thecivilrightsmovement.com/video-collection/2018/6/18/mark ing-history-in-philadelphia).

2

COMMUNITY FORMATION IN
THE COLONIAL CITY

The Ghosts of Washington Square

N
o plantations. No cotton fields. No makeshift cabins clustered at a distance from the Greek Revival–style "big house."

Philadelphia had none of these signposts of American slavery. Enslaved people were, however, very much a part of the city's history. Though northern urban bondage operated differently from slavery in the South, it was both a widespread and a cruel institution.

Holy Visions and Hypocrisy

As in other colonies, slavery in Pennsylvania was established early on along racial lines. Pennsylvania was founded by William Penn, a Quaker idealist who envisioned his colony as a "Holy Experiment" that would be characterized by religious tolerance and friendly relations with the Lenape Indians. Although Quakers later became leaders in the movement to abolish slavery, many were enslavers during the city's early history.

In 1685, Penn wrote to the steward of his Pennsbury Manor estate instructing him to use African workers because, unlike European indentured servants, they could be held in bondage for life. Eventually, about twelve enslaved people worked on Penn's property. Some of them were freed by Penn, but others died enslaved. His correspondence reveals that he liked and admired some of those he enslaved, though this did not stop him, or his wife, from treating them as possessions. An enslaved man named Jack asked Hannah Callowhill Penn if he could see his wife, Parthenia, in bondage on another property, one more time before she was to be sold to Barbados. Callowhill Penn agreed as long as Parthenia did the Penn family's laundry during the visit.

Laying Down the Law

In 1693, the city authorities sought to tamp down on the "tumultuous gatherings of Negroes of the old town of Philadelphia on the first day of the week." They passed a law proclaiming that "the Constable of Philadelphia or any other person whatsoever is given power to take up Negroes, male or female, whom they should gather about the first days of the week, without a pass from their Master or Mistress, or not in their company, to carry them to the gallows, there remain that night, and that without meat or drink and to cause them to be publicly whipped the next morning with 39 lashes well laid on their backs."

A 1700 law stated that indentured servants guilty of stealing would be punished by an extension of their indenture equivalent to twice the value of the pilfered property. Enslaved people, however, were to be whipped in the most public place possible. Over the next three decades, race-based chattel slavery was firmly encoded in Pennsylvania laws.

At the same time, laws were promulgated restricting the lives of free Blacks. In 1726, the state legislature passed the Law for the Better Regulation of Negroes. This act, which declared that "tis found by experience that free negroes are an idle, slothful people and often prove burdensome to the neighborhood," required that free Blacks be able to show proof of employment or risk being hired out by the authorities. The penalty for interracial marriage was seven years of servitude for a white person; a Black person would be sentenced to a lifetime of slavery. The term *free* was thus only relative, and until the 1780s, the enslaved population far outnumbered the free.

Conditions of Enslavement

Isolation was a salient characteristic of slavery in Philadelphia. Enslavers typically owned only one or two individuals; those who owned more tended to lease them out (until that practice was banned by the General Assembly in response to the protests of white laborers who objected to the competition). Enslaved men usually worked at the port or in a shop or business alongside their owner; enslaved women generally did domestic work. They lived in small spaces such as kitchens or garrets within their owners' homes. Given the distribution of the enslaved as individuals or pairs across the city, acculturation into English-speaking society happened relatively quickly, even among those who had come to Philadelphia directly from Africa. Enslaved people in places such as Philadelphia and New York City may have been better fed and housed than their southern counterparts; they lacked, however, the camaraderie and support of family and community close at hand.

As in southern slavery, family separation was a constant threat. Married couples, even if living under the same roof, could see one or both partners sold away to different owners. Once children reached the age of about ten, they would be hired out to other households, often outside the city. Despite all the hardships and restrictions, connections developed among enslaved Philadelphians, and the city's free Blacks mingled socially among the enslaved. A strong network coalesced among Black Philadelphians, and a potter's field on the outskirts of the young city became the focal point of that resilient community.

A Gathering Place

Philadelphia was laid out in a grid pattern by William Penn and the surveyor Thomas Holme. Having witnessed the Great Fire of London in 1666, Penn imagined an expansive city with a green space in each quadrant. In the Quaker spirit of simplicity, what we now know as Washington Square was originally called Southeast Square. Penn and Holme expected balanced settlement on the banks of both the Schuylkill and Delaware rivers; however, the young city developed exclusively along the Delaware River.

During the first century of Philadelphia's existence, Southeast Square was distant from the city's bustling port. In 1706, the square was declared a potter's field in which strangers, suicides, victims of epidemic diseases, prisoners, soldiers, and both free and enslaved Black people were buried. It also became a gathering place for the Black community, a place where they could visit the dead and commune with the living during their limited free time. Given the frequent separation of family members into disparate households, the square was also a place where husbands could visit with wives and parents could interact with their children.

John Fanning Watson's book *Annals of Philadelphia and Pennsylvania in Olden Time* (1830) contains the following description: "It was the custom for the slave blacks, at the time of fairs and other great holidays, to go there to the number of one thousand, of both sexes, and hold their dances, dancing after the manner of their several nations in Africa, and speaking and singing in their native dialects, thus cheerily amusing themselves over the sleeping dust below!" Watson continues with this vivid recollection: "An aged lady . . . told me she has often seen the Guinea negroes in the days of her youth, going to the graves of their friends early in the morning and there leaving them victuals and rum!"

Watson's estimate of one thousand people is almost certainly an exaggeration. Nonetheless, Southeast Square was a focal point of interaction for the city's eighteenth-century polyglot Black community.

Dr. William Shippen, a founder of the Medical College of Philadelphia, which later became part of the University of Pennsylvania, used cadavers stolen from the potter's field in his lectures about anatomy. In 1782, a group of free Blacks petitioned the city to build a protective fence around their section of the field to stop the body snatching, but their request was denied. Much to Shippen's dismay, free Blacks organized to stand guard at night to protect the bodies of recently buried relatives from exhumation. In a 1787 letter to his son, Shippen complained about "the negroes . . . determined to watch all who are buried in the Potters field." He recounted how several grave robbers managed to "beat off the negroes" and obtain a corpse, but "the resolute impertinent blacks broke open ye house stole ye subject and reburied it."

By the Wayside

Washington Square today bears little resemblance to the potter's field and social gathering place of old. The upscale apartment buildings on three sides of the leafy park have few Black residents. The office buildings, trendy restaurants, individual homes, and small organizations situated around Washington Square give no hint of the African American past. Within the square itself, a plethora of plaques and markers categorize the park's trees, commemorate the park's protectors, and explain the park's history. Of the more than forty varied plaques and markers, there is a single two-foot-high wayside marker that describes the eighteenth-century square. It was erected as one of five similar markers in 2002 when stewardship of Washington Square was transferred from Philadelphia to the National Park Service. Entitled "Sorrow and Joy," it reads, in part:

> Philadelphia supported a thriving African American community that celebrated its rich heritage in festivities in Washington Square. Until the 19th century, this was often a sorrowful place. Many people knew it as a potter's field, a "publick burying place for all strangers," for soldiers, sailors, convicts, and the "destitute whose remains are walked over." A lonely Acadian refugee found eternal rest here, along with epidemic victims, Catholics and African Americans. Only free and enslaved African Americans brought a measure of mirth to this square which, according to oral tradition, they called "Congo Square."

Although the term *Congo Square* has not been documented in writing, it has become a shorthand way of linking Washington Square to the Black community. Historians at the National Park Service and elsewhere are increasingly aware that, to understand African American history, nontraditional sources must be considered.

Arts Continue the Connection

While there is little visible in the current landscape to keep the idea of Congo Square alive, members of the Philadelphia arts and culture community have tried to fortify the bond between African Americans and Washington Square. In recent years, the square was the site of Juneteenth celebrations. In the week following the 2020 police killing of Walter Wallace Jr. in West Philadelphia, activists from Spiral Q, an activist, community-based arts organization, staged a daybreak dance performance. The goal of the event was "to illuminate Black Philadelphia space, lives and legacies in Washington Square Park, once known as Congo Square." In 2012, the African American poet Lamont B. Steptoe published *Meditations in Congo Square*. The titular poem evokes a vivid, albeit imaginary, picture of eighteenth-century Southeast Square:

> *There are children here running in and out of their mother's skirts dusky feet of joy pearly white smiles in African masks of sorrow*

There are old ladies bowed puffing on corn cob pipes heads
wrapped in scarlet bandanas whiskered like old men
Someone's speaking in Ba-kongo another answers a question
asked in English with a phrase of Wolof
Someone is telling a joke in Mandingo a young man—salt
water African—becrys his fate in Swahili
A right shout is underway someone whose taken too much rum
bewails the absence of drums
Bushy black curls and frenzied feet move in rhythm to a Congo
beat
House slaves tip they hats to free-men-of-color another day of
jubilee with some of us free
When dark begins to fall we'll leave this weekly ball pray that
another sun will bless us pray for the death of those that
oppress us
We ain't got no gold but the riches we have money can't buy
We just grin and groan laugh and moan.

To Do

▶ Visit Washington Square and find the "Sorrow and Joy" way-side marker in the northeastern quadrant.

▶ Watch a video of Spiral Q's dance performance "Rise and Reconcile—Congo Square" (https://spiralq.org/uncategorized/rise-and-reconcile-congo-square-philadelphia).

▶ Tour Pennsbury Manor in Morrisville, Pennsylvania (or visit the Pennsbury Manor website [https:/pennsburymanor.org]), and assess the interpretation of William Penn's ownership of about a dozen enslaved people at this Pennsylvania home.

▶ Watch *Jack and Parthenia's Story*, a short reenactment that is part of the series *People Not Property: Stories of Slavery in the Colonial North*, available at https://peoplenotproperty .hudsonvalley.org/letter-from-pennsbury.php.

3

ENVISIONING DINAH

Stenton's Ongoing Challenge

[With a Reflection by Karyn Olivier]

It is a chilly, damp late November night in 2019. Individually and in small groups, people make their way up a long, dark path of uneven bricks. An elderly woman using a walker needs assistance scaling the low set of steps at the path's end. Once inside, the people make their way to a meeting room and seat themselves on folding chairs arranged in a circle. A few of them are white—a young woman with a pierced nose, an aging hippie in a peasant skirt and beret, an older gentleman in a tweed blazer. Most, though, are Black women, middle aged and above. Thirty-eight people in total have gathered in this now crowded room on this wintry Wednesday evening. They have come to Stenton, a house museum in Northwest Philadelphia, to talk about how to best represent the story of Dinah, a Black woman who lived and died here more than two hundred years ago.

Stenton

Stenton was built in the 1720s as a country house for James Logan and his family. Logan came to Pennsylvania in 1699 to serve as provincial secretary for the colony's founder and fellow Quaker, William Penn. As Pennsylvania developed, Logan became a powerful politician, a wealthy merchant, and a respected scholar. He had the largest private book collection in North America and often lent volumes to his close friend and protégé, Benjamin Franklin. Some of Logan's writing was published by Franklin, and Franklin sought Logan's support in founding the University of Pennsylvania.

The Logan family continued to inhabit the Georgian-style mansion at Stenton, using it as either a summer or primary residence, for six generations. In 1899, the National Society of the Colonial Dames of America assumed responsibility for Stenton, a stewardship arrangement that continues to this day. Until the twenty-first century, tours of Stenton focused mainly on the life of James Logan, and visitors were encouraged to admire the sumptuous textiles, authentic Dutch tiles, and beautiful Chippendale and Queen Anne furniture that filled the meticulously re-created period rooms. No mention was made that James Logan's fortune came in part from the rum trade, which depended on Caribbean sugar cultivated by enslaved workers.

Recently, however, attention has shifted to the people who worked at Stenton, which, in addition to being a home, was a plantation where crops such as barley, corn, and potatoes were grown. The Stenton labor force included indentured servants, hired servants, and enslaved people. When Stenton was built, slaveholding was common among wealthy Philadelphians. After the 1720s, ownership of enslaved people declined, particularly among Quakers.

By the time James Logan died in 1751, opposition to slavery among Quakers was on the rise, but his son William inherited both his father's estate and his human property. William's wife, Hannah Emlen, brought an enslaved girl named Dinah, who was perhaps ten years old, to their marriage in 1740. Like most enslaved people, Dinah had no last name, and there is no image of her likeness. Nonetheless, Dinah has emerged as the focus of a major project at Stenton, an undertaking that epitomizes a reorientation from top-down history to an emphasis on those who have most often been left out of the dominant narrative.

Dinah

Much of Dinah's life remains shrouded in obscurity, but a paper trail does exist and allows us to glean pertinent details about her. She left the home of her enslaver George Emlen when his daughter Hannah married William Logan, but Dinah later married an enslaved man from the Emlen household. After George Emlen died, Dinah's husband was sold and then took ill. When his new owner decided to sell him, Dinah's husband begged William and Hannah Logan to purchase him so that he could be with his wife. The Logans did so in 1757, thus reuniting Dinah, her husband, and their daughter Bess. But by this time, owner-ship of enslaved people was frowned on among Quakers. Members of the Philadelphia Quaker Meeting investigated the situation and ruled that the Logans' purchase had been a humanitarian act due to Dinah's husband's poor health. According to the Logan family, Dinah's husband refused their offer of manumission because he feared that his illness would render him unable to support himself.

William Logan's will, dated 1772, indicated that both Dinah and her grandson Cyrus would be left to his wife Hannah upon his death. The will also mentions that Dinah's daughter Bess had already been set free by the Logan family. Months before William's death in October 1776, however, Dinah successfully petitioned for her freedom. Cyrus was granted freedom several months after William Logan's death. De-spite her manumission, Dinah stayed on at Stenton as a paid servant. Perhaps her motivation was to stay close to Cyrus, who was required to remain at Stenton until the age of twenty-one.

Much of what we know of Dinah comes from the records kept by Deborah Norris Logan, the wife of Dr. George Logan, a son of William Logan and grandson of James Logan. Following William's death, Deb-orah and George Logan became the next occupants of Stenton.

Dinah Saves Stenton

During the Revolutionary War period, the Logan family vacated Sten-ton for stretches of time. The estate served as headquarters for George Washington and, later, for British General William Howe leading up to the Battle of Germantown. A famous story demonstrates both heroism and quick thinking on Dinah's part. Following the Battle of German-town in October 1777, the house and grounds had been left in Dinah's care. Two British soldiers informed her that they were charged with burning the homes of patriots and intended to set Stenton alight. They told her to remove any items she wanted from the house and asked where they could find hay to serve as kindling. She pointed to the barn. Soon, though, a British officer in search of deserters arrived at Stenton. Dinah indicated that two deserters were hiding in the Stenton barn, and the hay-gathering soldiers were promptly arrested. Dinah, thus, is cred-ited with saving Stenton.

In 1912, the National Society of the Colonial Dames, in partnership with the Site and Relic Society of Germantown and private subscribers, commissioned a plaque commemorating Dinah's actions. It reads:

> In memory of
> DINAH
> the
> Faithful Colored Caretaker
> of Stenton
> who by her quick thought
> and presence of mind
> saved the mansion
> from being burned
> by British Soldiers
> in the winter of 1777

The plaque was initially placed in adjacent Stenton Park, but it later spent years languishing in the mansion's basement. The sentiment of honoring the brave deeds of an enslaved woman resonates in our current era, but the wording on the plaque sounds dated and even offensive to twenty-first-century ears. The desire to commemorate Dinah in a monument more appropriate to our own time motivated Stenton's administration to create a new memorial.

An additional inspiration to refresh Dinah's presence at Stenton was provided by the inconvenient gift of an obelisk-like monument honoring James Logan. When James Logan died, he donated his vast book collection to the citizens of Philadelphia. The Loganian Library did not survive the eighteenth century as an independent entity, and the books were transferred to the Library Company of Philadelphia, an institution founded by his friend Benjamin Franklin that continues to the present day. In 1939, a cast bronze memorial to Logan was created for the Library Company's Ridgway Building by Thomas Gym Cope, a Logan descendent. It sat on the steps of the Library Company's South Broad Street location (the building that currently houses the Philadelphia High School for Creative and Performing Arts, alma mater of Boyz II Men, Christian McBride, Leslie Odom Jr., and Questlove) until 1969, when the Library Company moved to Locust Street. The monument was stored in the basement of the Philadelphia Museum of Art until it was given to Stenton by the Association for Public Art in

2018, a time when opposition to public recognition of enslavers intensified dramatically.

Inequality in Bronze

The efforts to place the James Logan memorial in context and to honor Dinah anew developed into much more than the rewording of a plaque or the design of a new monument. Through an extensive community engagement process entitled "Inequality in Bronze," Stenton staff engaged in a multiyear effort to invite and include Stenton's African American neighbors in conceptualizing the form a new Dinah memorial would take. Residents of Nicetown, Germantown, and Logan were recruited through the offices of local politicians, churches, and various other networks and organizations. With funding from the Pew Center for Arts and Heritage, community representatives and Stenton staff participated in a series of facilitated gatherings to determine which aspects of Dinah's life and story should be emphasized and to delineate criteria for selecting an artist.

The community engagement process was both fruitful and fraught. Many neighborhood participants had never set foot on Stenton's grounds and perceived the property's chain link fence and dogs as intentional barriers to entry. Others questioned why they were invited to weigh in on the Dinah memorial rather than on questions of interpretation more broadly. Some had heard the Dinah story before and felt a sense of connection to a woman they perceived as a heroine. Others wondered why a formerly enslaved person would save the home of her owners and bristled at the "faithful servant" narrative inherent in the Dinah story.

The meeting I attended on a chilly Wednesday in November 2019 was one small part of this process. Once the group had assembled that evening, Stenton's executive director, Dennis Pickeral, explained that the meeting was to be the final chance for community input before the proposal would be presented to the Philadelphia Art Commission.

Karyn Olivier, the artist the community had selected, presented a slideshow with detailed images of *Right Here*, her proposed monument. Olivier, a self-described gay, Black, Caribbean immigrant and a Germantown resident, exuded enthusiasm. "I feel so blessed that we can memorialize our foremothers," she declared. Olivier called her work on the Dinah memorial "a dream project [because] this really, really matters."

A Complicated Legacy

The story of Dinah and her memorial provides a case study in the complexity of uncovering the history of marginalized groups in general and enslaved people in particular.

Most of the firsthand information we have about Dinah comes to us through the eyes of Deborah Norris Logan, the wife of George Logan, the third generation of Logans to live at Stenton. Fortunately for historians, Deborah was a prolific keeper of diaries (she wrote almost daily for four decades) and writer of letters. When Deborah married George Logan in 1781, Dinah would have been about fifty years old and working as a paid servant rather than as a slave.

The portrait that emerges of Dinah through Deborah's eyes is that of a kindly elder, beloved by—and faithful to—the Logan family. In letters to her husband, Deborah refers to "good old Dinah." A letter from George to Deborah requests, "Please Remember me to the Servants particularly to Dinah." To her son, Albanus Logan, Deborah writes, "Old Dinah begs not to forget her love." Her death and final resting place are described in an 1805 pocket almanac belonging to Deborah Norris Logan: "July 21st at about 3 in the afternoon our very faithful and good old Dinah breathed her last. Was buried the 23rd in my garden—she had requested during her lifetime to be interred at Stenton."

It is certainly possible that there were warm relations between Dinah and the Logan family. After all, it appears that it was she who decided to remain at Stenton even after she had been granted her freedom. But it is impossible to glean Dinah's true feelings about the family who enslaved her and at least three generations of her family. And were it not for the voluminous writings of Deborah Norris Logan, Dinah would have been all but erased from history—mentioned only as a piece of property in account books, legal documents, and Quaker records—as were so many among the enslaved.

Even the story of Dinah saving Stenton from British soldiers bent on arson comes to us originally via Deborah Norris Logan. The first written record of the tale appears in the manuscript of a biography Deborah wrote of her late husband, George, in 1822. Deborah had not yet married George in 1777 when the incident occurred, and her description attributes the saving of Stenton to "an old domestic," never mentioning Dinah by name.

the Home of the Sage of Stenton ...

... Saved by quick-witted Caretaker

WHILE William Penn and his secretary James Logan were traveling to America in 1699, their ship, according to legend, was attacked by pirates. Penn's principles forbade resistance but Logan successfully defended the vessel.

As Penn's confidential adviser, the scholarly Logan wielded great influence in Pennsylvania, in time becoming governor of the colony and mayor of Philadelphia. His home in what is now Germantown was started in 1728 and was named Stenton after his father's birthplace in Scotland. In his own words, he was obliged to spend much time at home, "being wholly reduced to a pair of crutches and Sedentary Life by a fall off my feet." Nevertheless, the curtailment of his physical activity enabled him to devote himself to writing and to his remarkable library.

Logan was exceedingly friendly with the Indians who used to stay at Stenton for long periods, lining the staircase at night or camping in the maple grove. Because of his admiration for Logan, Chief Wingohocking proposed that they exchange names in the Indian custom. Instead, Logan suggested that the chief's name be given to the stream that flowed through the property so that "while the earth shall endure" it would be called Wingohocking. The creek, incidentally, has long since gone underground.

Owned by the Logan family for many years, Stenton was Washington's headquarters before the battle of Brandywine. At the battle of Germantown the house fell into British hands and was occupied briefly by General Howe.

Later in 1777 two dragoons arrived in Germantown for the purpose of carrying out orders to burn the homes of patriots in the neighborhood. While they were in the stable gathering straw to start a fire in Stenton, a party of soldiers came looking for deserters. Dinah, the Negro caretaker, promptly told them that two suspicious men were lurking in the barn and despite their indignant protests the two dragoons were seized. Seventeen houses had been burned, but thanks to Dinah, Stenton was saved. Now the property of the city of Philadelphia and under the custody of the Pennsylvania Society of The Colonial Dames of America, this important landmark is open to public view.

A 1952 advertisement for home insurance that recounts and illustrates the story of Dinah saving Stenton. (Germantown Historical Society/Historic Germantown)

Over time, other writers picked up the story and filled in details. Dinah's name was inserted in some of these much later accounts, though it had been left out of Deborah's. For example, an 1897 version from an article in the *Philadelphia Press* includes dialogue written in dialect that sounds offensive to modern ears. This retelling provides Dinah's words when asked by British soldiers if she has seen any deserters:

"'Oh, yes, Massa' said the quick witted negro woman. 'You is just got heah in time. Der's two of the miserable critters a-hiding out day in de barn now.'" Although details may have been embroidered onto the story of Dinah saving Stenton, we can assume that something resembling Deborah Norris Logan's secondhand version of events did occur, and it is notable that Dinah was trusted to maintain Stenton on her own when the family was elsewhere.

Dinah's full story will never be known, but thinking about her actions and the way she is described by Deborah Norris Logan poses meaningful questions about her feelings and her motivations. The community engagement process revealed that Black neighbors of Stenton wanted a memorial that would explore the ambiguity of Dinah's relationship with the Logan family and would ask visitors to consider Dinah as a full-fledged person with emotions, preferences, family connections, and dreams.

The Women of Germantown mural on Germantown Avenue includes Dinah; a local actress who has often brought Dinah's story to life served as the model. In 2022, a mural of Dinah was completed at the recreation center and playground next to Stenton. The artist, the Nicetown native Russell Craig, was dismayed to realize that he grew up unaware of Stenton's problematic history. He depicts Dinah pointing the way toward the mansion. His goal, he explained, was to "let the community know there is a plantation in North Philadelphia that we never knew about."

A New Lens

It is notable that a house museum that was known for presenting the possessions and accomplishments of the prominent family that called it home has now turned its attention to honoring a woman that family enslaved and to exploring their connection to the institution of slavery. Visitors to Stenton can still learn about Logan family history and heirlooms, objects with which all who lived and labored at Stenton inter-

Dinah Memorial as proposed by the artist Karyn Olivier in 2019. As installed, the color, form, placement, and details evolved with community input and to address practical requirements. (Courtesy of the National Society of the Colonial Dames of America in the Commonwealth of Pennsylvania at Stenton)

acted, but they are also challenged to think about the workers, both enslaved and free, who performed the labor needed to sustain daily life in the mansion. Although the enslaved and indentured laborers did not leave behind written records, their existence and their humanity are being brought to light. The new Dinah memorial is a way to mark the landscape to demonstrate that shift in focus.

Olivier's design includes two semicircular benches that face each other across a small reflecting basin. Tablets that rise out of each bench feature a woman's silhouette. Superimposed on one silhouette is a list of questions for Dinah (e.g., What was your full name? How did freedom feel? Did you ever wish you had let it burn?); the opposite panel has questions for the viewer (e.g., What is your name? Do you feel free? Would you have saved Stenton?). We will never know Dinah's full story; nor will we know what she looked like. Thanks to the recent efforts of Stenton staff, neighbors, and supporters, however, her presence will not be forgotten; nor will the existence of scores of other people who labored at one of Philadelphia's former plantations.

Reflection

Karyn Olivier, *the designer of* Right Here, *is a Philadelphia-based artist who creates public art, sculptures, installations, and photography.*

I believe Dinah's memorial (which is also a monument) should allow for multiple perspectives, histories, and narratives to come to the fore as a site for inquiry, interpretation, and imaginings of the future. The best monuments are instruments—offering a mirror to witness ourselves, our community, our city, and our country. They are active, shifting, temporal, and contemporary. And though little is known about Dinah, this commemoration of her legacy—this physical marker, this evidence—must strive to be more than solely a symbolic gesture. I believe it can be imbued with the power to craft a continually evolving American history, adding Dinah's story to the narratives that become our collective "heritage."

To Do

► Visit the Friends of Stenton website (https://www.stenton.org) to find an up-to-date tour schedule and to learn about special events such as the annual garden party and Fourth of July picnic. The website also contains extensive information about the Dinah story, the Inequality in Bronze project, the Logan family, and the history of Stenton.

► Watch a video of the play *Remember My Name: Dinah's Story* at https://www.stenton.org/remember-my-name. This twenty-minute, two-person performance envisions a conversation between a young and an older version of Dinah.

► View the "Women of Germantown" mural on the side of the Germantown YWCA at 5722 Greene Street. The image of Dinah is based on Irma Gardner-Hammond, who plays Dinah in the *Remember My Name: Dinah's Story* video.

► Visit the Stenton Park Recreation Center to see a mural of Dinah that was completed in 2022. Plans for the Dinah mural developed separately from those for the Dinah memorial at Stenton; however, this coincidence of timing led to ongoing collaboration and cooperation between Stenton Museum and the Stenton Park Advisory Council.

► Tour Cliveden at 6401 Germantown Avenue to learn how another house museum in Northwest Philadelphia has worked to confront the history of slavery.

► To learn about an enslaved man named Sampson who fled from his owner, James Logan, at Stenton, watch "Franklin's Spark (1720–1765)," part of the *Philadelphia: The Great Experiment* series produced by History Making Productions, at https://www.youtube.com/watch?v=5vLw_xGtXYI.

► Visit Mount Pleasant in East Fairmount Park. A historical marker that was erected outside of this mid-eighteenth-century summer home and plantation in 2023 mentions the estate's enslaved inhabitants. The house, managed by the Philadelphia Museum of Art, is open to the public for special events.

4

~⌒~

RICHARD ALLEN AND ABSALOM JONES

Leadership in the Center of Free Black Life

[With a Reflection by State Representative Chris Rabb]

In just two decades, the makeup of Philadelphia's Black population changed drastically. According to the historian Gary Nash, in 1765 the city was home to about 1,400 enslaved people and one hundred free Blacks; by 1783, there were one thousand free Blacks and only about four hundred enslaved people. This relatively speedy reversal in proportions was due to a number of factors:

- *Quaker conscience kicked in—at last.* In 1776, the Society of Friends agreed to banish owners of enslaved people from membership in Quaker Meetings. This followed decades of pressure from antislavery Quakers such as Benjamin Lay (who once filled a Bible with berry juice and then stabbed it with a knife during Meeting for Worship to demonstrate his fury at Quaker enslavers) and the gentler Anthony Benezet (who tried to persuade his coreligionists to abandon slavery on moral grounds and educated scores of Black children at his groundbreaking school).
- *Revolutionary rhetoric.* The Age of Enlightenment concept of natural rights pervaded 1770s Philadelphia, as did comparisons of British colonial power to the institution of slavery. Thomas Paine and Benjamin Rush published pamphlets pointing out the inherent contradiction between the ideals of the

Declaration of Independence and the holding of people in life-time bondage. Enslaved people were influenced by what they heard and read, as were some of their owners. Manumissions increased dramatically, including among non-Quakers.

- *The fog of war.* Many enslaved people in Philadelphia escaped bondage in the early years of the Revolutionary War, taking advantage of the chaos as Patriot families fled the city during British occupation. Some gained freedom by serving on American naval ships; many more fought with the British, who had promised freedom to those who joined them in their fight. When the Continental Army reclaimed Philadelphia, numerous formerly enslaved people fled with the British.

- *Preference for wage labor.* In addition to moral and political reasons for manumitting enslaved people, it also made economic sense. Uncertainty in the lead-up to war made it preferable for employers to hire and dismiss workers as conditions shifted. Reluctant or recalcitrant laborers, unlike enslaved help, could easily be fired. And enslaved people were more likely to intentionally break tools, commit arson, or run away than their indentured or hired counterparts.

- *Constant resistance.* Although it is implicit in each of the points above, it is worth stating explicitly that Black people took action to end the institution that held them in bondage. Whether through persuading a master to set them free, sharing information about revolutionary ideals, assessing their best chance for freedom during wartime, or making slave labor an expensive proposition, Black people were agents of their own emancipation.

In addition to these reasons, some credit for the steep decline in slavery was due to the passage of Pennsylvania's Act for the Gradual Abolition of Slavery in 1780, the first such law in the United States. When I taught African American history, however, I always said that the emphasis should be on the word *gradual* in the legislation's title. It did nothing for people born before the act's passage on March 1, 1780; men born afterward would be held in slavery until age twenty-eight and women would be held in slavery until age twenty-four, a significant chunk of one's productive years, given the health conditions and life expectancy of the time. The act did, however, ban the importation of enslaved people into Pennsylvania. It also required that owners register the people they owned; several enslaved people were able to sue successfully for their freedom when their owners neglected to take this required step.

The Free Black Capital

As slavery waned throughout Pennsylvania, Philadelphia was in position to become the nation's center for free Black life. What was left of Philadelphia's Black community after the War for Independence was augmented substantially by newly freed people from New Jersey, New England, and, especially, other parts of Pennsylvania. Runaways and recently manumitted individuals from places such as Maryland and Delaware were also drawn to the city, the first big city north of the Mason-Dixon Line.

In addition to being the national capital, Philadelphia was a hotbed of abolition activity. In a virtuous cycle, free Black institutions such as schools and churches were formed in Philadelphia, attracting more Black people who were then able to participate in and solidify those institutions. In *The Philadelphia Negro*, W. E. B. Du Bois reports that the Black population of Philadelphia County skyrocketed from 2,489 in 1790 to 6,880 in 1800.

A critical mass of Black people, however, may not have sufficed for the community to make the remarkable progress that it did during the last decades of the eighteenth century and first decades of the nineteenth. Two remarkable men, Absalom Jones and Richard Allen, led Black Philadelphia with courage, determination, and intelligence. Institutions they created shaped the African American experience long after their deaths and far beyond the City of Brotherly Love.

Parallel Lives

Absalom Jones was born into slavery in 1746 in Delaware. At sixteen, Jones, his mother, and his siblings were sold to Benjamin Wynkoop, who soon moved to Philadelphia to become a merchant. His other family members were sold to a different owner. In Philadelphia, Jones—who had already learned to read—briefly attended the school founded by Anthony Benezet. He worked as a clerk and handyman in Wynkoop's store, and in the evenings he was able to work for others and keep his

Portrait of Absalom Jones by Raphaelle Peale, ca. 1810. The dignity of Jones in this depiction was remarkable for the time period. (Print Department Collection, Boston Public Library)

earnings. Jones married an enslaved woman named Mary King and purchased his wife's freedom to ensure that their offspring would be free. He asked his master repeatedly to free him, as well, but Wynkoop refused until Absalom, having earlier taken the last name Jones, was at last allowed to purchase his freedom at age thirty-eight.

Richard Allen was also born in bondage. He was owned by Benjamin Chew, the first chief justice of the Pennsylvania Supreme Court and a member of a prominent Philadelphia family. Known as "Negro Richard," he was sold to Stokely Sturgis, a farmer in Delaware, along with his mother and siblings. Sturgis, however, sold off part of the family for financial reasons. Richard, who taught himself to read and write, was able to buy his freedom, and in 1780 he was manumitted and took the name Richard Allen.

The similarities, however, do not end there. Both men were deeply spiritual people who had found Methodism to be the religion that ignited their faith. After traveling for some time as a preacher, Richard Allen came to Philadelphia. Both Jones and Allen became lay preachers at St. George's United Methodist Church, an interracial congregation at Fourth and Vine streets that still exists today.

Black Firsts

In 1787, Allen and Jones, along with other community leaders, founded the Free African Society, the first independent Black organization in the United States. Members, who were required to live "an orderly and sober life," paid dues to ensure that their widows and children would be cared for following their deaths. It was, however, much more than a mutual aid society. Members gathered for nondenominational religious services; petitioned the government to abolish slavery; sought to help people transitioning from bondage to freedom; and, perhaps most important, developed a sense of shared identity and collective strength.

Even after the founding of the Free African Society, Jones and Allen continued to preach at St. George's and to attract a growing audience of Black worshipers. As the congregation grew, Black members helped to construct a balcony to accommodate increasing attendance. At a Sunday service in 1792, African Americans including Jones and Allen were told that they were in the wrong place and ordered to leave the balcony, even as they kneeled in prayer. They responded by walking out en masse.[1]

The Free African Society then doubled down on its religious function. Although Jones and Allen had both chosen Methodism, the majority of the society's members preferred the Episcopalian church. Jones became the leader of this group and the founder of the First African Church which opened its doors on Fifth Street south of Walnut Street in 1794.

Richard Allen, however, remained committed to Methodism. In 1791, he purchased land at Sixth and Lombard streets. Allen's Bethel

---

1. Some historians give 1787 as the date of the walkout. A researcher, however, found evidence in the St. George's archives that the balcony was not constructed until 1792.

Church held its first services in a converted blacksmith shop in 1794. The blacksmith shop was later moved to the Sixth and Lombard location.

Yellow Fever

An important chapter in Jones and Allen's collaboration took place in between the founding of the Free African Society and the opening of their respective churches. In the summer of 1793, yellow fever was ravaging Philadelphia. Wealthy Philadelphia residents, including George Washington and most of the federal government, abandoned the city for their own safety. Dr. Benjamin Rush, who had become an advocate for Black rights and a friend of Jones and Allen, asked whether they could organize members of the Free African Society to nurse the sick and bury the dead. Black people, Rush assured them, were immune to yellow fever.

Seeing an opportunity to prove themselves to white Philadelphia, Jones and Allen agreed to Rush's request. During a time when the cause of yellow fever was unknown, and some people refused to help friends and family members for fear of infection, Black Philadelphians stepped into the void. It soon became clear that they were not immune to the disease, and even Richard Allen became ill. By the time a frost ended the epidemic in November, one out of ten Philadelphians had perished, with Blacks dying at nearly the same rate as white residents.

Matthew Carey, a prominent publisher and bookseller, produced a widely read pamphlet that accused Black nurses of price gouging and stealing from the dead and dying during the epidemic. Jones and Allen wrote a point-by-point response entitled *A Narrative of the Proceedings of the Black People, during the Late Awful Calamity in Philadelphia in the Year 1793 and a Refutation of Some Censures, Thrown upon Them in Some Late Publications*, an illustration of both men's leadership and of their commitment to defending their brethren.

Institution Building

As Philadelphia emerged as the center of free Black life, numerous institutions were founded to nurture, protect, and support this vital but vulnerable community. Jones and Allen were central to much of this activity. They were founding leaders of Philadelphia's Prince Hall Masonic Lodge. Both Jones and Allen opened schools for Black children. Jones led the Female Benevolent Society and the African Friendly Society. Allen organized the Free Produce Society, dedicated to boycotting goods made with enslaved labor. Both men, as well as many of their congregants, continued to participate in abolition work, and Mother Bethel Church became a stop on the Underground Railroad. The American Colonization Society, which advocated for free Blacks to relocate to Africa, picked up African American adherents in some cities. In Philadelphia, however, the Black community expressed a collective dedication to building lives of dignity and purpose on American soil.

A Continuing Legacy

The groundbreaking religious institutions founded by Jones and Allen nearly 230 years ago have endured. After joining the Episcopal diocese of Pennsylvania, Jones's church was renamed the African Episcopal Church of St. Thomas. In 1802, Absalom Jones became the first Black person ordained as an Episcopal priest. The African Episcopal Church of St. Thomas has occupied several different sites and is now located on Lancaster Avenue in the Overbrook Farms neighborhood of Philadelphia. In 1984, a historical marker was placed at the church's original location.

In 1816, Allen's Bethel Church allied with other Black Methodist congregations to establish the African Methodist Episcopal (AME) Church, the first independent Black denomination in the United States. Considered the founding home of the AME sect, Allen's church is known as Mother Bethel. There are AME churches throughout Philadelphia and the United States and in thirty-nine countries on five continents.

In 1941, Philadelphia's first federally funded housing project was named for Allen. The Richard Allen Homes, made up of low-rise apartments surrounding courtyards, were initially seen as an example of forward-thinking design. By the 1980s, the homes were plagued by crime and deteriorating conditions. The original buildings were torn down, and in 2003 the area was redeveloped as single-family suburban-style houses. Although the appearance of the area has changed, the name Richard Allen Homes remains. In addition, the Richard Allen Preparatory Charter School opened in Southwest Philadelphia in 2001.

Allen's most significant, lasting impact on the Philadelphia landscape is the church he founded, which still sits on the property he purchased in 1791. Mother Bethel remains at Sixth and Lombard on land that has the longest continuous Black ownership in the United States. The current building, completed in 1890, is a formidable edifice. Allen and his second wife, Sarah, are buried in a crypt in the building's ground floor, a space that also houses a history museum. A seven-foot statue of Allen was erected adjacent to Mother Bethel in 2016 to celebrate the bicentennial of the founding of the AME denomination. Historical markers for both the Free African Society and the church itself sit in front of the building, and a small commemorative street sign at Sixth and Lombard streets is labeled Richard Allen Avenue. Mother Bethel congregation members helped to paint a mural of Allen on the side of the Medical Arts Building at Thirty-eighth and Market streets that same year.

An additional mural depicting Richard Allen and Mother Bethel was unveiled in October 2022. In 1830, the last year of his life, Allen organized the first Colored Convention, a meeting of Black leaders to strategize for improving the lives of African Americans. Colored Conventions continued to be held until the 1890s, and eight of them took place in Philadelphia. The mural depicts Richard Allen perched atop a triangle-shaped pantheon of Colored Convention leaders and participants. A second mural, across from the Colored Conventions mural, highlights continuing Black activism, including the widespread Black Lives Matter protests of 2020. Both murals are on the sides of buildings at the Courtyard Apartments at Riverview, a low-rise affordable-housing complex on the edge of the South Philadelphia neighborhood of Queen Village.

A Burial Ground Rediscovered

Allen's legacy will soon become even more visible in Queen Village. The area was formerly the Southwark District, an independent municipality that was home to many members of the growing free Black community of the early nineteenth century. In 1810, Richard Allen and the trustees of Mother Bethel Church purchased land at Fourth and Catherine streets to be used as a burial ground. At that point, it was forbidden to bury African Americans in graveyards within city limits. More than five thousand Black people were interred at Bethel Burial Ground over the next five and a half decades. About two-thirds of those buried were children, many of whom died of typhoid or tuberculosis.

Burials ceased in 1864, and the property was sold to the City of Philadelphia in 1889 when Mother Bethel faced financial hardship. In the early twentieth century, the former burial ground was transformed into an urban garden and park. In 1950, the park was expanded to a full city block and became home to Weccacoe Playground.[2] In 2010, plans were afoot to renovate the playground when Terry Buckalew, a retired University of Pennsylvania facilities manager and amateur historian, informed the groups involved of the probable existence of the burial ground. An archaeological study confirmed Buckalew's theory. A small building housing toilet facilities sat directly atop human remains.

In the wake of these discoveries, African American groups including the Avenging the Ancestors Coalition and the newly formed Friends of Bethel Burial Ground protested the plans for a revamped playground.[3] The Bethel Burying Ground Coalition was established to figure out how to proceed. After gathering input from a variety of stakeholders (including at a standing room only meeting at the African American Museum of Philadelphia), the coalition suggested building a memorial, and the City of Philadelphia agreed to support the effort. The current pastor at Mother Bethel, Reverend Dr. Mark Kelly Tyler, explained the importance of creating a memorial at the Bethel Burial Ground site: "We must remember our history by creating a fitting commemoration. And we must interpret our history by culturally enlightening everyone."

Through a process of public engagement, numerous proposals were submitted to the City of Philadelphia's Office of Arts, Culture and the Creative Economy, and a winning design was chosen. Karyn Olivier, the artist selected for the Dinah Memorial, was also awarded this commission. Her design for the memorial includes granite and concrete pavers that cover the footprint of the old burial ground. Some will be engraved with brief biographies of the interred; others will remain blank to symbolize the many stories that have been lost to time. Some of the inscriptions will be visible only in wet or humid weather, lending an eerie, otherworldly aspect to the site.

An area adjacent to the memorial will continue to serve as a playground. Although some people might find the placement of a playground next to a burial ground to be unsettling, Reverend Tyler views the juxtaposition as an opportunity for teachable moments. When children ask about the memorial, says Tyler, "I think that would be a wonderful way to honor the ancestors who are buried there [and] to help these children write a new and better American story."

---

2. Weccacoe, meaning "pleasant place," is what the Lenni Lenape called this area.

3. The Avenging the Ancestors Coalition is led by Michael Coard. Joe Certaine organized the Friends of Bethel Burial Ground. Coard has provided a Reflection statement in Chapter 5 of this book.

Ceremony on October 6, 2022, renaming the Allen Lane Station for Richard Allen. State Representative Chris Rabb (*left*) and Reverend Dr. Mark Kelly Tyler (*right*) look at an informational panel. (Photograph by Amy Jane Cohen)

Fitting Tributes in 2022

In February 2022, a block of Allens Lane in West Mount Airy was officially renamed Richard Allen Lane, thanks to the efforts of local Black elected officials. Allens Lane was originally named for William Allen, a Philadelphia mayor and an enslaver. At the dedication ceremony for the newly named block, State Representative Chris Rabb declared: "When we take time to research our history, it gives us a chance to reflect and correct choices made with the inclusion or consideration of a diversity of stakeholders. We must closely examine the history we choose to memorialize and honor, especially versions of the past validated by false narratives that marginalize the value of Black people and other communities of struggle."[4]

---

4. Rabb also spoke at the dedication of the Colored Conventions Mural, where he read a speech that his great-great-great-grandfather had given at an 1841 Colored Convention in Portland, Maine.

Building on the positive reaction to the renamed street, Rabb and others initiated the process to rename the train station located on Richard Allen Lane in the bishop's honor, as well. On a sunny Thursday in early October 2022, about one hundred people gathered for the dedication of Richard Allen Lane Station. Explanatory placards tell the history of Richard Allen's life and the founding of the AME Church. The renamed block of Allens Lane and the Richard Allen Lane Station, fortuitously, are a mere quarter-mile from the top of Chew Avenue, a street named for young "Negro Richard's" enslaver.

Reflection

*These are remarks made by **State Representative Chris Rabb** at the dedication ceremony for the Richard Allen Lane Station.*

One of the reasons this is such an important moment to me is because I've benefited from the proud legacy of Black abolitionists. I descend from a number of Black abolitionists, one of whom worked very closely with Frederick Douglass and actually worked with the Vigilance Committee over 180 years ago in Germantown. So this is personal. This isn't just a renaming. This is a reimagining of what community looks like.

It's a journey. This is a journey that we're all on collectively. Where do we want to go collectively? We're not going to stop at a street sign. We started there. And people said, "What about the bridge?" And we said, "Let's do that." "And what about the SEPTA [Southeastern Pennsylvania Transportation Authority] station?" "Let's do that, too!" But it's not just about the name. The symbolism behind the name matters. It matters.

We're in a moment of great trauma. There are so many things that seek to destroy and divide us on so many levels, locally, statewide, nationwide, internationally. There are wars going on. And people say, "Y'all just spending time and money changing names. What you need to do is . . . fill in the blank." I want to address that because, like [State] Senator [Art] Haywood, our job is to create, amend, and repeal state law. Why? Because we believe in shared prosperity; we believe in community safety; we believe in giving everyone an equal chance to thrive.

Well, what does that have to do with this name? Everything! Everything! Because we chose as a community to change the name from the name of an enslaver with deeply problematic values to [the name of] a freedom fighter. And that adds value to everyone. What are we fighting for? We're fighting for all the things that keep us safe and allow us to grow and prosper and come together like we're doing right now. But for everyone! That's what we do on the local, state, and federal level if we're doing our jobs right.

And we're not doing it alone. We're doing it with community because the reality is that all the details that we will unveil—all the beauty, all the progress behind the scenes—were done by the community. We didn't give it to you; you made it happen. This is what we're capable of, and this is so small and yet so meaningful. What are we going to do next? What are we going to do next? What are we going to do with this inspiration that leads us to a higher level? That's the question, and it's up to us as a community to answer it together.

So I'm going to leave you with this: I am so moved that this is happening [within] walking distance from my home, in the center of my legislative district, in a neighborhood that has been so good to me, and that you all have made this happen, and that I can be a part of this moment, and celebrating what potential we have to unleash on so many more things.

To Do

► Attend services at either the African Episcopal Church of St. Thomas or Mother Bethel AME Church. The websites of the African Episcopal Church of St. Thomas (http://www.aecst.org) and Mother Bethel AME Church (https://motherbethel.org) contain abundant information about their respective founders.

► Visit the museum at Mother Bethel Church to learn more about Allen, Mother Bethel, and the AME denomination. While you're there, see the statue of Richard Allen in the parking lot and the historical markers outside for the Mother Bethel Church and the Free African Society.

► See the Richard Allen mural at Thirty-eighth and Market Streets.

► Watch "Fever (1793–1820)," part of the *Philadelphia: The Great Experiment* series produced by History Making Productions, at https://www.youtube.com/watch?v=P7L5olIfYcI&t=121s.

► View *Richard Allen: Apostle of Freedom*, a seven-minute biographical film available at https://www.youtube.com/watch?v=9Zd-PuQZVFE&t=1s.

▶ Explore the Library Company of Philadelphia's "Black Founders: The Free Black Community in the Early Republic" online exhibition at https://librarycompany.org/blackfounders.

▶ Learn more about the Colored Conventions project at https://coloredconventions.org and visit the twin murals at the Courtyard Apartments at 315 and 351 Washington Avenue.

▶ See the historical marker at Bethel Burial Ground that was installed in 2019 and check on the progress of the Bethel Burial Ground memorial.

▶ Follow the ongoing research about the Bethel Burial Ground Project at the website maintained by Terry Buckalew (https://bethelburyinggroundproject.com).

▶ Learn more about the Bethel Burying Ground Memorial Project at the Office of Arts, Culture and the Creative Economy's website (http://www.creativephl.org/public-art/bethel-burying-ground).

▶ Visit the Richard Allen Lane Station and see the two panels on Cresheim Street describing his life and the history of the AME religion.

5

THE PRESIDENT'S HOUSE MEMORIAL

P.S. George Washington Slept Here

[With a Reflection by Michael Coard]

In 1790, the national capital moved from New York City to Philadelphia. Robert Morris, a financier of the American Revolution, offered his home at Sixth and Market streets as the Executive Mansion.[1] Morris's wealth was accumulated in part through his involvement in the slave trade, and most of the house's previous residents (including Benedict Arnold) had been owners of enslaved people. Although Morris's home was one of the largest in the city, President Washington expanded it even further to accommodate his household, which included First Lady Martha Washington, two grandchildren, five office staff, and twenty-four "servants." Washington did not use the term *slave*; nonetheless, nine enslaved people worked and slept in Washington's Philadelphia residence.

It is widely known that our first president owned enslaved people. Mount Vernon relied on the labor of hundreds of people in bondage. Enslaving people in Philadelphia, however, was a different matter. It was not merely an immoral act. By 1790, it was also a crime.

---

1. Portions of this chapter appeared as the article "A History of Slavery: President's House Monument Turns 10," *Hidden City Philadelphia*, December 17, 2020, https://hidden cityphila.org/2020/12/a-history-of-slavery-presidents-house-monument-turns-10.

Presidential Scofflaw

When the Washingtons moved to Philadelphia, Pennsylvania's Gradual Abolition Act was ten years old. According to this law, enslaved people brought from out of state were to be freed after six months. Owners of the enslaved skirted this stipulation by sending their human property across state lines just as the six-month mark was approaching and then starting the clock over again upon their return to Pennsylvania. In 1788, the state legislature closed this loophole, stating explicitly that "all and every slave and slaves who shall be brought into this state, by persons inhabiting or residing therein, or intending to inhabit or reside therein, shall be immediately considered, deemed and taken to be free, to all intents and purposes."

President Washington flagrantly violated both the spirit of the 1780 law and the letter of the 1788 amendment. He claimed that he was still a resident of Virginia and made sure that neither he nor any of the people he enslaved stayed in Pennsylvania for more than six months in a row. In 1791, the Pennsylvania General Assembly considered a bill that would allow all federal officials to own enslaved people as a means of promoting Philadelphia as the nation's permanent capital. The bill was rejected.

George Washington signed the Fugitive Slave Act in 1793, almost certainly with several enslaved people close at hand. The U.S. Constitution, written at Independence Hall, just a short distance from the President's House, required free states to return freedom seekers from slave states. The law set up explicit procedures to make this happen. Any person, Black or white, assisting runaways would be punished. The Fugitive Slave Act guaranteed that people who escaped bondage would be fugitives for life; it also encouraged the kidnapping and sale of free Black people by unscrupulous slave catchers.

Nine Souls

Of the nine people enslaved at the President's House, we know the most about Ona Judge. She was born into slavery at Mount Vernon and served as Martha Washington's personal maid in both New York and Philadelphia. She was trusted by the Washingtons and was thus able to mingle with members of the burgeoning free Black community of Philadelphia when doing errands for the household. She joined Martha Washington on social calls and shopping trips; Judge even attended the circus.

When Ona Judge learned she was to be given as a wedding gift to a temperamental granddaughter of Martha Washington, she fled the President's House at twenty-two with the help of the free Blacks she had befriended. Aboard Captain John Bowles's sloop *Nancy*, Judge escaped to Portsmouth, New Hampshire, where she lived the rest of her life out of bondage yet never officially free. Washington was stung by this perceived betrayal, decrying "the ingratitude of the girl, who was brought up & treated more like a child than a servant" in a letter to Oliver Wolcott Jr. dated September 1, 1796. At one point, Judge told an intermediary that she would willingly return to the Washingtons if they guaranteed that she would be freed upon their deaths. They refused her request, fearing the example it would set for the other people they owned. George Washington continued to pursue Ona Judge until his death.

In 1845, Ona Judge, now seventy-two, was interviewed by Reverend Benjamin Chase, who described the encounter in a letter to the editor of the abolitionist newspaper *The Liberator*. She revealed that her life in Portsmouth had been difficult. Her husband had died only seven years after their marriage, and she could not afford to support her three children, two of whom predeceased her. Yet she never regretted fleeing her relatively comfortable enslavement in the Washington household for a life of poverty and toil in New Hampshire. "I am free," declared Ona, "and have, I trust, been made a child of God by the means."

Hercules Posey, an enslaved chef whom the Washingtons brought from Mount Vernon to Philadelphia, also successfully escaped from the first president's household. As with Ona Judge, the flight of Hercules enraged Washington, who believed that his chef had been treated well. Posey was allowed to sell leftovers and keep his earnings; the Washingtons agreed to bring his son to Philadelphia to help in the kitchen. After returning to Mount Vernon in 1797, however, Posey took off. Perhaps his exposure to Philadelphia's free Black community inspired him to take the enormous risk of liberating himself from so powerful an owner.

We know less about the other enslaved residents of the President's House. And even our information about Ona Judge and Hercules Posey comes—apart from Judge's late-in-life interview—through the eyes of white people. Official government documents, personal correspondence, and visitors' accounts of their time at the Washingtons' Philadelphia residence give us snippets of information to piece together an understanding of the lives of the enslaved.

Even living under the same roof as the president of the United States did not alter the basic, wretched facts of slavery. Austin, the half-brother of Ona Judge, died in his early thirties after falling off a horse in 1794. Giles, a wagon driver, sustained an injury in 1791 that also led to an early death. Paris, who misbehaved on a tour of the southern United States, was not allowed to return to Philadelphia. While still in his twenties, he took ill at Mount Vernon and died in 1794.

History Forgotten

When Washington left office in 1797, John Adams became the next resident of the President's House. Adams and his son John Quincy Adams were the only two of the first twelve U.S. presidents who did not own enslaved people. Although the national capital was supposed to move to the banks of the Potomac, leaders in Pennsylvania tried mightily to keep the capital in Philadelphia. A mansion three times the size of the President's House was constructed on Ninth Street as a luxurious abode for the nation's chief executive. Adams, however, could not be enticed to decamp to this grand residence, even when the city doubled the rent on the President's House to force the move. In December 1800, Adams became the first president to inhabit the White House in Washington, DC.

The Philadelphia President's House was sold and initially became a hotel. As the surrounding area became increasingly commercial, the once elegant dwelling was gutted and converted into three stores on the ground level, with a boardinghouse on the floors above. Although the façade of the building was significantly altered, some of the original walls were still in place until 1951 when the entire structure, along with hundreds of other long-standing buildings, was demolished to make room for Independence Mall, a vast lawn on the blocks north of Independence Hall. A public restroom was built on the President's House site. A small plaque indicated that the toilet facility sat atop the former home of presidents.

A Jarring Juxtaposition

In late 2000, an archeological dig on Independence Mall revealed that a proposed new home for the Liberty Bell, a symbol long associated with freedom, overlapped some of the outbuildings of the President's House. By January 2002, construction of the Liberty Bell Center was well underway when a bombshell revelation about the location of the new structure came out in the winter issue of the *Pennsylvania Magazine of History and Biography*. An article by the independent historian Edward Lawler, "The President's House in Philadelphia: The Rediscovery of a Lost Landmark," meticulously presented information about the architecture and appearance of the President's House. Among his findings, "The last thing that a visitor will walk across or pass before entering the Liberty Bell Center will be the slave quarters that George Washington ordered added to the President's House."

Spurred on by Lawler's article, the historian Gary Nash contacted the Independence National Historical Park (INHP) to see how the story of the President's House and its enslaved residents would be told in the new Liberty Bell Center. Nash was told that interpretive plans were nearly complete and that the permanent Liberty Bell exhibition would focus squarely on the history and lore of the beloved American symbol. By 2002, however, the INHP's simplistic and celebratory approach had become anachronistic. Local historians were outraged by the INHP's plans and banded together as the Ad Hoc Historians. They were able to garner the interest and outrage of the public. Nash spoke about the issue on a radio talk show, and several articles and op-eds appeared in the *Philadelphia Inquirer*. The consensus among engaged city residents was clear: twenty-first-century Philadelphians were ready to wrestle with the complexities of freedom and slavery existing side by side.

Under pressure, the INHP's leadership agreed to negotiate the interpretation plan for the Liberty Bell Center. In spite of their initial reluctance, INHP officials, in consultation with members of the Ad Hoc Historians, reworked the center's entire interpretation plan. New descriptive material was written to challenge visitors to contemplate the ways in which the lack of freedom for some was interwoven in the fabric of the nation.

A Memorial to the Enslaved

Once agreement between historians and the INHP leaders was reached regarding the Liberty Bell Center, attention turned to the President's House site. Grassroots activism by Black Philadelphians was central to this next phase. On July 3, 2002, hundreds of African Americans gathered at the Liberty Bell Center to demand a monument to Washington's slaves. The Avenging the Ancestors Coalition (ATAC), led by the attorney Michael Coard, organized a petition drive and a letter-writing campaign with this same objective. Charles Blockson and other Black historians supported these efforts. Chaka Fattah, a Black member of the U.S. Congress, spearheaded legislation to appropriate funds for the National Park Service (NPS) to develop a plan to commemorate the President's House and its enslaved residents.

Developing and funding a plan for an entirely new memorial on NPS land was a more complex challenge than rewriting exhibition text for the Liberty Bell Center. An initial design for the President's House Memorial was presented by the NPS at a public meeting at the African American Museum of Philadelphia in January 2003. Members of the Black community had not felt included in the design process, and the slave quarters were not included in the plans. The design was rejected, and turbulent consultations with historians ensued. A public forum on the President's House organized by the INHP attracted hundreds of participants. Annual July 3 gatherings continued, keeping the issue in the public eye and building the membership and visibility of ATAC.

In the meantime, Philadelphia's Mayor John Street pledged $1.5 million to the President's House Memorial at the opening of the Liberty Bell Center in October 2003. In September 2005, Representatives Chaka Fattah and Bob Brady secured a federal grant of $3.6 million for the project. In February 2007, the Black-led architectural firm Kelly/Maiello was selected, this time with public input, to design the President's House site. Mayor Michael Nutter's administration raised additional funds, and in 2009 the Delaware River Port Authority contributed $3.5 million. The first slavery memorial on federal property was on track to be built in Philadelphia.

A Meaningful "Jumble of Bricks"

Finally, on a bitterly cold December morning in 2010, The President's House: Freedom and Slavery in the Making of a New Nation was dedicated. Emanuel Kelly's innovative, open-air monument broadly represents the structure and dimensions of the President's House. Historical reenactments are displayed on video monitors perched on brick walls above faux fireplaces. Actors playing Ona Judge, Hercules Posey, and Richard Allen, as well as George Washington and John Adams, are

The President's House: Freedom and Slavery in the Making of a New Nation—the memorial was dedicated in 2010. (Photograph by Michael Bixler, Hidden City)

featured in the vignettes. A granite wall lists the name of each person enslaved at the President's House. Explanatory panels describe topics such as the archaeology of the site, the emergence of Philadelphia's free Black community, George Washington's meetings with Indian leaders, John Adams's signing of the Alien and Sedition Acts, and conditions of slavery at the President's House and elsewhere. Colorful drawings illustrate some of this information. A set of bronze footsteps set in concrete represent Ona Judge's flight to freedom. A plexiglass vitrine leaves part of the archaeological excavation visible.

Critics panned the new monument's form and content. Inga Saffron, writing for the *Philadelphia Inquirer*, called it "a confused jumble of bricks." Edward Rothstein of the *New York Times* described it as "lacking both intellectual coherence and emotional power." In the *Pennsylvania Magazine of History and Biography*, Steven Conn wrote of the video monitors mounted on chimney walls, "Rather than evoke one of the grandest houses in eighteenth-century Philadelphia, these make the place feel . . . more like twenty-first century McMansions." *Commentary Magazine* published a review by the *Wall Street Journal*'s architecture critic Michael Lewis, who found the monument characterized by "one-sided tendentiousness"; he described it as "misguided in execution and offensive in its omissions." Lewis concluded, "It should be dismantled . . . and the site rebuilt from scratch." In addition, in the first months after the memorial's dedication, the video screens malfunctioned frequently, and the vitrine exposing the archaeological dig leaked.

But even the critics—at least, the less ideologically driven among them—acknowledged the challenge of telling so many competing stories in a relatively small space. Conn asserted, "It isn't that there is too much material crammed into too small a space, though that is probably true. More than that the material itself is enormous: slavery in the midst of freedom; the creation of a new nation and the patterns of governance that would distinguish presidents from kings; to say nothing of the history of the city itself at the end of eighteenth century, the extraordinary stories of these individuals, and more besides." As Saffron noted in her *Inquirer* review, "As the first federal site to acknowledge the congenital defect of slavery . . . the project's very existence is special. It's not until you are inside the space that you understand the memorial as a full-throated expression of pain and rage. Sure, Washington's tenure there is virtually reduced to a footnote, but at least that story can be found in books. This is the rare memorial where history's collisions can be experienced firsthand."

The President's House monument neatly fits the description of at least one constituency involved in the memorial's planning. The Avenging the Ancestors Coalition sought a design that was a "culturally-dignified, historically-complete, prominently-conspicuous, physically-dramatic, formally-official, and timely-installed commemoration on the grounds of the President's House to honor, primarily, the nine enslaved African descendants." Though some would argue that "historically-complete" is too high a bar, The President's House: Freedom and Slavery in the Making of a New Nation otherwise fulfills ATAC's criteria beautifully.

Love it or hate it, the President's House Memorial is a manifestation of a sea change in how Black history is represented in Philadelphia. In 2002, leaders of the INHP sought to maintain the fiction of heroic Founding Fathers creating a glorious nation characterized by "liberty and justice for all." They eschewed input from academics and the general public. Over the course of less than a decade, however, the orientation of the NPS changed dramatically. The history presented to locals and tourists, at the President's House Memorial and elsewhere, has become significantly more challenging, more complex, and more inclusive. Adjacent to the Liberty Bell Center—where officials once resisted in-

The attorney and activist Michael Coard speaking on the anniversary of the President's House memorial, December 15, 2022. (Photograph by Amy Jane Cohen)

cluding information about slavery—sits an entire structure whose purpose is to make visitors contemplate the people whose bondage helped to build our country.

Reflection

Michael Coard is a defense attorney, radio host, columnist, educator, and activist. As the leader of the Avenging the Ancestors Coalition, he was instrumental in the reimagining of the President's House site.

Thanks to eight consecutive years, from 2002 to 2010, of instigating agitation and relentless activism of a grassroots organization called ATAC (of which I am a proud founding member), and thanks to the initial funding and governmental leadership of Mayor John Street; the powerful influence, persuasive assistance, and financial assistance of Congressmen Chaka Fattah and Bob Brady; and the surprising open-mindedness and "woke" collaboration of the Independence National Historical Park, history was made on December 15, 2010.

The spectacular slavery memorial, designed by a Black-owned Philadelphia architectural firm, consists of a massive open-air, 24/7/365-accessible permanent exhibition with several motion-activated television monitors displaying reenactors in the roles of the enslaved; a lengthy story wall explaining the history of the site; a large vitrine allowing viewers to look at the actual foundation of part of the house untouched since our enslaved ancestors and Washington resided there in the late eighteenth century; and a "slave quarters" area just about ten feet away from the main entrance to the new Liberty Bell Center. Think about that ten-foot proximity for a minute. As you enter this heaven of liberty—the Liberty Bell Center—you literally have to cross the hell of slavery: the "Slave Quarters." If that's not the height of historical hypocrisy, nothing is.

The nine Black men, women, and children enslaved by Washington in Philadelphia were just that—men, women, and children. They had hopes. They had dreams. They had aspirations. They weren't mere "slaves." Instead, they were enslaved human beings.

America's psychotic desire to, at worst, enslave Blacks or, at the very least, hold Blacks down in a condition of slavery-like servitude didn't end in 1865 with the passage of the Thirteenth Amendment, and it didn't end in 2010 with the installation of the Slavery Memorial at America's first "White House." That psychotic desire is also evidenced, as the Brennan Center for Justice at New York University Law School points out, by the fact that "between January 1 and July 14, 2021 more than four hundred bills that included provisions that restrict voting access have been introduced in forty-nine states. And during that same time, eighteen states have already enacted thirty laws that make it harder for people to vote."

By "bills," the Brennan Center obviously means the legislative initiatives of racist Republican state senators and representatives. And by "people," the Brennan Center obviously means Black people.

So what's the solution to America's psychotic, historic, and relentless racism? Well, first, visit the Slavery Memorial and pour libation. But if you're unable to physically go there, go there spiritually and acknowledge those nine enslaved ancestors from your home on that day and pour libation.

Second (and forever): "Never forget. Always avenge."

To Do

▶ Visit Independence National Historical Park to tour the President's House Memorial, the Liberty Bell Center, Independence Hall, and other attractions. The Deshler-Morris House in Germantown is also part of the INHP; it is sometimes called the Germantown White House because the Washingtons stayed there in the summers of 1793 and 1794.

▶ Read Erica Armstrong Dunbar's National Book Award–winning *Never Caught: The Washingtons' Relentless Pursuit of Their Runaway Slave, Ona Judge* (2017). There is also a young readers' edition by Dunbar and Kathy Van Cleve entitled, *Never Caught, the Story of Ona Judge: George and Martha Washington's Courageous Slave Who Dared to Run Away* (2019).

▶ Watch a five-minute clip from the opening of the documentary *Sisters in Freedom*, which tells the story of Ona Judge, at https://www.historymakingproductions.com/sistersinfreedom-1.

▶ Watch the nine-minute video *Ona Judge Virtual "Walking" Tour* on the Museum of the American Revolution's website (https://www.amrevmuseum.org/ona-judge-virtual-walking-tour).

▶ Visit the website https://www.ushistory.org/presidentshouse to learn more about the President's House and the President's House Memorial.

▶ Visit Historic Strawberry Mansion in East Fairmount Park, a summer home built by Judge John Lewis, a lead author of the Gradual Abolition Act of 1780.

PART II

Nineteenth Century

6

PENNSYLVANIA HALL

City of Brotherly Love?

In 1838, the growing conflict over slavery erupted in Philadelphia in a dramatic conflagration that shocked the nation.[1] This astonishing chapter in our city's history, however, has largely been forgotten and is barely recognized in our current landscape.

A Sisterhood of Abolition

As residents of the Quaker City, many of us know that our town was a hub of abolitionist organizing and a busy station on the Underground Railroad. The Pennsylvania Abolition Society, founded in 1775, is the oldest such organization in the country. The American Anti-Slavery Society was established here in 1833. When women were forbidden to join, they formed the Philadelphia Female Anti-Slavery Society (PFASS), an interracial abolitionist group.

Although Lucretia Mott may be the best-known member of the PFASS, several notable Black women were also founders and leaders of the group. The Forten family was the wealthiest Black family in Phila-

---

1. Portions of this chapter appeared as "Bigotry in the Quaker City and the Burning of Pennsylvania Hall," *Hidden City Philadelphia*, March 16, 2020, https://hiddencityphila.org/2020/03/bigotry-in-the-quaker-city-and-the-burning-of-pennsylvania-hall.

delphia in the early nineteenth century. The Revolutionary War veteran and sailmaker James Forten and his wife, Charlotte, had three daughters: Margaretta Forten, Harriet Forten Purvis, and Sarah Forten Purvis. All four of the Forten women were founders, generous funders, and active members of the PFASS.

Grace Bustill Douglass, the daughter of a prominent baker and herself a milliner, was a founding member of PFASS and served as the group's vice president. Her daughter, Sarah Mapps Douglass, was also an original member. Sarah Mapps Douglass went on to found and lead a school for Black girls and became the first Black woman to attend the Female Medical College of Pennsylvania. Both mother and daughter were frequent speakers at national abolitionist conventions and dedicated their lives to ending slavery and improving the lives of Black people.

Another Side of Philadelphia

Although Philadelphia comfortably associates itself with the history of abolition, the city was also a hotbed of pro-slavery sentiment. As the first big city north of the Mason-Dixon Line, Philadelphia had well-established social ties to the South. Its medical schools trained southern doctors. Philadelphia elites mixed with southern gentry in Cape May and at other tony resorts. As the city industrialized, owners of textile mills grew rich by selling items manufactured with southern cotton. Many Philadelphians feared that abolitionists would divide the country over the issue of slavery. In 1835, a white mob dumped abolitionist literature into the Delaware River as the city's mayor stood by.

Along with pro-slavery sentiment, anti-Black racism grew throughout the 1830s. Members of the growing Irish immigrant community vied with Blacks for unskilled jobs and feared that the end of slavery would lead to increased competition. Poor whites resented the small but significant Black middle class who had attained economic security in spite of anti-Black racism. As Philadelphia attracted increasing numbers of free Blacks, rioting and destruction of Black homes and institutions increased.

Anti-abolitionist feeling had become so strong in the city that by the early 1830s, antislavery groups faced difficulty even finding places to meet. A coalition of these organizations decided that the best solution was to build their own venue. The Pennsylvania Hall Association raised $40,000 (more than $1 million today) fairly quickly by selling shares at

An 1838 lithograph of Pennsylvania Hall before it was burned down by a pro-slavery mob. (Library Company of Philadelphia)

$20 apiece. The women of the PFASS were instrumental in this fund-raising effort, which made it possible to build a grand three-story building on the west side of Sixth Street between Arch and Race streets.

A Temple of Liberty

A late nineteenth-century history of suffrage written by Elizabeth Cady Stanton and Susan B. Anthony described Pennsylvania Hall as "one of the most commodious and splendid buildings in the city." It had polished woodwork, tall glass windows, and all the modern amenities. According to Stanton and Anthony, the hall was "scientifically ventilated and brilliantly lighted with gas." The first floor contained offices for antislavery organizations and the *Pennsylvania Freeman*, an abolitionist newspaper. There were conference rooms; reading rooms filled with antislavery literature; a bookstore; and a shop selling "free" produce, the term for food items made without enslaved labor. The second floor had a lecture room with three hundred seats.

The pièce de résistance of the so-called Temple of Liberty was the Grand Saloon, a large room that could accommodate three thousand people. Stanton and Anthony describe a platform with "superb chairs, sofas, and desks covered in blue silk damask; everything throughout the hall was artistic and complete." Above the dais were the words "Virtue, Liberty, and Independence" in large gold letters. It was the among the first buildings in the city to have gas lighting.

In May 1838, the second Anti-Slavery Convention of American Women was to be the newly finished building's inaugural event. Abolitionists from throughout the North gathered in Philadelphia. Adding to the excitement was the pre-convention wedding of two of the nation's most prominent abolitionists, Theodore Weld and Angelina Grimké. Originally from Charleston, South Carolina, Angelina and her sister Sarah had rejected their slave-owning family and became famous as persuasive orators in the fight against slavery. Before a mixed-race group of friends, and presided over by both a Black and a white minister, Weld and Grimké swore their devotion to each other using egalitarian language. Naturally, the wedding meal featured delectable fare made and served without slave labor. Although both Weld and Grimké were white, rumors spread that their union was interracial, stoking the anger of many Philadelphia residents.

A Time of Tension

The opening of Pennsylvania Hall took place during a period of conflict within the abolitionist movement over philosophy and tactics. Colonizationists advocated for an end to slavery followed by mass migration to Africa by the newly freed. Gradualists sought a protracted end to the hated institution to respect property rights and give time to prepare the enslaved for freedom. Others, led most notably by William Lloyd Garrison, called for an immediate and complete end to slavery; they also advocated for full rights for Black people and no compensation for the owners of enslaved people. The "immediatists" were viewed as radical, even by many of their fellow antislavery activists.

Abolitionist tactics were also up for debate. Some promoted "moral suasion," convincing the owners of enslaved people that their actions were wrong and sinful. The Great Postal Campaign of 1835, in which abolitionist literature was shipped in bulk to the South, exemplified the moral suasion approach. Others thought slavery could be ended only through political action and believed that running for office and circulating petitions were the most effective strategies.

In addition, there was much disagreement about the role of women.

Despite the significant contributions of women in raising funds for Pennsylvania Hall, some abolitionists thought it would be unseemly for women to speak in front of "promiscuous" audiences, as mixed-gender groups were called at the time. Thus, despite the cooperation needed to fund the construction of such a grand building, tensions within and among abolitionist organizations bubbled just below the surface.

Mob Action

Pennsylvania Hall's debut infuriated pro-slavery Philadelphians. The day after the convention got underway, posters appeared throughout the city stating:

> Whereas a convention for the avowed purpose of effecting the immediate abolition of slavery in the Union is now in session in this city, it behooves all citizens, who entertain a proper respect for the right of property, and the preservation of the Constitution of the United States, to interfere, forcibly if they must, and prevent the violation of these pledges, heretofore held sacred. We would therefore propose to all persons, so disposed, to assemble at the Pennsylvania Hall in 6th street, between Arch and Race, on to-morrow morning (Wednesday 16th May) at 11 o'clock, and demand the Immediate dispersion of said convention.
>
> Signed, Several Citizens

A crowd gathered as requested. They threw the odd rock or brick at the windows, jeered the abolitionists as they left the hall, and beat up a few of the departing Black attendees. The members of the overwhelmingly young, male crowd were not only opposed to the antislavery beliefs of the conventioneers. They were also galled by the spectacle of women speaking from a podium and, most of all, by "amalgamation," the social mixing of Blacks and whites.

By the convention's third day, tensions had built as the crowd around the hall grew larger and more aggressive. The newlywed Angelina Grimké Weld, whom the crowd mistakenly believed had just wed a Black man, took the stage as a steady barrage of rocks vibrated against the windows and the volume outside increased. The phrases "great noise" and "stones against the window" were repeated several times in the transcript of her fiery talk. Weld addressed the North's complicity with the slave system and recounted her eyewitness observations of the lives of the enslaved. "What if the mob should now burst in upon us, break up our meeting, and commit violence against our persons? Would this be anything compared with what the slaves endure?" she asked the increasingly nervous audience.

Undeterred by the roiling crowd outside, Weld spoke for more than an hour. As the audience departed, white women and Black women walked out arm in arm, hoping to prevent the crowd from targeting the Black women.

A Fateful Day

The next morning, the managers of Pennsylvania Hall met with Mayor John Swift to seek protection for the conventioneers. An accord was reached under which the managers would cancel the speeches scheduled for that night, and the mayor would address the increasingly volatile anti-abolitionist mob. Such trust did the managers put in Swift that they acceded to his request to turn over to him the keys to the building. Perhaps they should have realized that their trust was ill placed when he admonished them: "It is public opinion that makes mobs! And ninety-nine out of a hundred with whom I converse are against you!"

In the evening, Swift walked from his office at the State House (now called Independence Hall) two blocks north to Pennsylvania Hall. After locking the building, he addressed the crowd: "The Managers had the right to hold their meeting; but as good citizens they have, at my request, suspended their meeting for the evening. We never call out the military here! We do not need such measures. Indeed, I would, fellow citizens, look upon you as my police . . . , and I trust you will abide by the laws. And keep order. I now bid you farewell for the night!"

Thus, with a large pack of rabid foxes left in charge of the brand-new henhouse, Mayor Swift took his leave. Although the throngs that gathered the previous two nights had been composed mostly of young members of the laboring class, the crowd this night was different. It included men of means: merchants, professionals, and not a small number of southern enslavers.

Expecting that the mayor would turn a blind eye, the crowd became a mob intent on destruction. Dockworkers from the nearby Delaware

River post brought axes, crowbars, and wooden beams that were used as battering rams to knock down the doors so recently locked by the mayor. Streetlamps were extinguished to obscure the illegal activity. The contents of the reading room and bookstore provided effective kindling for fires set in the Grand Saloon. The gas lamps in the interior of Pennsylvania Hall intensified the flames. By the time Mayor Swift was alerted to the chaos and returned with his police force in tow, they were vastly outnumbered.

In a foreshadowing of the MOVE disaster nearly a century and a half later, the firemen on the scene turned their hoses away from the burning building, refusing to help extinguish the flames. Unlike the MOVE incident, however, the firemen did prevent the fire from spreading to neighboring buildings.[2] Pennsylvania Hall, opened only days earlier, was ruined. The mob, encouraged by its "victory," spent the next few days threatening and attacking Black homes, churches, and even an orphanage. A few men suspected of being the Pennsylvania Hall arsonists were arrested and quickly released.

The Aftermath

The police report on the incident put the blame firmly on the abolitionists themselves. It accused Pennsylvania Hall's managers of "openly promulgating and advocating in it *doctrines repulsive to the moral sense* of a large majority of our community." Elaborating on the nature of these morally repulsive doctrines, the report continues, "The mass of the community could *ill brook the erection* of an edifice in this city, for the *encouragement of practices believed* by many to be *subversive to the established orders of society*, and viewed by some as repugnant to that separation which it has pleased the great Author of nature to establish

---

2. In 1985, at the request of Philadelphia Police Department, a Pennsylvania State Police helicopter dropped a satchel full of explosives onto the home of the radical back-to-nature group MOVE on West Philadelphia's Osage Avenue. Eleven MOVE members were killed, including five children. Only two MOVE members survived. The Philadelphia Fire Department stood by as fire spread to sixty-one adjacent residences and destroyed more than two city blocks. No officials were ever held criminally responsible for the bombing and its aftermath, and the tragedy irrevocably stained the reputation of Philadelphia's first African American mayor, W. Wilson Goode. Thanks to a group of eighth-graders at the Jubilee School, a historical marker was placed on Cobbs Creek Parkway across from Osage Avenue in 2017.

among the various races of man." In other words, the abolitionists had violated God's plan for racial segregation.

Undeterred by the violence of 1838, the Anti-Slavery Convention of American Women returned to Philadelphia in 1839, this time gathering in a former horseback riding school. Mayor Swift asked attendees to avoid walking through the city in racially mixed groups. They did not honor his request.

The managers of Pennsylvania Hall left the charred remnants of the once grand building as a visual reminder of the mass hysteria, widespread intolerance, and government inaction that destroyed the "Temple of Liberty." Relics of the remains of Pennsylvania Hall were sold at antislavery fairs for years to come. In 1846, the managers sold the property to the Oddfellows, whose building remained on the site through the early twentieth century. Although no physical trace of the resplendent, short-lived Pennsylvania Hall remains, there is a historical marker at its Sixth Street location in front of the studios of the WHYY radio station.

Honoring the Sisters in Freedom

A better place to reflect on the legacy of the city's antislavery movement, particularly the movement's women, is at a Quaker graveyard. Murals depicting a group of the PFASS women and another mural showing a few key leaders are located on each side of an empty lot beside the Fair Hill cemetery, the final resting place of numerous abolitionist leaders, including the PFASS founders Lucretia Mott and Harriet Forten Purvis. Harriet's husband, Robert Purvis, is also buried at Fair Hill and depicted on one of the murals.

Although murals can easily be painted over or covered by an adjacent building project, the Fair Hill Burial Ground in its current form is a fitting place to honor the women of the PFASS. In one of the poorest neighborhoods of Philadelphia, an interracial coalition made up mostly of women has worked together since the 1990s to beautify the site, develop educational programs, establish gardens and libraries in surrounding schools, and advocate for neighborhood improvements. Like Pennsylvania Hall, Historic Fair Hill, Inc., illustrates how much can be accomplished when a diverse group of social justice activists, including a large contingent of women, combine their energy.

A portion of the Female Anti-Slavery Society mural depicting the burning of Pennsylvania Hall and members of the Philadelphia Female Anti-Slavery Society. The mural is across the street from the Fair Hill Burial Ground. (Photograph by Amy Jane Cohen)

To Do

► Explore the Historic Fair Hill website (https://historicfairhill .com) to learn more about the programs, mural tours, and special events coordinated by Historic Fair Hill, Inc.

► Visit the Fair Hill Burial Ground at 2901 Germantown Avenue.

► Watch "Disorder (1820–1854)," part of the *Philadelphia: The Great Experiment* series, at https://www.youtube.com/watch ?v=lTOUquhPKWc.

► Read *History of Pennsylvania Hall That Was Destroyed by a Mob on the 17th of May 1838*, by Samuel Webb. A digital copy is available online at https://www.books.google.com/books /about/History_of_Pennsylvania_Hall_which_was_D.html?id =J1E2AQAAMAAJ.

▶ Watch a ten-minute reenactment of the burning of Pennsylvania Hall from the documentary *Sisters in Freedom* at https://www.historymakingproductions.com/sistersinfreedom-1.

▶ See the Pennsylvania Hall historical marker at 150 North Sixth Street on Independence Mall and the nearby Philadelphia Female Anti-Slavery Society marker at North Fifth Street and Arch Street in front of the U.S. Mint.

7

A PANTHEON OF HEROES

Uncovering Philadelphia's Underground Railroad

[With a Reflection by Dr. Naomi Johnson Booker]

The Underground Railroad is one of very few topics in African American history that is guaranteed to be included in American history courses. This is not surprising: the Underground Railroad exemplifies Black-white cooperation and features exciting tales of daring escapes. It can be taught in a safe, comfortable way by white educators, even to elementary school students.

Although the Underground Railroad is likely familiar to most readers, Philadelphia's crucial role in the enterprise may not be. This clandestine network mainly of African Americans and Quakers helped about nine thousand fugitives as they stopped in Philadelphia, either to stay in the city permanently or, much more often, to flee farther north to New York, New England, or Canada. And although you have no doubt heard of Harriet Tubman, the Underground Railroad's most famous "conductor," you may not know of Robert Purvis, sometimes called the "President of the Underground Railroad." You also may never have heard of James Forten, William Whipper, William Still, or Stephen Smith.

Purvis, Forten, Whipper, Still, and Smith are on a long list of remarkable Philadelphia-based Black figures whose biographies astounded me when I began teaching African American history in 2005. Although I have lived in Philadelphia nearly all my life, and I have both a bachelor's and a master's degree in history, their names were new to me. I use their stories as a means of illuminating Philadelphia's role in the

Underground Railroad, not only because of their centrality to the Underground Railroad, but also because during their long lives they intersected with so many other important people, events, and institutions in nineteenth-century Philadelphia.

Robert Purvis

Dido Badaracka, Robert Purvis's maternal grandmother, was kidnapped in Morocco around 1766 and sold into slavery in Charleston, South Carolina. After nine years in bondage, Badaracka was freed upon the death of her owner. According to Purvis, his grandmother then married Baron Judah, a Jewish merchant. Purvis's mother, Harriet Judah, was their third child. Harriet married William Purvis, a prosperous English-born merchant and cotton dealer. The second of their three sons, Robert, was born in Charleston in 1810. Robert was close to his grandmother, and she encouraged him to take pride in his African roots. Though only one-quarter Black and appearing white to many observers, Purvis identified as a Black man for his entire life. In spite of his involvement in the cotton trade, William Purvis despised slavery and instilled antislavery beliefs in his sons.

The family moved to Philadelphia in 1819, and the Purvis boys attended the Clarkson School, run by the Pennsylvania Abolition Society. When his father died in 1826, Robert Purvis inherited a substantial fortune. After completing his education in Massachusetts, he returned to Philadelphia and invested money in real estate and small businesses. Two of Philadelphia's wealthiest Black men—the sailmaker James Forten and the lumber merchant William Whipper—were mentors to Purvis. He joined Forten and Whipper in criticizing the colonization movement that aimed to move free Black people to Africa.

In 1831, Robert Purvis married James Forten's daughter, Harriet. Robert and Harriet Forten Purvis were a formidable couple and, eventually, were parents to eight children. Together and separately they were active in a wide array of antislavery and other human rights causes. Soon after marrying, they began hiding freedom seekers in their Lombard Street home. When the need arose, runaways went through a trapdoor to a hidden basement beneath the Purvis children's in-home schoolroom. Throughout the 1830s, increasing numbers of runaways fled to Philadelphia. Robert Purvis, along with his father-in-law, James Forten, founded the Vigilance Association in 1837 to assist these freedom seekers. Dues-

Photograph of Robert Purvis, ca. 1840s.
(Print Department Collection, Boston Public Library)

paying members of the association elected a Vigilant Committee (also known as a Vigilance Committee) that carried out their secretive work of hiding, clothing, feeding, and transporting fugitives.

The Vigilant Committee oversaw a local network of people willing to take great risks to aid freedom seekers. They arrived by boat, on foot, on horseback, and sometimes even on literal railroads. Young men were the most likely to flee enslavement, but women, the elderly, and children also took the risk to run away. Most fugitives were hidden in the homes of Black families. Churches such as Mother Bethel were also frequent "stations" on the Philadelphia section of the Underground Railroad. "Conductors" led fugitives from station to station. Black and white women worked together to sew clothing for the freedom seekers. A network of barbers and dressmakers helped to disguise the runaways as they continued their flights to freedom. As a wealthy man, Purvis was an important "stockholder," or financial supporter, of the Underground Railroad in addition to frequently opening his home as a place of refuge.

Robert Purvis was also a founding member and officer of the Pennsylvania Anti-Slavery Society and the American Anti-Slavery Society; Harriet Forten Purvis was a founding member of the Pennsylvania Female Anti-Slavery Society. Naturally, they both attended the second Annual Convention of Anti-Slavery Women at Pennsylvania Hall in 1838. Given that they appeared to be an interracial couple, their presence outraged the assembled pro-slavery mob when Robert helped Harriet out of their carriage, and they entered the building arm in arm.

Earlier that same year, the Pennsylvania legislature drafted a new state constitution stripping Black men of their voting rights. Purvis wrote an "Appeal of Forty Thousand Citizens, Threatened with Disenfranchisement, to the People of Pennsylvania" to convince the state's voters to vote down the new constitution. His words, however, failed to persuade his fellow Pennsylvanians that most Black people were tax-paying, law-abiding, hardworking contributors to society who deserved to keep the franchise. Black suffrage in Pennsylvania was not restored until decades later.

Purvis became president of the Vigilant Committee in 1839, and his Lombard Street home served as the unofficial headquarters of city's Underground Railroad during a time of escalating racial animosity. In 1841, Purvis wrote a letter to the *Public Ledger* newspaper objecting to a new property tax, given that the right to vote had been taken away from Black men. In response to the letter, a mob surrounded the Purvis home and burned a Black church nearby. The following year, a white mob attacked members of the Young Men's Vigilant Association as they paraded on Lombard Street near Mother Bethel Church in celebration of West Indian Emancipation Day. Three days of anti-Black rioting ensued. African Americans were beaten and killed; their homes were burned; their stores were looted; and a church was set on fire. The Purvis home was twice more surrounded with threatening mobs. Disheartened both by the action of the mob and the inaction of the police and white community leaders, the Purvis family left Lombard Street.

Initially, they resided in their country home north of the city, in Bensalem. Then Purvis bought a farm in Byberry Township (now part of Northeast Philadelphia) where the family lived for the next several decades. Called Harmony Hall, the Byberry farm became an important stop on the Underground Railroad, sheltering approximately one fugitive a day for nearly two decades. A secret room had been constructed in

Harmony Hall even before the Purvis family moved in. Although Robert's day-to-day leadership of the Vigilant Committee ended, the Purvis family continued to provide significant financial support to the Underground Railroad and to antislavery and human rights organizations. In addition to scores of runaways, the Purvises hosted the nation's leading abolitionists, including William Lloyd Garrison, Theodore and Angelina Grimké Weld, James and Lucretia Mott, and Frederick Douglass.

Robert and Harriet Purvis also purchased a nearby lot and constructed Byberry Hall, a community center that hosted abolition meetings and speakers on a variety of women's and civil rights causes. Robert had a deep understanding of intersectionality (the concept that people can be oppressed based on multiple aspects of identity such as race, class, and gender) long before the term was coined. When most Black men advocated for a Fifteenth Amendment extending the franchise only to men, Purvis declared he would "rather that his son never be enfranchised, unless his daughter could be also, as she bore the double curse of sex and color."

William Still

With Purvis ensconced at his Byberry estate, William Still emerged as the leader of the Philadelphia Vigilant Committee. Still, who was born free, had come to Philadelphia from New Jersey in 1844. Still's father had purchased his freedom; his mother had escaped slavery in Delaware but was forced to leave two of her children behind. Still was hired by the Pennsylvania Anti-Slavery Society, under Purvis's leadership, first as a janitor and later as a clerk. Part of his job involved greeting and interviewing freedom seekers from the South. During one of these encounters in 1850, he realized that he was interviewing one of his own older brothers who had been left behind decades earlier.

Still's leadership coincided with the terrifying years that followed the passage of the Fugitive Slave Act of 1850. The act required police and even civilians to assist in the capture of runaways. Philadelphia was no longer safe for runaways, who were compelled to travel farther north. Even longtime Black residents of the northern states were in jeopardy of being kidnapped by enslavers. The South Philadelphia home of William Still and his wife, Letitia, sheltered many freedom seekers along their route farther north or to Canada. Some of the runaways who showed up on the Stills' doorstep were brought there by Harriet Tubman, a close associate of Still.

Among those sheltered by the Stills were Jane Johnson and her two sons. William Still and the white abolitionist Passmore Williamson, with the aid of Black dockworkers, helped Johnson to escape from her owner, who had intended to take her and her children with him to Nicaragua. Both Still and Williamson were imprisoned for their actions, garnering much sympathy for the cause of abolition. Another famous runaway assisted by Still was Henry "Box" Brown, who mailed himself from Richmond, Virginia, to Philadelphia in a wooden crate and then made a career of telling his story. Between 1853 and 1861, Still assisted approximately one thousand freedom seekers.

Still earned the moniker "Father of the Underground Railroad" for his work helping runaways and recording their stories. After the chance encounter with his long-lost brother, he began writing down key details about runaways in case it could help to reunite families. Knowing that recording this information put him, and others, at great risk, Still hid the records at Lebanon Cemetery, a Black burial ground located near present-day Nineteenth Street and Snyder Avenue in South Philadelphia.[1] After the Civil War and while running a successful coal business, Still turned his secret records into a book, *The Underground Rail Road*, which was published in 1872 and helped reunite many families. Still's nearly eight hundred-page book is the single best source of information about the eastern branch of the Underground Railroad. It is the only firsthand account written by a Black participant in the Underground Railroad, and it emphasizes the key role played by African Americans in helping their courageous brethren to flee enslavement.

William Whipper and Stephen Smith

Among the African Americans who participated in the Underground Railroad were Purvis's friend and mentor William Whipper and his business partner, Stephen Smith. They were highly successful lumber merchants with residences in both Philadelphia and Columbia, Pennsylvania. From the late 1840s through the beginning of the Civil War, Whipper and Smith provided substantial financial support to the Underground

---

1. Lebanon Cemetery closed in 1903, and remains were moved to Eden Cemetery in Collingdale, Pennsylvania. Opened in 1902, Eden Cemetery is the oldest ongoing Black-owned cemetery in the United States. People mentioned in this book who are buried there include Absalom Jones, James Forten, William Still, Frances E. W. Harper, Octavius Catto, Caroline Le Count, Julian Abele, and Marian Anderson.

The Belmont Mansion, ca. 1870. The house was completed for the Peters family around 1751; later served as a stop along the Underground Railroad; and became part of Fairmount Park in 1869. The Belmont Mansion now houses the Underground Railroad Museum. (Library Company of Philadelphia)

Railroad. During this same period, they helped freedom seekers hide in the false end of boxcars carrying their merchandise on the Columbia-Philadelphia Railroad. When the train reached the Belmont Plateau, the escapees would get off before the boxcar was lowered onto an inclined plane to cross the Schuylkill River Bridge. They would be greeted by a "conductor" who would escort them to the nearby Belmont Mansion, where the wealthy Peters family provided temporary shelter. Whipper and Smith did not keep precise records of those they assisted, but late in life Whipper wrote to William Still recollecting the people that he and Smith had hidden: "On their arrival they were generally hungry and penniless. I have received hundreds in this condition; fed and sheltered from one to seventeen at a time in a single night." Whipper's letter is included in William Still's *The Underground Rail Road.*

The Underground Railroad in the Philadelphia Landscape

Although the Underground Railroad was meant to be invisible, it is possible to find traces of its existence in current day Philadelphia. The Belmont Mansion is home to an Underground Railroad Museum run by the American Women's Heritage Society, an African American organization dedicated to preserving the site and telling the story of the Underground Railroad and the role of the Peters family in the abolition movement. The Johnson House in Germantown was owned by a family of Quaker abolitionists and became a frequent stop on the Underground Railroad. William Still attended meetings at the house. A historical marker was erected in front of the house in 1995, and two years later the Johnson House was named a National Historic Landmark.

William Whipper and Stephen Smith owned adjoining houses at 919 and 921 Lombard Street. A historical marker honoring William Whipper sits in front of 919 Lombard Street, and both structures were recently added to the Philadelphia Register of Historic Places. A historical marker honoring Stephen Smith was erected at 1050 Belmont Avenue in 1991, at the site of the former Stephen Smith Home for the Aged, of which he was the major benefactor.

A 1992 historical marker for Robert Purvis sits before a house on the corner of Sixteenth and Mount Vernon streets in the Spring Garden section of the city. The brick townhouse has spent decades alternately deteriorating due to owner neglect and being restored thanks to the efforts of local residents who value its connection to Purvis. This house is where he lived following the death of Harriet after forty-four years of marriage. Purvis resided there with his second wife, Tacie Townsend, from 1878 until his death at eighty-eight in 1898. The Purvis home in Byberry is gone, but Byberry Hall, the meeting place constructed by Robert and Harriet, still stands and is one of very few African American history sites in Northeast Philadelphia.

A historical marker for William Still was installed on Twelfth Street south of Locust Street in 1991. Although the marker sits in front of a Georgian-style brick townhouse at 246 South Twelfth Street, Still actually lived at 244 South Twelfth Street, which is now a modern townhome. Another house where Still and his wife lived and hid fugitives was recently rediscovered at 625 South Delphi Street, in the Bella Vista section of South Philadelphia. Records indicate that William and Letitia Still lived on what was then called Ronaldson Street from 1850 to 1855. It wasn't until the historian James Duffin came across an advertisement for Letitia Still's dressmaking business in an 1851 newspaper that the precise address was known. Still's records indicate that Harriet Tubman delivered fugitives to the house and that hundreds of runaways were hidden there.[2] The house was added to the Philadelphia Register of Historic Places in 2018, thanks to the efforts of local preservationists.

---

2. In January 2022, a statue entitled *Harriet Tubman: The Journey to Freedom* was installed temporarily on the north side of City Hall. The sculpture proved so popular that city officials announced that plans are underway for a permanent Harriet Tubman monument for the site.

Student Voice

Philadelphia and the surrounding area host many markers related to the Underground Railroad. This is due, in part, to the relatively uncontroversial nature of the topic. In addition, Charles Blockson, the author of a large group of marker nominations in the early 1990s, is an Underground Railroad expert and successfully proposed numerous historical markers on the topic.

In 2003, I used these markers as a teaching tool in an Underground Railroad unit in a history of Philadelphia course for high school seniors. After studying the Underground Railroad, we moved on to an exploration of the many racial and religious riots that took place in antebellum Philadelphia. One day in class I mused out loud, "I wonder why there are so many historical markers related to the Underground Railroad and none about all of these riots?" Fortunately, one of the students took the bait and declared, "We should apply for a historical marker about a riot." They did. It was accepted, and in fall 2005 a historical marker was installed on the southeastern corner of Sixth and Lombard commemorating an 1842 anti-Black riot—the event that led the Purvis family to leave Lombard Street and move to the country.

Perhaps we will one day reach a point where school curricula and historic sites reflect not just the interracial cooperation and heroics of the Underground Railroad but also some of the uglier aspects of our national history.

Reflection

Dr. Naomi Johnson Booker is the founder and chief executive officer of the Global Leadership Academy charter schools.

In 1986, Audrey Johnson Thornton, a Philadelphia living legend, visited a historic house in West Fairmount Park. The house had been slated to be demolished by the City of Philadelphia. A true woman of achievement, Audrey Johnson Thornton served as president, chairperson, director, and member of countless civic, community, and political organizations. However, there was never a place where these organizations could meet and call home. Most were meeting in one another's homes. She saved the Belmont Mansion from extinction in 1986 so it could be the vision she wanted: a place for African American organizations to meet and cherish as a landmark in African American history. She researched and restored the house as a national landmark and was the founder of the American Women's Heritage Society, the first women's organization to become stewards of a historical landmark. They managed the Belmont Mansion, the "Crown Jewel of Fairmount Park," for more than thirty years. Thornton also published the book *The Crown Jewel of Fairmount Park: Belmont Mansion*, chronicling three hundred years of history of the Belmont Mansion and its direct association with the antislavery movement and the Underground Railroad. Belmont Mansion has been identified as a National Underground Railroad Site.

In 2021, the Philadelphia City Council named the street that the Belmont Mansion is on Audrey Johnson Thornton Way. The Belmont Mansion stands as an icon with a museum that shares the history of the Peters family, who built it. Thousands of people have visited the Belmont Mansion Museum nationally and internationally. We must keep this icon alive so that our American and African American history can continue to be taught and shared. To that end, I have also dedicated my life, as Audrey Johnson Thornton's daughter, to making sure that her legacy continues by serving as president of the American Women's Heritage Society.

Audrey Johnson Thornton became an ancestor in 2019 at ninety-three.

To Do

▶ Visit the Underground Railroad Museum at Belmont Mansion in Fairmount Park and the Johnson House Historic Site in Germantown to learn more about how the Underground Railroad functioned in this region.

▶ See Byberry Hall, constructed by Robert and Harriet Purvis in 1846. You can also visit the Byberry Meetinghouse (1808) and Byberry Schoolhouse (1823) at 3001 Byberry Road in Northeast Philadelphia. An exhibition of eighteenth- and nineteenth-century books is housed on the second floor of the schoolhouse.

▶ Read *The Price of a Child* (1995), by the Philadelphia author Lorene Carey, a fictional account of the events surrounding the rescue of Jane Johnson.

▶ Walk along the Lombard Street corridor to see the Whipper and Smith homes and the historical marker for the 1842 riot. See the William Still marker on Twelfth Street.

▶ See the Colored Conventions mural at 315 and 351 Washington Avenue (as described in Chapter 4). William Still and William Whipper are both depicted, as is Frances Ellen Watkins Harper, Still's close friend. Harper was a poet, novelist, orator, and antislavery activist. Her home and historical marker are located at 1006 Bainbridge Street.

▶ Watch the film *Harriet* (2019) about Harriet Tubman, which features the Philadelphia native Leslie Odom Jr. as William Still.

▶ Read William Still's *The Underground Railroad*. The version available at https://www.gutenberg.org/files/15263/15263 -h/15263-h.htm has hyperlinks that enable you to easily move among different sections of the book.

▶ See the 2006 *Harriet Tubman and the Underground Railroad* mural on Germantown Avenue, across from Fair Hill Burial Ground. In addition to Tubman, the mural features Robert Purvis, William Still, and Henry "Box" Brown. Tubman is also depicted in *Breaking Chains*, a mural at 500 South Fifty-second Street in West Philadelphia.[3]

▶ Learn more about the remarkable careers of Robert Purvis, James Forten, Harriet Forten Purvis, William Still, William Whipper, and Stephen Smith. This chapter focuses on their role in the Underground Railroad. They were also active in the founding and leading of numerous other Black organizations, including the American Moral Reform Society, temperance groups, literary clubs, libraries, Colored Conventions, and many more.

---

3. A seventy-foot mural of Tubman on Ninth and Chestnut streets was demolished in 2002 to make way for a parking lot.

8

OCTAVIUS CATTO AND A QUEST FOR PARITY

A Monumental Statement

In the late morning of September 2017, hundreds of people gathered on the south side of Philadelphia's City Hall. The crowd was young and old, Black and white, and included school groups, extended families, curious city residents, local politicians, and a group of African American Elks. A band played; prominent people spoke from a podium. Finally, the big moment arrived. Mayor Jim Kenney and the sculptor Branly Cadet removed a draping black cloth, revealing the larger-than-life bronze figure of a Black man. The crowd cheered; some wept.

The unveiling of the statue of Octavius Valentine Catto was the culmination of a fourteen-year effort by Mayor Kenney and other civic and grassroots leaders. Catto's bronze likeness was the first on public land in Philadelphia to honor the life of an African American individual. Just months after participants in the Unite the Right rally in Charlottesville, Virginia, protested the removal of Confederate statues, the installation of the Catto statue took on an even greater symbolic meaning.

As you already knew or have learned in this book, Philadelphia's Black history contains the stories of many remarkable African Americans. This raises a question: Why was Octavius Catto chosen for such a significant honor?

Fortunately, Branly Cadet was charged with developing more than a single statue; the statue is part of a larger memorial he created, titled

Students walking home from a school encounter with A Quest for Parity, the Octavius Catto memorial, on September 28, 2017—two days after the unveiling of the statue. (Photograph by Amy Jane Cohen)

A Quest for Parity, which presents Catto's biography in words, images, and sculptural elements. Although some people may prefer more abstract works of art, Cadet's memorial to Catto does more than just represent his physical likeness. It encapsulates the achievements of a man who deserves his place of distinction on the south side of City Hall.

Early Years and the Institute for Colored Youth

Behind the Catto statue stand five pillars, four of which represent different aspects of Catto's life. A timeline is mounted on the pillar at the far left. It begins with Catto's birth on February 22, 1839, to free parents in Charleston, South Carolina. Nine years later, the Catto family came to Philadelphia, home to the largest free Black population in the North and a place of opportunity for a small but energetic group of Black elites, a social set the Catto family joined when they arrived in the city.

The next date on the timeline is 1854, the year that fifteen-year-old Octavius Catto became a student at the Institute for Colored Youth (ICY). The ICY was a Quaker-funded teacher training academy. During the time Catto was a pupil, it was located at 716–718 Lombard Street, the heart of Philadelphia's Black community. Admission was competitive, and students pursued a rigorous classical education. Students' grades were published in the *AME Christian Recorder*, the most widely read newspaper in the Black community, and final exams were conducted in public. About half of the ICY seniors failed each year and had to return for more study.

Catto was a star pupil and a school leader. After graduating in 1858 as valedictorian, he spent a year teaching Latin and Greek in Washington, DC. The next year he was back at the ICY as a teacher of English and math. As indicated on the timeline, Catto was named principal of the boys' division of the school in 1869. The ICY is also where he met the woman who would become his fiancée, Caroline Le Count. Ahead of its time, the ICY sought to educate girls as fully as boys—though they studied in separate classes.

A bronze relief plaque of the ICY building is affixed to one of the pillars. It depicts the building at 915 Bainbridge Street to which the school moved in 1866. The building still stands, although it now houses upscale condominiums. The school moved to Delaware County in 1902 and evolved to become Cheyney University.

Civil War

In 1861, the graduates of the ICY formed an alumni association. Catto, a natural leader, was elected its first president. His leadership was particularly evident when Pennsylvania was threatened by a Confederate invasion.

When the Civil War began in 1861, Black people were not permitted in the Union Army. The Emancipation Proclamation of January 1, 1863, however, invited Black men to enlist. There was, however, one catch: Pennsylvania military officials still refused to accept Black regiments. The situation changed again in May. Confederates were amassing near the Maryland-Pennsylvania border, and Philadelphia residents feared an impending invasion. Pennsylvania's Governor Andrew Curtin put out a plea for *all* able-bodied men to come to the defense of the state.

At this point, Catto; his father, Reverend William Catto; and fifty-two other Philadelphia "gentlemen of color" publicly encouraged Blacks to enlist to defend their home. Broadsides, huge advertisements for enlistment four feet wide by eight feet high, bore the names of the Cattos, other prominent Philadelphia Black men, and Frederick Douglass, the most famous Black person in the country at the time.

Catto, then twenty-four, worked with his best friend, Jacob White, to gather a contingent of ninety young men, many of whom were ICY students. In June 1863, the men gathered at Independence Hall, walked together to the City Armory on Broad Street, and from there boarded a train to Harrisburg, Pennsylvania, to offer their services to protect their state during what was called "the emergency."

Although Philadelphia's Mayor Alexander Henry had encouraged the temporary assistance of these Black troops, Major General Darius Couch insisted that Catto and the other Black volunteers agree to serve for three full years, a commitment that was not required of white men seeking to join the fight. Catto and his company of recruits were thus soon back in Philadelphia. Secretary of War Edwin Stanton later sent Major Couch a telegram insisting that he accept volunteers "regardless of race," but Catto did not make another attempt to become a soldier. Instead, he returned to his teaching position and continued working to recruit Black troops, hundreds of whom eventually served, thanks to Catto's encouragement.

Because of Catto's dedication to this work, and because he later achieved the rank of major in the Pennsylvania National Guard, one of the pillars in A Quest for Parity has a bronze engraving of Camp William Penn, the first training ground for United States Colored Troops (USCT), located just north of the city in Cheltenham.

As the Civil War came to an official close, Catto presented a ceremonial battle flag to the 250 members of Philadelphia's Twenty-fourth USCT. He described the Black soldiers as "trusting to a redeemed country for the full recognition of their manhoods in the future." The reality was not as bright as expressed in Catto's ceremonious words. Even with the abolition of slavery and the ending of the Civil War, many battles lay ahead for him and other civil rights activists of the mid-nineteenth century.

Streetcars

One of these battles, represented in another pillar, was about public transportation. The mass transit system of mid-nineteenth-century Philadelphia was a network of privately owned streetcars. Most prohibited Black riders, though some allowed them to pay a fare for the "privilege" of standing on the narrow, mud-splattered platform at the front of the horse-drawn conveyances.

Before Blacks began fighting for the Union Army, this discriminatory practice was aggravating, inconvenient, and insulting. William Still and Robert Purvis had both spoken and written on the topic. But once African American soldiers were putting their lives on the line, it became absurd. Soldiers and their families could not use the streetcars to travel to and from Camp William Penn. Nor could families ride streetcars to visit relatives convalescing from battle wounds in city hospitals. Frederick Douglass and the Civil War hero Captain Robert Smalls were among the best-known people kicked off Philadelphia streetcars.[1]

Even more upsetting than the barring of celebrities was what happened to Catto's friend and minister in July 1864. Reverend William Alston took his two-year-old son for a walk along the Delaware River when the boy suddenly stopped breathing and spiked a fever. Alston flagged down a passing horse-drawn streetcar, hoping to get his child home quickly. The conductor refused to allow Alston and his obviously ill son aboard—even though there were no other passengers.

Although his son recovered, Alston was enraged. A graduate of both Oberlin and Kenyon colleges, he wrote a letter that was published in the *Philadelphia Press*. "Is it humane," Alston asked, "to exclude respect-

---

1. In 1862, Smalls, an enslaved man, was the pilot of a Confederate transport ship. Disguised in the uniform of the ship's captain, he piloted the ship out of Charleston Harbor while the white officers were spending the night on shore. Smalls's family and the families of his fellow Black crew members had been brought aboard for this daring escape. Smalls then became an important source of intelligence for the Union Navy and, later, a U.S. congressman.

able colored citizens from your street cars when so many of our brave and vigorous young men have been and are enlisting to take part in this heavenly ordained slavery extermination?" His letter sparked action: Catto and sixty-five other Black leaders called a meeting. Some wanted to persuade the streetcar companies to change their policies. Catto and members of his generation had a different idea: pressure the state legislature to pass a law. But that process would take time.

In the meantime, a delegation of Black and white leaders met with the mayor and a group of streetcar owners. The owners agreed to a poll: white riders would vote on whether to allow Blacks on board. Not surprisingly in that era of widespread racism—and in a city in which unskilled white immigrants knew that access to streetcars gave them an advantage in getting to jobs—riders voted to maintain the whites-only policy by a huge margin.

Catto worked with a sympathetic state senator, Morris Lowry, on a bill to desegregate mass transit. As the slow process of lobbying for its passage got underway, Black Philadelphians continued to board streetcars, sometimes hiding in a group of white passengers as they boarded and sometimes in open defiance of the regulations.

By late 1866, the U.S. Congress was poised to pass the Fifteenth Amendment, which would grant voting rights to Black men. Senator Lowry sensed that the moment was right: on February 5, 1867, the bill that Catto had helped to write was approved by Pennsylvania lawmakers. The Republicans who dominated legislature hoped that their vote for desegregation would lead soon-to-be enfranchised Black constituents to reelect them and members of their party for years to come.

Laws, though, can be effective only if they are enforced. Caroline Le Count, Catto's fiancée and by then a twenty-one-year-old school principal, attempted to board a streetcar at Eleventh and Lombard streets. The conductor refused to allow her in his car. After Le Count showed a magistrate both a news article and the text of the new law Catto had helped to write, the conductor and his company were fined $100.[2]

One of the pillars of A Quest for Parity features a bronze plaque depicting a streetcar. The pillars themselves, moreover, represent street-

---

2. In 2021, Caroline Le Count was the top vote getter in an effort to rename Taney Street, a Grays Ferry/Fitler Square/Fairmount thoroughfare. Roger Taney was the Supreme Court justice who wrote the 1857 Dred Scott decision denying citizenship to African Americans. The Rename Taney coalition has been fighting to change the name to Le Count Street for several years.

cars. Visitors can enter the pillars on the far right and far left, as if stepping into an actual streetcar.

Baseball

Catto was a serious young man, but he did have a fun-loving side, as well. He enjoyed summer trips to Cape May (one of the few Jersey Shore communities that welcomed Blacks), and he loved the game of baseball. During the Civil War, men from all social strata were exposed to games played with balls and bats. Thus, once the war ended, the game that evolved into baseball became a widespread phenomenon. The number of baseball teams and baseball fans skyrocketed, and Catto, a natural athlete in addition to his many other talents, was clearly paying attention.

In 1866, Catto and friends formed the Pythians, the city's second Black baseball team. With Catto as captain and second baseman, the Pythians ended their first season with a 9–1 record, easily defeating nearly all the Black teams from Washington, DC, to New York City.

After the success of the Pythians' first season, Catto applied for team membership in the Pennsylvania chapter of the burgeoning National Amateur Association of Base Ball Players. Although 265 all-white teams were all admitted, the organization refused even to vote on the Black team's application.

Catto still had hope. The December 1867 meeting of the National Amateur Association of Base Ball Players was to be held in Philadelphia. Even though they had been rebuffed by the state chapter, the Pythians applied for national membership. This time their application at least came up for a vote, but the majority chose not to admit the Black team. The official explanation: "If colored clubs were admitted there would be, in all probability, some division of feeling, whereas, by excluding them no injury could result to anyone."

The next year, the Pythians had another stellar season: they went undefeated. Although they had been rejected by the game's governing body, the team's athleticism and skill did attract the attention of white sports journalists, ballplayers, and spectators. On September 3, 1869, the Olympics, Philadelphia's first baseball club, accepted a challenge to play against the Pythians.

Four thousand enthusiastic fans, both Black and white, filled the stands. The game was remarkable enough to attract national press. Soon, another white team played the Pythians. In the years following these interracial Pythian games, competitions between white and "Negro" leagues became common. During the many decades that Blacks and whites tended to live, work, socialize, worship, and study separately, the ballfield became one of the few places where the races mixed. Even in his choice of leisure activities Catto made a difference in terms of the quest for fair treatment, equality, and the opportunity for Black people to prove themselves to a racist society. A bronze plaque showing a team portrait of the Pythians is affixed to one of the pillars in the Catto memorial.

Voting Rights

The right to serve in the Union Army, access to Philadelphia streetcars, admission to the National Amateur Association of Base Ball Players: Catto had worked hard for each of these things. Of all the battles he fought, however, none was as important to him as his final campaign: the struggle for voting rights. Catto and his associates knew that access to the ballot box could potentially make all other rights fall into place.

During the post–Civil War period known as Radical Reconstruction, the U.S. Congress was led by men such as Thaddeus Stevens, a member of the House of Representatives from Pennsylvania, and others who believed that Black men should be able to vote. In the South, men newly emancipated from slavery were already voting and even holding elected office. In the North, however, many states still limited the franchise to white men.

With pressure from groups such as the Equal Rights League, another organization in which Catto played a leading role, the Fifteenth Amendment extending voting rights to Black men was passed by Congress in 1869 and ratified by the states in 1870. But the right to vote and the ability to safely cast a ballot were not the same thing—certainly not in Philadelphia.

Democrats, many of whom were working-class Irish Americans, knew that their influence, power, and economic well-being would be severely diminished should the Republicans, "The Party of Lincoln" to which blacks were overwhelmingly loyal, be elected to office in Philadelphia. A patronage system was firmly in place in the city. A Republican mayor would likely replace many Irish workers on the City Hall payroll, maybe even with Black people.

Once Black male suffrage was the law of the land, intimidation of Black voters became a strategy to maintain Democratic control. The first time newly enfranchised Blacks participated in an election in Philadelphia was 1870, and there was sporadic violence against Black voters.

On Election Day in 1871, such violence intensified. As always, Catto, a teacher first, began the day—October 10—at the ICY. While he was engaged in his work, reports began to trickle in that Black voters were being bullied at both the Tenth and Bainbridge and the Sixth and Lombard polling places. Soon rioting flared up along Lombard Street and spread as far south as Fitzwater Street. Fearing for the safety of the students, the ICY closed after lunch.

Catto, at that point a National Guardsmen, received word to arm himself and report to Fifth Brigade headquarters at Broad and Race streets. After stopping at a bank on Ninth and Lombard streets to withdraw money, his next stop was a pawnshop near Third and Walnut streets, where he purchased a gun. As he approached his home at 814 South Street, a man with a bandaged head shot Catto twice at close range. At thirty-two, Octavius Catto was dead. Although clearly the most prominent victim of Election Day violence, Catto was one of four Black men fatally shot that day.

In A Quest for Parity, the figure of Octavius Catto appears to be stepping forward toward a large silver ball encased in plexiglass atop a granite stand. The ball represents a nineteenth-century ballot box, and the stand is engraved with the word *Activist* and the text of the Fifteenth Amendment. In the memorial, as in Catto's life, voting rights are an issue of singular importance.

Death and Legacy

Catto's funeral, the largest ever for a Black man in Philadelphia, was attended by members of Congress and city officials, as well as scores of former students, colleagues, friends, and ordinary people. A procession of more than 125 carriages followed a three-mile route to Lebanon Cemetery in South Philadelphia.

Frank Kelly, widely known to be Catto's assassin, was able to escape. Six years later, he was found living in Chicago under an assumed name. A murder trial was held in April 1877. Though the prosecution presented many eyewitnesses who identified Kelly as the shooter, the all-white jury turned in a verdict of not guilty.

Jacob White, Catto's best friend and fellow educator, tried for years to raise money for a memorial, but he was unable to gather sufficient funds. Both Booker T. Washington and W. E. B. Du Bois wrote about Catto. A chapter of the Black Elks fraternal organization called the Octavius V. Catto Lodge was founded in 1903 and continues to this day. Like those of others interred in Lebanon Cemetery, Catto's grave was long ago moved to Eden Cemetery in Collingdale, Delaware County, where a commemorative marker labeling him "Forgotten Hero" was erected in 2007.

So why was this hero forgotten? For many years, the stories of Black heroes were forgotten because they were not taught in schools. Catto's name, however, was kept alive in the Black community, in part through the Elks and a disciplinary school (now Paul Robeson High School) named in his honor.

In 2003, City Councilperson Jim Kenney, who had spent his life in Philadelphia and represented the area that Catto called home, read Catto's story. He was fascinated and angry. Why had he never learned about this remarkable Philadelphian? Kenney began advocating for a memorial to Catto in a prominent Philadelphia location, and he was joined by a coalition of supporters both Black and white.

A Gathering Place

A Quest for Parity has become a gathering place for civic demonstrations, a backdrop for the press conferences of progressive politicians, a place of pride for African Americans to pose for photos, and an increasingly familiar landmark to Philadelphians. During the election of 2020, long lines of voters snaked by the Catto memorial as they waited to place their ballots in City Hall drop boxes. When the cloth was removed from Branly Cadet's statue in 2017, Octavius Catto was still unknown to most city residents. The Catto memorial has sparked a remarkable transition: the "Forgotten Hero" is now a household name in much of Philadelphia.

To Do

- ▸ Visit A Quest for Parity on the south apron of City Hall.

- ▸ See the historical markers for the Institute for Colored Youth at 915 Bainbridge Street and for Octavius Catto in front of his final home, 814 South Street.

▸ Watch the fifteen-minute documentary *Octavius V. Catto: A Legacy for the 21st Century* at https://222.historymakingpro ductions.com/ovc.

▸ Listen to "The Life and Times of Caroline R. Le Count: Part I" and "The Life and Times of Caroline R. Le Count: Part II," episodes 3 and 4 of the *Found in Philadelphia* podcast (https:// foundinphiladelphia.com/episode-no-3-the-life-and-times-of -caroline-r-le-count-part-1 and https://foundinphiladelphia .com/episode-no-4-the-life-and-times-of-caroline-r-le-count -part-2).

▸ Go to "Forging Citizenship and Opportunity—Octavius Cat- to's Legacy" (https://catto.ushistory.org) for history, primary sources, maps, essays, education guides, and other informa- tion related to Octavius Catto.

▸ Watch the nine-minute "Baseball: The Philadelphia Game," part of the *Philadelphia: The Great Experiment* series pro- duced by History Making Productions, at https://www.you tube.com/watch?v=uNCY1R-Lsqw.

▸ Visit *Remembering a Forgotten Hero*, a mural about Octavius Catto, his fellow nineteenth-century activists, and the context in which they lived on the side of the Universal Charter School at 1427 Catharine Street.

▸ Travel to the La Mott area of Cheltenham to see a historical marker at the site of Camp William Penn. Street signs in the area bear profiles of members of the United States Colored Troops. Learn about reenactments and other events at Camp William Penn at https://www.usct.org.

▸ Follow the progress of the efforts to rename Taney Street in honor of Caroline Le Count at https://www.renametaney.com.

9

W. E. B. DU BOIS AND THE SEVENTH WARD

Reviving *The Philadelphia Negro*

[With a Reflection by Reverend Dr. Charles Howard]

When William Edgar Burghardt Du Bois arrived in Philadelphia in 1896, he was one of the best-educated men in the United States. He had earned a bachelor's degree from the all-Black Fisk University in Nashville and a second bachelor's degree from Harvard University (which did not recognize his work at Fisk). He received a fellowship to do graduate work at the University of Berlin and returned to the United States to become the first African American to earn a doctorate from Harvard. In spite of these credentials, his only job offers came from Black colleges. While teaching at Wilberforce University in Ohio, Du Bois was invited to take a one-year position as an assistant in the Sociology Department at the University of Pennsylvania. Although this job title was well beneath his exemplary qualifications, Du Bois and his new wife, Nina, came to Philadelphia.

The newlyweds were housed at the College Settlement House at 617 Carver (now Rodman) Street. Their temporary home was just to the east of the area Du Bois had been hired to study. At the behest of Susan Wharton, a well-connected College Settlement activist, Penn had recruited Du Bois to investigate the "Negro problem" in the city's Seventh Ward, the corridor from South Street to Spruce Street running from Seventh Street to the Schuylkill River. At the end of the nineteenth century, nearly one-quarter of Philadelphia's forty thousand Black residents lived in the Seventh Ward.

W. E. B. Du Bois in a photograph by John Mosley, a prolific and prominent African American photojournalist who documented Black life in Philadelphia during the mid-twentieth century. (John W. Mosley Photograph Collection, Charles L. Blockson Afro-American Collection, Temple University Libraries, Philadelphia)

Du Bois came to a city that had experienced significant population growth in the previous decades. Large numbers of southern freedmen had migrated North following emancipation; Du Bois found that more than half of the Seventh Ward's Black residents had been born in the South. Most lacked job skills, education, and experience in living in an urban environment. Immigrants from Europe had also poured into the rapidly industrializing city. Longtime residents no longer recognized their city, and many thought that the Black population would doom Philadelphia to a bleak future. As Du Bois later recalled, "The fact was that the city of Philadelphia at that time had a theory . . . that this great, rich, and famous municipality was going to the dogs because of the crime and venality of its Negro citizens, who lived largely centered in the slum at the lower end of the seventh ward. Philadelphia wanted to prove this by figures and I was the man to do it."

During his brief stint as a University of Pennsylvania employee, Du Bois collected a staggering amount of quantitative data. His conclusions contradicted the common wisdom of the day.

The Study

There are numerous remarkable aspects of the work Du Bois did in Philadelphia. He surveyed virtually every Black household in the Seventh

Ward, eventually conducting five thousand interviews. He created—from scratch—the content of a questionnaire as well as record-keeping protocols and data analysis techniques. Although Du Bois had few models to work from, his Seventh Ward study, published in 1899 as *The Philadelphia Negro: A Social Study*, became an exemplar in the emerging field of sociology. Du Bois devotes seven chapters to the history of "The Negro in Philadelphia" from 1638 to 1896. The quality of his research and the thoroughness of his narrative have made *The Philadelphia Negro* a valuable resource for historians of local Black history to this day.

Du Bois's house-to-house canvass of the Seventh Ward was comprehensive. Except for a few brothels and a small number of families who refused to participate, he gathered data from every Black household about the age, sex, "conjugal condition," place of birth, education, occupation, health, and family structure of the residents. In addition to this general census of the population, Du Bois studied the "organized life" of the community (e.g., churches, beneficial societies), the "Negro criminal," "pauperism and alcoholism," housing conditions, and suffrage.

One of Du Bois's groundbreaking findings was that there was social stratification within the Black community. Whereas most white people thought of the city's African American population as an undifferentiated mass, Du Bois described four different levels:

Grade 1: The "Middle Classes" and those above
Grade 2: The Working People, Fair to Comfortable
Grade 3: The Poor
Grade 4: Vicious and Criminal Classes

A hand-drawn, color-coded map included in the book (as a foldout in the original publication) reveals a distinct pattern. Fewer than a third of Seventh Ward residents were Black, and very few lived in the western end, from Nineteenth Street to the Schuylkill River. The middle section, between Eighth and Nineteenth streets, was home to a mixture of the Black elite, the working class, and the poor. The dense alleyways between Seventh and Eighth, on either side of Lombard Street, made up a neighborhood that Du Bois repeatedly refers to as a "Negro slum."

Du Bois's study found that about 11 percent of Seventh Ward Blacks met his criteria for Grade 1. This relatively affluent group was made up mostly of Philadelphia-born caterers, clerks, teachers, and other professionals. The largest group, 56 percent of the total, were in Grade 2, the working class, described by Du Bois as "the mass of the servant class. The porters and waiters, and the best of the laborers." Du Bois considered about 30 percent of the Seventh Ward's Black population to be Grade 3, or poor. This group included "immigrants [from the South] who can not get steady work; good-natured, but unreliable and shiftless persons who cannot keep work or spend their earnings thoughtfully; those who have suffered accident or misfortune; the maimed and defective classes, and the sick; many widows and orphans and deserted wives."

Although Du Bois refers to members of Grade 4 as "the submerged tenth," his study reveals that fewer than 6 percent of the Black population of the Seventh Ward belonged to this group of "low, open idlers." Du Bois, an erudite, elegant, and cultured Victorian gentleman, viewed his slum-dwelling brethren as immoral, lazy, and in need of uplift. He does, however, devote considerable energy to trying to understand how this "lowest class of criminals, prostitutes, and loafers" ended up in their condition.

Nearly all the work of *The Philadelphia Negro* was done by Du Bois and Isabel Eaton, a College Settlement employee who served as his assistant. A special report on "Negro Domestic Service" written by Eaton is included as an appendix to the book. The one time Du Bois acknowledges the help of anyone else is when he uses a footnote to thank a group of students from the Wharton School who spent several evenings in 1897 counting and recording the gender and race of people entering and exiting Seventh Ward saloons. The students also noted how many carried liquor away and how many appeared drunk.

Findings

When Du Bois was hired to study the "Negro problem," the prevailing wisdom was that Black poverty, unemployment, criminality, and so on were the result of inherent racial inferiority. This explanation was consistent with the eugenics theories and social Darwinist ideas of the time. Du Bois's research, however, revealed other forces at work. White prejudice, he explained, was a major cause of Black suffering. Particularly in employment, the unwillingness of white bosses to hire African Americans and the refusal of white workers to toil beside Black people frustrated the ambitions and stymied the advance of skilled, educated, and motivated Black residents. Recently arrived immigrants from Europe, even those lacking qualifications, were able to find work in the industrial and commercial sectors, while Black people were routinely denied such positions.

Schools such as the Institute for Colored Youth provided a sound educational foundation for many of the city's young Black residents. To find a modicum of career success, however, the graduates of these schools had to leave Philadelphia. Ironically, many were able to find work in the former Confederacy more easily than in their home city. Describing graduates of the Robert Vaux Grammar School, Du Bois explained: "From one-half to two-thirds of these have been compelled to leave the city in order to find work; one, the artist [Henry Ossawa] Tanner, whom France recently honored, could not in his native land much less in his native city find room for his talents. He taught school in Georgia in order earn money enough to go abroad."[1]

Black people, relegated overwhelmingly to low-paid domestic work and to sporadic, menial employment, sometimes turned to alcohol, crime, prostitution, and gambling. To pay the elevated rents of the Seventh Ward, nearly 40 percent of Black households took in boarders, which the puritanical Du Bois found disruptive to the family structure. "In such ways the privacy and intimacy of home life is destroyed, and elements of danger and demoralization admitted," he lamented. Although many parts of the Seventh Ward were crowded and the rents were high, Blacks were not welcome in many other parts of the city, and their work often required them to live near their places of employment—usually the homes of white families in or near the Seventh Ward. The reasonably priced houses that sprouted up around factories were available to the white immigrant workforce, not to members of the struggling Black community.

---

1. Henry Ossawa Tanner (1859–1937) fell in love with painting during his childhood in Philadelphia. He studied with Thomas Eakins at the Pennsylvania Academy of Fine Art, where he was the only Black student. Frustrated with the racism that limited his prospects as an artist, Tanner moved to Paris, where he found great success and international acclaim. A historical marker in front of his former home at 2908 Diamond Street has been in place since 1991 and was one of Charles Blockson's original nominations. Although the house is a National Historic Landmark, it is in precarious condition. The National Trust for Historic Preservation named the Tanner House one of the eleven most endangered historic places in the United States in 2023. The Friends of Tanner House is working with the Preservation Alliance of Greater Philadelphia to stabilize the property and turn it into a community asset.

Conclusions

In the last chapter of *The Philadelphia Negro*, Du Bois lays out his views on the separate duties of Blacks and whites to improve conditions for the city's African Americans at the end of the nineteenth century.

Du Bois advises Black Philadelphians to collectively reduce their involvement in crime, increase their dedication to education, avoid wasting money on frivolous pursuits, and find some "rational means of amusement" to keep young people out of "saloons and clubs and bawdy houses." Above all, he encourages the community to focus on work: "Work, continuous and intensive; work, although it be menial and poorly rewarded; work, though done in travail of soul and sweat of brow, must be so impressed upon Negro children as the road to salvation, that a child would feel it a greater disgrace to be idle than to do the humblest labor."

Du Bois also advocates that "the better classes of the Negroes should recognize their duty toward the masses." *The Philadelphia Negro* contains the seeds of the notion that grew into the Du Boisian concept of "The Talented Tenth," the idea that the elite of the race were responsible for the destiny of all African Americans. "This is especially true," writes Du Bois, "in a city like Philadelphia which has so distinct and creditable a Negro aristocracy."

Not surprisingly, Du Bois calls on white Philadelphians to improve job opportunities for the city's Black residents: "There is no doubt that in Philadelphia the centre and kernel of the Negro problem so far as the white people are concerned is the narrow opportunities afforded Negroes for earning a decent living. Such discrimination is morally wrong, politically dangerous, industrially wasteful, and socially silly." He continues, "The cost of crime and pauperism, the growth of slums, and the pernicious influences of idleness and lewdness, cost the public far more than would the hurt to the feelings of a carpenter to work beside a black man or a shop girl to stand beside a darker mate."

In addressing white residents, Du Bois again underscores the key role of the Philadelphia-born Black elite in the uplift of their less well-off peers. He criticizes white Philadelphians for neglecting to make a suitable place in society for the Black upper crust: "It is a paradox of the times that young men and women from some of the best Negro families of the city—families born and reared here and schooled in the best traditions of this municipality—have actually had to go to the South to get work, if they wished to be aught but chambermaids and bootblacks."

Finally, Du Bois makes a call for human understanding and simple civility. *The Philadelphia Negro* concludes with the following request of white residents:

> A polite and sympathetic attitude toward those striving thousands; a delicate avoidance of that which wounds and embitters them; a generous granting of opportunity to them; a seconding of their efforts. And a desire to reward honest success—all this, added to proper striving on their part, will go far even in our day toward making all men, white and black, realize what the great founder of the city meant when he named it the City of Brotherly Love.

Reviving the Du Bois–Philadelphia Connection

Though the University of Pennsylvania did not consider Du Bois an official faculty member during his time in Philadelphia, the school now celebrates its connection to the renowned writer, scholar, and activist. In the late 1960s, Black students at Penn, like their peers at other American colleges, pressured the university to expand course offerings and find ways to support African American students. Penn's Afro-American studies program and the W. E. B. Du Bois College House were both launched in 1972. Located at 3900 Walnut Street, Du Bois College House is a four-story residential hall and a center for promoting scholarship, community, and opportunity for students of the African diaspora. In 2012, the university awarded Du Bois an honorary emeritus professorship in the departments of sociology and Africana studies.

Although *The Philadelphia Negro* was well known among sociologists, the book faded in importance during Du Bois's long career. In 1996, however, the University of Pennsylvania Press reissued the book with a new introduction by the sociologist Elijah Anderson. Two years later, *W. E. B. Du Bois, Race, and the City: The Philadelphia Negro and Its Legacy* was published, also by the University of Pennsylvania Press, in recognition of the centenary of *The Philadelphia Negro*. At the University of Pennsylvania, Dr. Amy Hillier and Dr. Stephanie Boddie launched The Ward, an initiative to develop teaching materials to make

Du Bois's work relevant to twenty-first-century students. Fortuitously, their efforts coincided with the School District of Philadelphia's mandate in 2005 requiring a year of African American history for high school graduation.

This renewed interest in *The Philadelphia Negro* is also reflected in the landscape. In 1995, a historical marker was installed in front of the Rodman Street building where W. E. B. and Nina Du Bois lived while in Philadelphia. In 2008, the team from The Ward partnered with the Mural Arts Program to create a mural commemorating Du Bois's work in Philadelphia. *Mapping Courage,* on the side of a firehouse on the northwestern corner of Sixth and South, also honors Engine Company 11, an all-Black fire company that was segregated by official Fire Department policy from 1919 to 1952.

The Seventh Ward Today

Du Bois's Seventh Ward, particularly the "Negro slum" area between Seventh and Eighth on Lombard Street, is nearly unrecognizable today, at least in terms of population. Due to the urban renewal efforts of the late 1950s and early 1960s, the neighborhood has been transformed from a deteriorating warren of dilapidated housing for Blacks and poor immigrants into an upscale neighborhood characterized by charming colonial houses and modern brick townhomes. From 1960 to 1970, the Society Hill neighborhood at the eastern end of the Seventh Ward went from being one of the poorest to one of the wealthiest areas in the city. Today, the neighborhood is 88 eight percent white and only 2 percent Black, statistics that would shock Du Bois.

The middle of the Seventh Ward, from Eighth to Nineteenth streets, also houses few Black families, and most of the Black churches and businesses along Lombard Street have shuttered or moved to other parts of the city.[2] Middle- and working-class Black residents left over time, for varied reasons, including finding better housing opportunities else-

---

2. St. Peter Claver, the city's first Black Catholic church, on the corner of Twelfth and Lombard streets, stopped holding regular services in 1984. It remained a center of Black Catholic life, however, and in 1991 a historical marker nominated by Charles Blockson was unveiled at the site. In late 2022, the Archdiocese of Philadelphia announced that the building would be permanently closed and put up for sale, much to the dismay of members of the Black Catholic community.

where and gradual gentrification. A planned crosstown expressway slated for South Street led to massive disinvestment in the southern portion of the Seventh Ward. Although the planned roadway was never constructed, many Black businesses and homeowners had already sold their property to avoid further depreciation while negotiations over the South Street expressway dragged on. The one part of the ward that remains demographically unchanged is the western end. South Street to Spruce Street west of Nineteenth Street is still a mostly white, affluent neighborhood, as it was in Du Bois's time.

Epitaph

Du Bois wrote *The Philadelphia Negro* quite early in his long and prolific career. When the book was published in 1899, he believed that detailed evidence of the impact of racial prejudice and gentle admonishments of both Blacks and whites could alleviate racial tension and improve the trajectory of African Americans. This optimism did not last. In *The Souls of Black Folk* (1903), Du Bois advocated protest and political action and criticized Black leaders such as Booker T. Washington, who thought hard work and a temporary acceptance of second-class status were the best path forward. In his role as a founder of the National Association for the Advancement of Colored People (NAACP) in 1909 and editor of its magazine, *The Crisis*, from 1910 to 1934, Du Bois continued to advocate for aggressive tactics to pursue civil rights for Black people.

Du Bois also emerged as a leader of Pan-Africanism, the idea that all people of African descent shared a common heritage and destiny, and Black nationalism, the notion that Black people should develop economic self-reliance and a separate body of arts and literature. Later, Du Bois moved toward socialist and Marxist interpretations of history and current events. In 1961, Du Bois became a member of the Communist Party and left the United States for Ghana. He died at ninety-five as a Ghanaian citizen on August 27, 1963. The next day, from the stage of the March on Washington for Jobs and Freedom, NAACP President Roy Wilkins announced Du Bois's death and declared, "Regardless of the fact that in his later years Dr. Du Bois chose another path, it is incontrovertible that at the dawn of the twentieth century his was the voice that was calling to you to gather here today in this cause."

Reflection

Reverend Dr. Charles Howard is the university chaplain and vice president for social equity and community at the University of Pennsylvania. His grandfather, Charles Preston Howard Sr., was a friend and fraternity brother of, and worked closely with, both W. E. B. Du Bois and Paul Robeson.

It is a very short list of individuals who have buildings named in their honor on Ivy League campuses. And the list of individuals of African descent whose names are on buildings is even shorter. Thus, one can understand how moving it is for young Black scholars on the campus of the University of Pennsylvania to walk into the W. E. B. Du Bois College House named after Dr. Du Bois, who—among many other remarkable and world-changing efforts during his near-century of life—worked at the university. In fact, it was at Penn where he researched and wrote the ground-breaking and perspective-changing text *The Philadelphia Negro*.

I lived in Du Bois College House during my undergraduate years at Penn. It was a home, and it felt like family in more ways than one. The other students in the house were more than just classmates; they were siblings. The house dean and faculty director were like parents. We laughed together, celebrated milestones, grieved losses, dreamed of a better world, studied, rested, protested, sang, danced, ate, and grew in this home.

It also felt like home in another way. My grandfather (also named Charles Howard) was a friend of Dr. Du Bois's and maintained regular correspondence with him even after Du Bois moved to Accra toward the end of his life. Walking into this building that bears the name of my grandfather's friend—well, it felt safe. It felt strong. It felt wonderfully Black.

To Do

- ▶ Read *The Philadelphia Negro*. Du Bois is an excellent writer, and it is a book that one can either skim or read carefully. The full text is available online at https://openlibrary.org/books/OL6961266M/The_Philadelphia_Negro.

- ▶ Check the W. E. B. Du Bois College House's website (https://dubois.house.upenn.edu/front) to find events that are open to the public.

▶ Follow the progress of 7th Ward Tribute, an initiative to honor the rich history of the Seventh Ward by marking the borders of the area with artistic installations. You can learn more about this project of Little Giant Creative, the Philadelphia Archives, and Philadelphia Mural Arts by visiting https://www.7thwardtribute.com.

▶ Visit the *Mapping Courage* mural at Sixth and South streets and the nearby Du Bois historical marker on Seventh and Rodman streets.

▶ Take a self-guided walking tour of the Seventh Ward using a map provided at http://www.dubois-theward.org. This website also includes videos, oral histories, curriculum materials, and other resources about Du Bois and *The Philadelphia Negro*.

▶ Watch the three-minute "Crosstown Expressway," part of the *Philadelphia: The Great Experiment* series produced by History Making Productions, at https://www.youtube.com/watch?v=ycEf0ID-jqA&t=1s.

PART III

~

Twentieth Century

10

～

FIRST AFRICAN BAPTIST CHURCH

Sacred Sacrifices and Real Estate Realities

In the summer of 2006, a historical marker in front of a church on Sixteenth and Christian streets caught my eye. I pulled my car over to read it:

> FIRST AFRICAN BAPTIST CHURCH
>
> Founded in 1809 as one of the first Black Baptist churches in America. Later two members sold themselves into slavery to free a slave to serve as pastor.

I was stunned.

Beyond this tale of extraordinary sacrifice, the story of First African Baptist Church is remarkable. For more than two centuries, visionary leadership has maintained the continuity of a religious community, even when that has meant following the congregation to new locations.

The Early Years

Early nineteenth-century Philadelphia saw rising migration to the city by people fleeing or freed from enslavement in the South. This led to increasing economic competition between less-skilled Blacks and similarly less-skilled Irish workers and to intensifying animosity toward Black people by a growing cross-section of white residents. The city's

Black community reacted by building up institutions, particularly religious institutions.

The First African Baptist Church was founded in 1809 by thirteen men who had come to Philadelphia from Virginia. The group's formerly enslaved leader, Henry Simmons, worked as a rag dealer to save money to purchase a small plot of land near Tenth and Vine streets on which to build a church. As the congregation grew, the church moved several times within a few blocks of the original site. From 1867 to 1906, First African Baptist Church was located on Cherry Street near Tenth Street—thus, its nickname Cherry Memorial Church. First African Baptist was also called the Mother Church because of its history as the first Black Baptist congregation in Philadelphia.

Reverend James Burrows, who would lead the church from 1832 to 1844, had been enslaved in Northampton County, Virginia, but nonetheless experienced the call to preach. Burrows persuaded his owner to allow him to go to Philadelphia as a pastor and to work to purchase his freedom. The owner consented only after two cousins of Burrows, John and Samuel Bivins, agreed to temporarily be put in bondage as human collateral. After a year, Burrows had earned enough to purchase his freedom, and the Bivins brothers returned to Philadelphia.

In the eight years that Burrows led the First African Baptist Church, the congregation grew from sixty members to 252, and a Sunday School program was started. The cemeteries used by the church at this time were discovered in the 1980s when digging for the Vine Street Expressway began. The remains of 225 bodies were reinterred at Eden Cemetery in Collingdale, Pennsylvania.

Reverend James Underdew was another notable leader of the church. He served from 1859 to 1863. Underdew left the pulpit to enlist in the United States Colored Troops, where he was assigned as chaplain to an infantry regiment on the front lines of the Civil War.

Moving on Up

The term of Reverend William Abraham Creditt, from 1897 to 1915, was a time of relocation and expansion for First African Baptist Church. Creditt was born in Baltimore in 1864 and earned a Bachelor of Arts from Lincoln University in Chester County, Pennsylvania, the nation's first degree-granting Black college. He then studied at the Newton Theological Institute in Massachusetts, where he graduated as class orator despite

The First African Baptist Church was based here from 1909 to 2015. It is now home to the Deacon, a boutique event space and hotel, and the Aspen Grove School, a childcare center. The First African Baptist Church is now located at 6700 Lansdowne Avenue. (Photograph by Amy Jane Cohen)

being the only Black student. He was later among the first and youngest individuals to earn an honorary doctorate from Lincoln University.

Before coming to Philadelphia, Creditt served as pastor for several churches, including Berean Baptist Church in Washington, DC, where Frederick Douglass, Blanche K. Bruce (the second Black U.S. senator), and John R. Lynch (a Black congressman from Mississippi) were frequently in attendance.

Under Creditt's leadership, the congregation increased its membership to the point that the Cherry Street building no longer sufficed. Creditt made the bold and seemingly prescient decision to move the church to Sixteenth and Christian streets, an area that, at the time, was dominated by middle-class Irish American families. When the cornerstone of the imposing limestone building was laid in 1906, Blacks made up less than a quarter of the neighborhood's residents.

By the time First African Baptist Church was ready to commemorate the congregation's one-hundredth anniversary in 1909, there was much to celebrate beyond the new Gothic Revival building. The congregation of nearly two thousand members was enthusiastic and engaged. Church organizations worked on fundraising, building maintenance, helping with religious services, and visiting shut-ins. There were youth groups, women's groups, men's groups, Bible study groups, and choirs. Indeed, the church was such a significant institution that Booker T. Washington, arguably the most famous Black man in the country at the time, spoke at the one-hundredth anniversary celebration.

The trustees of the church were mostly professional men who had been born in the South and had worked their way up the social and economic ladder in Philadelphia. John S. Trower, a successful caterer and major benefactor of Baptist charities, was president of the Board of Trustees at the time of the church's centennial. Along with Reverend Creditt, Trower founded the Downingtown Industrial and Agricultural School, an African American trade school that operated from 1905 until 1993.[1]

Charles H. Brooks, another member of the Board of Trustees, was a Kentucky-born graduate of Howard University Law School who worked in real estate and insurance. In 1922, Brooks published a detailed history and description of the First African Baptist Church. In a chapter titled, "The Business Features of the Church," Brooks opined: "A religion without industry may take us a long way in the world to come; but it won't help much here." Accordingly, the church ran the thriving Reliable Mutual Aid and Insurance Society and the Cherry Building and Loan Association, a groundbreaking mortgage lending enterprise that helped members to become homeowners. These organizations and other subsidiaries were housed at 1440 Lombard Street, a

---

1. In 2021, a historical marker for John Trower was unveiled on Germantown Avenue in front of the former site of his catering business.

building owned by First African Baptist Church. Adding to its real estate holdings, the congregation also purchased a parsonage on the 1800 block of Christian Street.

Brooks described the First African Baptist Church as "one of the most intelligent and fashionable congregations of colored Baptists to be found anywhere in the United States." He continued:

> The culture and combined wealth of this congregation are not equaled by any other Church of color in America. Besides the large number of well-ordered families which regularly attend the service, many physicians, dentists, lawyers, teachers, musicians, business men and students often swell the congregation to more than 1500 persons. Carefully collected statistics show that the property owned by the members of this Church is worth nearly $2,000,000. The Church edifice is among the finest buildings owned by colored congregations in this country; it is a model of elegance and beauty; fitted up with all modern appliances for the comfort and pleasure of worshipers, thereby attesting the fine esthetic and artistic taste of the people.

A Neighborhood Transforms

When First African Baptist Church opened in its new location in 1909, the surrounding blocks were on the verge of becoming a new "Black Main Street." For the remaining decades of the twentieth century, First African Baptist was located in a Black community, albeit a community of diminishing means. (More on twentieth-century Christian Street in the next chapter.)

Around the turn of the twenty-first century, however, the neighborhood went through a period of rapid transformation. What had once been considered a blighted section of South Philadelphia became the Graduate Hospital area, an increasingly desirable—and pricey—extension of Center City. Named for a now defunct hospital at Twentieth and South streets, Graduate Hospital, also known as Southwest Center City, experienced extreme gentrification. A study released in 2016 by Pew Charitable Trusts showed that the median price for homes on Christian Street and the blocks to its immediate north and south had soared from $25,500 in 2000 to $311,250 in 2014, the steepest increase in all of Philadelphia. Median household income rose by 98 percent during the same period. The percentage of Black residents on Christian Street and nearby blocks had plummeted from 90 percent in 2000 to 38 percent fourteen years later.

Pastor Terrence Griffith saw this rapid change as an opportunity for First African Baptist Church. As the Black population of the neighborhood fell and membership declined, the expense of maintaining a century-old building continued to climb. The bell tower had been torn down in 1999 after Hurricane Floyd exacerbated damage from an earlier lightning strike. By 2015, the Sixteenth Street wall was crumbling, and the building was deemed unsafe by the city's Department of Licenses and Inspections. Griffith planned to sell the First African Baptist Church to developers, knowing that he could charge a steep price for such a large parcel of land in a hot market. He expected to sell the building for more than $3 million—money that could be used to purchase a new property in a less expensive area with a larger Black population.

Griffith's efforts were thwarted when a faction of the church membership opposed the plan. Working with the preservationist Oscar Beisert, they successfully had the church added to the Register of Historic Places by the Philadelphia Historical Commission. This not only ensured the survival of the church structure but also made the property less desirable to developers who would almost certainly have demolished the ailing building to replace it with pricey condominiums or townhouses. In the final days of 2015, the First African Baptist Church was sold for a lower price of $2 million, bringing in enough revenue for the congregation to purchase and renovate a former Catholic church on a two-acre campus in Overbrook.

A Happy Ending?

Today, the congregation of the First African Baptist Church (renamed the FAB Church) is again thriving. Membership has increased, and Pastor Griffith has emerged as a leading member of Philadelphia's clergy. A historical marker outside of the new building is larger and more detailed than its Christian Street predecessor. It reads:

> Founded in 1809, it is one of the first black Baptist churches in America and the oldest in P[ennsylvani]a. In 1832, two members, John and Samuel Bivins, sold themselves into slavery to free an enslaved man, James Burroughs, to serve as pastor. After a year,

A guest room at the Deacon with stained glass designed by
Reverend William A. Creditt. (Photograph by Amy Jane Cohen)

Burroughs paid the slaveowner and [the] Bivinses were freed.
F.A.B. Members helped found the Downingtown Industrial
School and many Philadelphia-area churches. Booker T. Wash-
ington spoke at the church centennial.

The First African Church building on Sixteenth and Christian still
stands. A large exterior sign saying First African Baptist Church remains affixed to the exterior, and the historical marker that stopped me
in my tracks is still posted outside. The inside of the building, however,
is thoroughly transformed. The Deacon, a boutique hotel and event
space, occupies most of the former church. Stained glass windows designed by Reverend William A. Creditt grace the well-appointed guest
rooms that also feature Sonos speakers and luxury bedding. A chande-

lier that lit the church sanctuary hangs from the vaulted ceiling of the expansive central area used now for wedding parties, corporate retreats, and family reunions. Another portion of the former First African Baptist Church houses the Aspen Grove School, a "nature-based" day care and preschool. Kindergarten tuition exceeds $16,000 per year.

The current owners have ensured the structural soundness of the building and put it to innovative new uses. How one feels about the Deacon and the Aspen Grove School occupying this once sacred space depends on one's perspective. Given my initial encounter with First Baptist Church, I am glad that the historical marker remains outside and continues to inform passersby of the sacrifice made by two parishioners to enable an enslaved pastor to come to Philadelphia to preach.

To Do

▶ See the historical marker for the First African Baptist Church member John S. Trower at 5706 Germantown Avenue or sign up for a Deep Rivers Tour of Ebenezer Maxwell Mansion in Germantown to learn more about Trower and other Black leaders of late nineteenth-century Philadelphia.

▶ Visit the site of the onetime First African Baptist Church Cemetery, at Eighth and Vine streets, to see the historical marker.

▶ Watch *Ground Truth: Archeology in the City* (1988), a dated but interesting thirty-five-minute documentary about the discovery of remains from the First African Baptist Church cemetery, available online at https://archive.org/details/ground trutharcheologyinthecity.

11

JULIAN FRANCIS ABELE

The Unlikely Figurehead of Black Doctors Row

Julian Francis Abele (1881–1950) was born into a prominent Black family in Philadelphia. He graduated from the venerable Institute for Colored Youth and studied architectural drawing at the Pennsylvania Museum School of Industrial Art, now University of the Arts. At seventeen, Abele enrolled in the University of Pennsylvania's architecture program, which followed the École des Beaux-Arts system of architectural education.

The École des Beaux-Arts system involved numerous competitions, and Abele garnered more first-place awards than any student in his class. As a junior he won a competition to design the Pretty Memorial Alumni Award, a commemorative tablet that hangs on the first floor of the University of Pennsylvania's Van Pelt Library. His design was selected for the Conklin Memorial Gateway that graces Haverford College, and he won the Arthur Spayd Brooke Memorial Prize, which is awarded to the student showing the most promise. Most significant, he was elected *by his classmates* to be the president of the Architectural Society. When he graduated in 1902, he was the third African American in the nation to earn a degree in architecture.

Abele's success at Penn was particularly astounding given the racist ethos of the university, the city, and the nation at the start of the twentieth century. The only other African American likely to have been in College Hall, the program's home, would have been the janitor.

A professor at Penn's School of Architecture described the École des Beaux-Arts program in a way that reveals the casual, virulent racism that pervaded elite institutions of the era:

> In an atelier one of the causes for the rapid development of the new student is the tradition already mentioned as one of the features of the [É]cole system—the older, more advanced pupils helping the younger; and what goes with it, the younger men working for the older. This latter is called "n*****ing" and consists of doing anything the advanced man asks.

My great-granduncle Louis Magaziner was the older student with whom Abele was paired, no doubt because he, too, was an outsider at the school. Magaziner was the first Jewish student to get a degree in architecture from the University of Pennsylvania. Abele and Magaziner became best friends and remained so for the rest of their lives.

Abele spent nearly his entire architectural career in the firm of Horace Trumbauer, quickly rising to the position of chief designer and eventually taking over the firm with a colleague following Trumbauer's death in 1938. Because Trumbauer's employees did not sign their work and scant correspondence among Trumbauer's employees remains, and because of the racial implications of denying Abele his due, there is much debate about Abele's role in various projects. The architectural historian David Brownlee has, however, determined Abele's pivotal role in several major projects.

In 1911, Trumbauer assigned Abele the job of designing the main branch of the Free Library of Philadelphia along the city's newly constructed Benjamin Franklin Parkway. Abele presented a proposal to the city's Art Jury on April 2, 1912. Two weeks later, the *Titanic* sank, taking with it the streetcar magnate George Widener and his son Harry. Work on the Free Library was put on hold when the bereaved family hired Trumbauer's firm to build the Widener Library at Harvard, Harry's alma mater. Abele was the project's lead designer, and the building was dedicated in 1915. The Free Library of Philadelphia was not completed until 1927 due to funding shortfalls, cost-cutting changes in materials, and other delays. A historical marker installed in front of the building in 2002 credits both Trumbauer and Abele, a dual attribution that makes sense given that Trumbauer was the head of the firm.

Beginning in the 1970s, articles appeared in the local Black press claiming that Abele also designed the Philadelphia Museum of Art. In 1991, a historical marker for Abele (nominated by Charles Blockson) was erected on the art museum's site. The idea that Abele was *the* architect for the museum is inaccurate. The design and construction of the museum took decades and was the product of a contentious collaboration between the Trumbauer firm and the firm of Zantzinger and Borie. According to the extensive research done by David Brownlee and Abele's biographer Dreck Wilson, it seems that Abele did numerous initial designs for the building. For several years, though, Howell Lewis Shay, another Trumbauer designer, took the lead within the firm. Toward the end of the project, Abele stepped back in. Although he surely played a role in creating the glorious building, no one individual deserves singular credit.

Abele almost certainly had a hand in designing some of Center City's other iconic buildings, including the Widener Building (across from City Hall), the Jefferson University Medical Building on Walnut Street, the Ritz Carlton Hotel on Broad Street, and the second tower of the Land Title Building (which housed the Trumbauer firm), also on Broad Street. During Abele's tenure, the Trumbauer firm was commissioned to build homes for the region's wealthiest families, including Ardrossan, the Montgomery family's fifty-room mansion in Villanova. The firm built the Fifteenth Street addition to the Union League, the Philadelphia Racquet Club, and the YMCA on Arch Street—all places from which Abele was excluded.

Although the details are murky, Duke University now proudly claims Abele as the lead architect of its campus, including Cameron Indoor Stadium, the Duke Chapel, and many classroom and dormitory buildings. Abele's central role, however, was generally ignored until brought to the university's attention by Abele's great-grandniece Susan Cook in 1986. Since 1989, the Julian Abele Awards have been given out to honor achievements by Black individuals and groups at Duke. In 2015, Duke named a central passageway on campus Abele Quad and engraved a cornerstone of the Duke Chapel with his name. It is unknown whether Abele ever visited this project, but it is doubtful that he would have made himself visible on the campus that did not accept Black students until 1962. Nor would he have willingly made himself vulnerable to the indignities of the Jim Crow South.

Dignity was of paramount importance to Julian Abele. His relatives and few close friends described him as cultured, quiet, fastidious, and dapper. His hobbies included needlepoint, woodworking, painting, and

Julian Francis Abele in the backyard of his home at 1515
Christian Street with his daughter Nina. (Courtesy of the Free
Library of Philadelphia, Print and Picture Collection)

playing the piano. He attended operas and symphonies. The closest he
ever came to uttering profanity was using the words *confounded* and
darn. Abele's pride and dignity contributed to the lack of clarity about
his role in various projects. When he finally applied to the American
Institute of Architects in 1942, long after his body of work should have
ensured his acceptance, the only buildings he listed as his own were a
house he built for his sister soon after completing his studies and the
Duke University buildings completed after Horace Trumbauer's death.

Although Abele no doubt experienced discrimination and prejudice,
racial issues were not his focus. He was light-skinned, and people he
encountered were often unsure of his race. His wife, Marguerite Bulle,
was white. According to Dreck Wilson, "For all intents and purposes,
Julian did not consider himself black. He was almost aracial. He buried
himself in being an artist."

When Abele died in 1950 at sixty-eight, he was known in architectural circles but was obscure to the public. The twenty-first century, however, has seen a marked increase in attention to Julian Abele. In addition to Duke, Harvard University, Haverford College, the University of Pennsylvania, and Monmouth College have recently taken steps to promote their connection to him. Articles about Abele have appeared in *Smithsonian Magazine*, *House Beautiful*, the *Philadelphia Inquirer*, and numerous other publications.

Philadelphia has been particularly enthusiastic about promoting Abele's legacy. In 2002, the Free Library of Philadelphia's seventy-fifth anniversary celebration included a weekend of events devoted to Abele. Julian Abele Park on Twenty-second Street, near Abele's longtime home at 1515 Christian Street, was dedicated in 2008. In May 2020, the University of Pennsylvania launched a Julian Abele Fellowship to support Black students of architecture. In September 2021, the Philadelphia Museum of Art hosted an hour-long online presentation about Abele's role in designing the building. Abele is one of fourteen Black Philadelphians featured in the Charles Blockson Collection's 2022 publication *BLAM! Black Lives Always Mattered! Hidden African American Philadelphia of the Twentieth Century.*

Black Doctors Row

Renewed interest in Julian Abele may have played a role in the creation of Philadelphia's first historic district based on Black history. In July 2022, the Philadelphia Historical Commission approved the creation of the Christian Street/Black Doctors Row Historic District stretching from Broad Street to Twentieth Street along Christian Street. The designation is based on the Christian Street corridor's significance in the Black community from about 1910 to 1945.

Abele purchased a three-story brick row home at 1515 Christian Street in 1919 and lived there until his death three decades later. During that period, Christian Street was home to a critical mass of Philadelphia-born African American professionals, including about a dozen doctors who worked at the nearby Black medical centers, Douglass Hospital on Fifteenth and Lombard Street and Mercy Hospital on Seventeenth and Fitzwater Street. The moniker "Doctors Row" was attached to Christian Street, though most inhabitants were working-class African Americans, often migrants from the South. Following Abele's death,

This photograph from April 2022 shows the row house adjacent to Abele's former home being replaced with new construction. The Christian Street/Black Doctors Row Historic District will prevent similar demolitions. (Photograph by Amy Jane Cohen)

the Black elite dispersed to North, West, and Northwest Philadelphia. Decades of population decline, deterioration, and disinvestment followed but was reversed by rapid gentrification beginning at the turn of the twenty-first century. The neighborhood that Abele had called home transitioned rapidly from mostly Black and struggling to mostly white and affluent.

During the period of decline, Barbara Candia, the longtime resident of Abele's former home, purchased several row houses along Christian Street. In the summer of 2020, Candia sold 1513 Christian Street to a developer. Although the building was in good repair and being used as a boardinghouse, the developer applied for a demolition permit and proposed replacing the nineteenth-century brick townhouse with a modern four-story luxury condominium building with four units. The house at 1513 was demolished, as was the house at 1507. Similar permits were approved for buildings on nearby blocks of Christian Street. Abele's house, and many others, were clearly at risk of a similar fate.

At the suggestion of the Preservation Alliance for Greater Philadelphia, City Councilman Kenyatta Johnson gained approval for a moratorium on demolitions from Broad Street to Twentieth Street along Christian Street in June 2021. This gave the Preservation Alliance time to write an application to create the Christian Street/Black Doctors Row Historic District as the thirty-seventh historic district in the city, a designation that permanently prevents demolitions and requires official permission for major alterations to the exteriors of existing structures.

Preserving Abele's Street

Kevin Block and Adrian Trevisan, the authors of the 486-page nomination packet for Christian Street/Black Doctors Row Historic District, made a strong case that, both architecturally and culturally, the Christian Street corridor is significant and deserves protection. Christian Street's remaining Victorian townhouses, with wooden cornices and arched lintels above doorways and windows, are worth preserving on aesthetic grounds. The social history of the area is even more compelling.

At the time the Christian Street row houses were built, most residents were middle-class Irish Americans. As these residents moved to areas such as West Philadelphia and Delaware County, Black people flocked to the Christian Street corridor. The African American presence on the 1400–1900 blocks of Christian Street grew from 24 percent in 1910, to 57 percent in 1920, 92 percent in 1930, and 97 percent in 1940.

The influx of southern Black people into Philadelphia in the first wave of the Great Migration (1910–1920) accelerated both the neighborhood's transition and the development of separate Black institutions. Although members of the Black elite had previously been welcome at Center City restaurants and theaters, discrimination against them rose along with the number of Black people in the city. Similarly, Black residents who had been able to patronize white-owned law practices, hospitals, and stores found that they would no longer be served. As a result, Black Philadelphians turned to African American providers; thus, some Black lawyers, medical professionals, and businesspeople were able to thrive economically, and many of them became Abele's neighbors on Christian Street.

A banner headline in the December 20, 1919, edition of the *Philadelphia Tribune* declared "Colored Citizens Own Much Property: Don't Have to Live in Slum Dives and Dilapidated Shacks." The article describes Christian Street from Broad Street to Twentieth Street as "the social centre of colored wealth and pride." In addition to attracting affluent professionals, Christian Street was home to numerous African American institutions. The Christian Street YMCA opened in 1914 as the first Black branch of the YMCA with its own building. The Quaker City Lodge, a chapter of the fully Black-run and Black-funded Improved Benevolent and Protective Order of the Elks, opened a Christian Street headquarters in 1930. Jack and Jill, a club for the children of the Black elite, was founded in 1938 by a dozen neighborhood mothers and had its first meeting in a home across the street from First African Baptist Church (see Chapter 10).

Although the African American population of Christian Street was always of mixed socioeconomic status, the percentage of affluent professionals decreased over time. Nonetheless, Christian Street's reputation as "Doctors Row" persisted. Ninety-four-year-old Sylvia Harrod Blackwell, an African American woman who lived, attended school, went to church, and witnessed her father's businesses thrive along Christian Street, told the Historic Commission in 2022 that "calling Christian Street 'Doctors Row' celebrates the early contributions made in Philadelphia by Black people."

A Strong Dissenting Voice

Although some of the strongest supporters of the Christian Street/Black Doctors Row Historic District are African Americans, so is its most vocal critic. Faye Anderson, a Philadelphia preservationist, activist, and public historian, believes that many other areas of the city are more deserving of becoming the first historic district based on Black history. In a June 2021 tweet, Anderson pointed out that Julian Abele is the only resident of "Black Doctors Row" on Wikipedia's list of "notable Black Philadelphians of the twentieth and twenty-first centuries." Anderson also mentioned that not a single listing in the Green Book for Black travelers, published from 1936 to 1966, had an address on Christian Street.

Anderson's larger criticism, however, is that the designation of the Christian Street/Black Doctors Row corridor as historic is elitist. Although some Black professionals lived along Christian Street, Anderson asserts, most residents were struggling migrants who were not welcome in the social milieu of their light-skinned, Philadelphia-born counterparts. In a letter to the Committee on Historic Designation in June 2022, Anderson declared, "It is ludicrous to suggest the cultural life and identity of African Americans, half of whom were unemployed during the period of significance, were shaped by *poseurs* who held them in contempt. . . . Fact is, they exemplify the legacy of slavery, and the rape of Black women and girls. The descendants of enslaved victims of sexual assault—the 'light, bright, and damn near white' Christian Street 'elite'—had access to educational opportunities that were denied Negroes with darker skin tones."

Anderson is particularly contemptuous of Abele: "Architect Julian Abele is the most accomplished of this largely unknown colored 'elite.' His significance is already memorialized in a historical marker at the Philadelphia Museum of Art. According to his biographer, Dreck Spurlock Wilson, Abele did not consider himself Black. He would have followed in the footsteps of his brother Joseph Bolivar Abele who passed for white, but his skin tone was too dark. So he chose an existence that was neither black nor white. He was 'beige.' Wilson notes that Abele 'did not appreciate beauty in sepia skin women.'"

Summing up her opposition to the Christian Street/Black Doctors Row Historic District, Anderson writes, "The nomination is not about Black history and culture. It's not about the past; instead, it's about the present and next level white privilege. . . . The nomination is about protecting the streetscape of six blocks from which African Americans have been displaced in the most gentrified neighborhood in Philadelphia."

In spite of Anderson's objections, the confirmation of Christian Street/Black Doctors Row Historic District in July 2022 was greeted with delight by many preservationists, historians, and community members. The work done by Block and Trevisan in their detailed application provides the groundwork for future historical markers, walking tours, and new discoveries about Black community life and notable individuals in early twentieth-century Philadelphia.

One wonders what Julian Abele would have made of the debate about the destiny of the street that he called home. My hunch is that, as an architect, he would have liked to see the well-built Victorian row homes kept intact. As to the deeper questions about race, elitism, gentrification, and privilege, he might well have preferred to keep his perspective to himself, focusing instead on music, art, and architecture.

To Do

- ▶ Visit the Free Library of Philadelphia and the Philadelphia Museum of Art and find Abele's historical markers.

- ▶ Watch a seventy-five minute video, *A Profile of African American Architect Julian Abele: The Shadows are All Mine*, presented by Institute of Classical Architecture and Art at https://www.classicist.org/articles/a-profile-of-african-american-architect-julian-abele-the-shadows-are-all-mine.

- ▶ Stroll the Christian Street corridor from Sixteenth to Eighteenth streets. In addition to the First African Baptist Church building, you will see a Jack and Jill historical marker at 1605 Christian Street and the Christian Street YMCA and historical marker at 1724 Christian Street. At 1710 Christian Street you will see a marker for John C. Asbury, a prominent Black Republican who was one of the founders of Eden Cemetery and Mercy Hospital.

- ▶ Visit Julian Abele Park on Twenty-second Street between Carpenter and Montrose streets.

- ▶ Read a comic book-style biography of Julian Abele in *BLAM! Black Lives Always Mattered! Hidden African American Philadelphia of the Twentieth Century.*

12

ALAIN LOCKE

Triple Minority and Native Son

A lain LeRoy Locke (1885–1954) had much in common with other prominent twentieth-century Black men with ties to the Philadelphia area.[1] Like the architect Julian Francis Abele, Locke was dapper, an aesthete, and a member of the Black elite. Similar to the painter Henry Ossawa Tanner, Locke found liberation from pervasive racism while spending time in Europe. Both Locke and the singer Paul Robeson have Philadelphia public schools named in their honor, even though they were followed by the Federal Bureau of Investigation (FBI) due to their openness to communist ideas. Like another FBI target with a school named in his honor, West Chester's Bayard Rustin, Locke was gay.

Although Locke had similarities to these men, he was also one of a kind. As a queer Black man and follower of the Baha'i faith, Locke was a triple minority. At four feet eleven inches tall, his stature further marked him as outside of the mainstream. In spite of, or perhaps because of, these challenges, Alain Locke lived a remarkable life, earning the moniker "Father of the Harlem Renaissance." Although Locke, who spent decades teaching at Howard University, may be more closely associated with Washington, DC, and Harlem, he was a product of Philadelphia.

---

1. Portions of this chapter appeared as "Alain LeRoy Locke: Father of the Harlem Renaissance and Philly LGBTQ Hero," *Hidden City Philadelphia*, June 2, 2021, https://hiddencityphila.org/2021/06/alain-leroy-locke-father-of-the-harlem-renaissance-and-philly-lgbtq-hero.

Alain Locke in a 1940s photograph by the photojournalist John Mosley.
(John W. Mosley Photograph Collection, Charles L. Blockson Afro-American Collection, Temple University Libraries, Philadelphia)

Heritage and Early Years

Alain Locke's grandfather, Ishmael Locke, was the first principal of the Institute for Colored Youth (ICY), whose intellectually gifted Black students included Octavius V. Catto; Julian Abele; Alain's father, Pliny Locke; and his mother, Mary Hawkins Locke. While a student at the ICY, Pliny Locke befriended Catto, and they were teammates on the Pythians baseball team.

After completing his studies at the ICY, Pliny Locke taught at the school and at a Freedman's Bureau school in Tennessee. He later graduated in the first class of Howard University Law School, and after becoming the first Black person to take and pass the federal civil service exam, he became the first African American to work for the U.S. Postal Service. Despite his intelligence and credentials, though, Pliny Locke's career path was constrained by his skin color: there was little demand for Black attorneys in late nineteenth-century Philadelphia.

After a sixteen-year engagement, Pliny and Mary were married in 1879. They, along with their mothers, lived on Nineteenth Street near Addison, a neighborhood that housed members of Philadelphia's Black elite. Arthur LeRoy Locke was born in 1885 (he changed his name to Alain as a teenager). Pliny took a job as a night janitor so he could spend his days with their son. While Pliny was home reading Virgil and Homer to the boy, Mary taught at an all-Black school in Camden, New Jersey. Along with both of Alain's grandmothers, the family moved to Sixth and Tasker in South Philadelphia in 1890.

The following year, when Alain Locke was just six years old, Pliny died. By this point, he had already become frustrated with his son's effeminate tendencies. His father's death only strengthened Alain's bond to his mother. Mary Locke's commitment to education and culture had a powerful influence on Alain. Together they took advantage of Philadelphia's many integrated cultural institutions. They attended concerts at the Academy of Music, heard Greek myths read aloud at the Free Library of Philadelphia, took in exhibits at the Pennsylvania Academy of Fine Arts, learned about science at the Franklin Institute, and went to lectures at the Ethical Society.

Alain Locke was a studious child who loved to read. At thirteen he was admitted to Central High School, then located on the west side of Broad and Green streets, today the site of Benjamin Franklin High School and the Science Leadership Academy. When he graduated in 1902 (Class 107 for you Central Lancers out there), he was ranked second. Locke was then first in his class at the Philadelphia School of Pedagogy, a teacher training school for Central grads that he attended for two years.

Leaving Philadelphia

Locke realized that his options would be limited if he tried to teach in Philadelphia, where Black teachers could teach only Black students. Integrated schools such as Central hired only white teachers. Locke left Philadelphia to study philosophy at Harvard. His closest college friends, all white, were fellow Central grads. His small size finally an advantage, Locke was the first Black coxswain for the Harvard crew team.

Continuing to excel academically, Locke graduated magna cum laude and Phi Beta Kappa from Harvard in 1907. He became the first

Black Rhodes scholar, gaining the opportunity to study at Oxford University. There was not another African American Rhodes scholar until 1963, when the author John Edgar Wideman won the prestigious award.

After three years at Oxford, Locke studied an additional two years at the University of Berlin, reveling in the more open social and sexual atmosphere of the cosmopolitan city. When he returned to the United States, Locke taught at Howard University and later completed his doctorate in philosophy at Harvard. He returned to Howard but was dismissed for three years in the mid-1920s after advocating for pay equity between white and Black professors, a policy that did not yet exist even at this flagship Black university.

It was during this hiatus from teaching that Locke moved to New York and wrote his most famous work: *The New Negro: An Interpretation*. An anthology of poems, essays, drawings, musical pieces, stories, and music by Black artists, the volume made Locke a national figure. He was able to explain the flowering of the arts then taking place in Harlem to both whites and African Americans. Locke believed that Black people had a special ability to draw on their pasts to create personal works of art that conveyed universal themes. He became the preeminent authority on African American culture and promoted the works he found most worthy. Langston Hughes, Countee Cullen, Claude McKay, Jean Toomer, and Zora Neale Hurston were among the many Black creatives mentored, and sometimes courted, by Locke.

In 1928, Locke was lured back to Howard by the university's first Black president. He stayed there as chair of the Philosophy Department until 1953. The actor Ossie Davis was among the many students with whom Locke developed a close bond. By the time Locke died in 1954, he was a world-renowned scholar, writer, speaker, editor, and critic.

Once Locke headed to Harvard, Philadelphia was never again his primary residence. Indeed, when he first arrived in Cambridge and was seeking a place to board, he wrote to his mother: "If I could get a nice bunk up here, Phila would never see me again." However, even after Mary Locke moved to Washington, DC, to be closer to her son, Alain continued to visit the city of his birth.[2]

---

2. Though Mary Locke was delighted to be living near Alain, she missed shopping at John Wanamaker's. Blacks were banned from Garfinkel's, the leading department store in Washington, DC.

Hometown Connections

In 1924, Locke was summoned to the Merion estate of Albert Barnes, another Central grad, though one who had graduated at the bottom of the ninety-second class. The two had met in Paris and shared a passion for African art, albeit for different reasons. While Barnes saw African art as the inspiration for his beloved European modernism, Locke hoped it could provide a source of pride and motivation for African American artists. Both Barnes and Locke were known for their exceptional taste and their outsize egos. Not surprisingly, they had a falling out. Barnes accused Locke of plagiarizing his ideas, and their brief connection was forever ruptured.

But Locke's ties to Philadelphia remained intact. In 1927, he wrote a brief introduction for the first edition of the *Black Opals*, a series of pamphlets for Philadelphia's Black public school students; in the essay, "Hail Philadelphia," Locke celebrates his hometown with obvious pride as a place where "the tradition of breeding and respectability in the race lingers in the old Negro families of the city." As the originator of the term "New Negro," he also exhorted Philadelphia youth to engage in "vital creative thinking" and to avoid "self complacency and smugness." The essay concludes: "I want to sing a 'Hail Philadelphia' that is less a chant for the dead and more a song for the living. For especially for the Negro, I believe in the 'life to come.'"

Locke was in Germantown for Negro Achievement Week in April 1928, a celebration of Black contributions in the arts. The event was an interracial collaboration between local organizations and notable national figures, including W. E. B. Du Bois and the writer and activist James Weldon Johnson. Locke was the keynote speaker at the opening meeting and spoke on Literature Night three days later.

In the early 1940s, after decades of heartbreak, Locke found love in his native city. Maurice Russell was forty years Locke's junior, but the affection and attraction between the men seems to have been mutual. Russell had a civil service job at the Philadelphia Naval Yard, yet Locke impressed on him the importance of education, writing to him: "Training is imperative for everyone nowadays, particularly for the younger Negro. Philadelphia youth haven't seemed to realize this as realistically as they should. The town is full of nice, untrained, but complacent people." Russell sent Locke the 1942 summer schedule for Philadelphia

Orchestra concerts at the Robin Hood Dell. Locke expressed particular interest in attending performances by two Black singers: the Philadelphia native Marian Anderson and the future Philadelphia resident Paul Robeson.

Locke in the Landscape

Locke traveled the world, but Philadelphia was his birthplace and the city in which he came of age. Although five American schools have been named for him, Philadelphia's Alain Locke School at Forty-sixth and Haverford was the first. The school opened without controversy in 1965. At that point, his homosexuality was virtually unknown to the public. In contrast, the school board of West Chester, Pennsylvania, briefly rescinded its decision to name a high school for the civil rights activist Bayard Rustin in 2002 when community members objected to honoring a gay man in this way, particularly one who had associations with communism.

In 1991, a historical marker was installed in front of 2221 South Fifth Street, the home purchased by Mary Locke following her husband's death. She and Alain lived in this two-story row house between Jackson and Wolf from 1892 to 1899. Once Mary Locke sold the home, it was purchased eight more times—mostly by people with Jewish or Italian last names. The current residents are from Cambodia.

Unfortunately, the historical marker is no longer standing. According to a representative of the Pennsylvania Historical and Museum Commission, "It was continually hit by vehicles on the narrow streets of South Philadelphia." Malcolm Lazin of the Equality Forum led an effort to erect a new marker honoring Alain Locke in 2021, this time in front of the African American Museum of Philadelphia.[3]

Like many gay men in his generation, Locke lived in the closet in an atmosphere Lazin describes as a "tsunami of homophobia" but is celebrated today as a gay icon. In 2018, a mural of Locke was painted at

3. Malcolm Lazin, founder and executive director of the Equality Forum, has played the Charles Blockson role for the LGBTQ community. His first successful application was for a marker unveiled in 2005 commemorating demonstrations for gay rights that took place at Independence Hall on July 4 from 1965 to 1969. There are currently more than a dozen markers recognizing the LGBTQ experience in Philadelphia—more government-approved LGBTQ historical markers than in any other city in the world. That's quite a feather in the cap of the City of Brotherly Love and Sisterly Affection.

Mural of Alain Locke on Juniper Street in the Gayborhood. (Photograph by Michael Bixler)

Juniper and Spruce, the heart of Philadelphia's gayborhood—a fitting honor for a noteworthy native son.

To Do

► Learn more about Negro Achievement Week by reading *The Battles of Germantown*, by David W. Young (Temple University Press, 2019).

► Visit the Alain Locke mural at Juniper and Spruce Streets.

► Read Locke's groundbreaking essay "Enter the New Negro" in the March 1925 issue of *Survey Graphic* magazine (http://nationalhumanitiescenter.org/pds/maai3/migrations/text8/lockenewnegro.pdf).

► See the Alain Locke historical marker in front of the African American Museum of Philadelphia at Eighth and Arch streets.

MARIAN ANDERSON AND
SADIE ALEXANDER

A Tale of Two Cities

[With a Reflection by Jillian Patricia Pirtle]

etween the end of the nineteenth century and the beginning of the 1920s, Philadelphia experienced escalations in both discrimination and racial violence.[1] One of the worst episodes of racial violence in the city's history took place in 1918. To understand the context of the events of July 1918, it helps to examine the early lives of two of Philadelphia's most noteworthy African American women. Both Marian Anderson, born into the struggling working class, and Sadie Alexander, a member of the Black elite, were affected by the increasing racial animosity that exploded in the summer of 1918.

South Philadelphia Roots

The world-renowned singer Marian Anderson (1897–1933) was born in South Philadelphia during an era of relative racial peace in the city. At the start of the twentieth century, the Black population was small (only about sixty thousand people in a city of more than 1.2 million residents) and led by an educated, intellectually engaged elite that had coalesced in the late nineteenth century, the group that W. E. B. Du Bois had

---

1. Portions of this chapter appeared as "Examining Class and Racial Dynamics on the Anniversary of the 1918 Riots in South Philadelphia," *Hidden City Philadelphia*, July 25, 2019, https://hiddencityphila.org/2019/07/examining-class-and-racial-dynamics-on-the-anniversary-of-the-1918-riots-in-south-philadelphia.

Marian Anderson (*center*) with her mother, Anna, and sisters, Alyse (*left*) and Ethel (*right*), ca. 1910. (Marian Anderson Collection of Photographs, ms. coll. 198, vol. 1, p. 2, item 1, Kislak Center for Rare Books, Manuscripts and Special Collections, University of Pennsylvania, Philadelphia)

dubbed "Grade 1" in *The Philadelphia Negro*. Members of this community attended the prestigious Institute for Colored Youth, mixed among themselves at exclusive Black social clubs, and frequented restaurants and theaters alongside white Philadelphians.

The Anderson family was not of this ilk. Like many poor Black Philadelphians, Marian's grandparents had been enslaved, and her parents were recent migrants from the South. Although Marian's mother,

Anna, had been a teacher in Virginia, she was unable to find work in her profession once she came to Philadelphia. So despite her education, she took in laundry and worked in a tobacco factory. Once she had her three daughters, of whom Marian was the eldest, Anna Anderson worked outside the home only when extra money was needed. Marian's father, John, delivered coal and ice and worked in the refrigeration room at Reading Terminal Market. In her autobiography, Marian Anderson recalls that that he would bring home pound cake from the market as an occasional treat.

John, who was also a church officer with the Union Baptist Church, was proud that his daughter was able to join the choir at six. Known as the "baby contralto," Marian Anderson was soon invited to sing at events, thus bringing in a much needed bit of money. When she was twelve, her father died as a result of a work injury. The family moved into her paternal grandmother's home, first on Fitzwater Street and later on Christian Street, and Marian's mother did domestic work and took in laundry. Without her father's income, the family struggled financially. Members of Union Baptist Church and other neighborhood groups took up a collection to help Marian pay for music lessons and clothing for performances. Her budding talent gave the family a sense of specialness within their community, albeit a less elevated community than that of their wealthier and more established African American peers.

After attending E. M. Stanton Elementary School, an integrated school at Seventeenth and Christians streets, Marian moved on to William Penn High School on North Broad Street and transferred to South Philadelphia High School on South Broad Street because of its superior music program.

Lofty Pedigree and Distinguished Degrees

Sadie Tanner Mossell Alexander (1898–1989) was born a year after Anderson. The extended Tanner Mossell family epitomized Philadelphia's Black elite. The famed painter Henry Ossawa Tanner was an uncle on her mother's side. Her father, Aaron Mossell, was the first African American to attend the University of Pennsylvania's Law School, and his brother, Nathan Mossell, was Penn's first Black medical school graduate.

After earning a Bachelor of Arts from the University of Pennsylvania's School of Education in 1918, Sadie Tanner Mossell stayed on at

Sadie Tanner Mossell Alexander (*far right*) with members of the Delta Sigma Theta sorority, the first Black sorority at the University of Pennsylvania. (Image courtesy of University of Pennsylvania, Archives and Records Center, Philadelphia)

Penn to become the first African American woman in the country to earn a doctorate in economics. As a graduate student, she established a chapter of the Delta Sigma Theta sorority at Penn and became the first national president of the organization. She married the attorney Raymond Pace Alexander, another descendant of the Black aristocracy. In 1927, Sadie Alexander became the first Black female graduate of the University of Pennsylvania Law School and the first Black woman admitted to the Pennsylvania Bar.

Interestingly, to understand both a key turning point in the life of Marian Anderson and the racial violence of 1918, we must turn to the work of the young Sadie Mossell. Her thesis, written in pursuit of a master's in economics, was titled "The Standard of Living among One Hundred Negro Migrant Families in Philadelphia." Completed in 1919, her research documented the quickly shifting racial dynamics that existed in early twentieth-century Philadelphia and their effects on families like Anderson's.

Changing Racial Dynamics

Marian Anderson's family lived in several South Philadelphia locales, neighborhoods that were characterized by a mix of African American, Jewish, Irish, and Italian residents. Racial tension existed, and Anderson recalled instances when trolley cars would pass by without stopping to pick up Black passengers. Overall, though, these diverse communities of recent arrivals to the city struggled and strived in proximity and generally in peace.

But, as Alexander explained, the rapid influx of southern migrants during the era of World War I changed the racial mood of the city. As European immigration screeched to a halt, poorly educated and low-skilled Black families were lured to Philadelphia and other industrial cities of the North by the prospect of employment and a better life. Philadelphia's Black population skyrocketed, causing consternation among the city's white residents. The increase was particularly steep from 1916 to 1918, when an estimated 150 Black migrants arrived from the South each week.

Finding a place to live became the biggest challenge for the new arrivals. Alexander described the reception given the typical Black migrant: "If we may judge the attitude of the whites by their efforts to segregate him, it would seem that he was highly unwelcome. The housing problem was itself a result of the determination on the part of the white people that the migrant should live only in that part of the city in which Negroes had previously lived. Vacant houses in other sections were not for rent or sale to the Negroes."

The Black elite, also known as the Old Philadelphians (OPs), were also wary of the new arrivals, who posed an enormous threat to their comfortable, genteel way of life. According to Alexander, "The increase in Negro population greatly stimulated the movement. . . . to segregate children in schools. Also, such social privileges as the service of eating houses and the attending of white churches and theaters by Negroes were practically withdrawn after the influx of Negro migrants into Philadelphia."

It is in this context that we must understand a watershed moment in young Marian Anderson's life. In 1914, with the encouragement of her community and a high school degree, she walked from her South Philadelphia home to the Philadelphia Musical Academy at 1617 Spruce Street (later the Garden Restaurant and now a condominium). She hoped to audition for a place at the school. After hours of being passed over as aspiring white musicians took their turns, Anderson returned home in despair. Nearly five decades later, Anderson still recalled the sting of that rejection. Given the more racially tolerant Philadelphia of her early years, she claimed that this was when she first experienced a "painful realization of what it meant to be a Negro."

Racial Hatred Unleashed

Unfortunately, a woman named Adella Bond learned about changed racial attitudes in more dramatic fashion. In 1918 she bought a home in Gray's Ferry, at 2936 Ellsworth Street. Mossell describes Bond as "a colored probation officer of the Municipal Court, a woman of refinement and training and an old citizen of Philadelphia." But amid growing racial hostility, being a member of the OP class did not insulate Black people from anti-migrant anger. In fact, Bond's affluence may have been a factor in stirring up anger in the neighborhood. The real estate agent who sold the house to Bond told the *Philadelphia Tribune* that white residents in the area were perpetually behind on their rent. "We got tired of dealing with these people," he explained. "Yes, I employed a negro agent and sought to dispose of the eight houses I owned there. . . . We were glad, of course, to sell to the desirable colored people he found."

On July 26, 1918, a crowd of about one hundred white men and boys, many of them armed, congregated in front of Bond's new home. After a rock was thrown through her parlor window, she shot a rifle through her second-story window, which alerted the police. Bond was arrested, and several days of rioting ensued. Large swaths of the area from Dickinson Street to Washington Avenue and Twenty-third to Thirtieth streets were engulfed in violence. A police officer was shot by a Black man; subsequently two Black men were killed while in police custody. Sixty Black people and three white people were arrested during the days of violence. Many witnesses thought the police exacerbated the situation, antagonizing and arresting the African American men and protecting the white men. Overall, four people died, hundreds were injured, and Black neighborhoods were severely damaged. It was the first race riot the city had experienced since 1871.

During the years of World War I, racial attitudes in Philadelphia had changed. Increased hostility and discrimination affected not only struggling Black people, like the Andersons, but also members of the established Black elite, like the Mossells and the Alexanders. As Sadie Alexander described in her thesis, "As in the case of the probation officer (Adella Bond) so in numerous other occurrences, the colored people of every class received harsh treatment at the hands of the white public." No wonder Anderson chose to leave the city to pursue her career; and no wonder that Alexander chose to stay—as an attorney and leading civil rights advocate.

Sadie Alexander was tapped to write the civil rights legislation that was included in Philadelphia's Home Rule Charter, adopted in 1951. Her provisions codified bans on discrimination in a wide range of city government activities and required the establishment of a Human Relations Commission. Alexander was the first leader of the new organization, which was charged with carrying out the city's present and future antidiscrimination laws, investigating accusations of violations of those laws, and educating the public to counteract religious and racial bias.

Anderson and Alexander in the Landscape

While both women were highly regarded during their lifetimes, Anderson, of humbler origin, is the one who became internationally renowned. At seventeen, Anderson won a contest to sing with the New York Philharmonic. She then toured Europe, where she sang in front of royalty and at leading opera houses. In 1936, she became the first Black person to perform at the White House and famously gave a live performance at the Lincoln Memorial at the invitation of First Lady Eleanor Roosevelt when the Daughters of the American Revolution refused to allow her to sing at Constitution Hall. In 1955, she was the first African American to perform with the Metropolitan Opera. President Dwight Eisenhower named her a delegate to the General Assembly of the United Nations, and in 1963, President Lyndon Johnson awarded her the Presidential Medal of Freedom. Anderson's final performance was at Carnegie Hall in 1965—

quite an impressive career, particularly for a Black girl from South Philadelphia who had to overcome severe discrimination to succeed.

In 1924, Anderson purchased a three-story brick row house on Martin Street, around the corner from the current location of Union Baptist Church. She used her Philadelphia home as a place to rest between tours and to entertain in the finished basement. Like many Black people, she preferred to host friends at home rather than risk rejection at white establishments. Although Anderson traveled widely and frequently, the house she purchased at twenty-seven was her primary residence for the rest of her life. Julian Abele was among her many friends in the neighborhood. The building now houses the National Marian Anderson Museum, and the block of Martin Street has the honorary name of Marian Anderson Way. The museum interprets Anderson's life and career and sponsors educational programs and musical performances.

The area around the museum is marked by banners that call it the Marian Anderson Heritage Village. A few blocks away, a recreation center is named in Anderson's honor, and she has a plaque on South Broad Street's Walk of Fame. A historical marker in front of the Union Baptist Church at 1910 Fitzwater Street mistakenly states that Anderson sang there as a child. Union Baptist Church moved to its current location in 1916, when Anderson was nineteen. The church building in which she sang as a child was located on Twelfth Street, near Bainbridge. In 2015, that building, then home to New Hope Temple Baptist Church, was demolished and replaced with an apartment building, a fate shared by numerous Black churches as gentrification has transformed large swaths of South Philadelphia.

In June 2023, the Chester A. Arthur Elementary School at Twentieth and Catharine streets was renamed the Marian Anderson Neighborhood Academy. Fifth-grade students initiated the push to make the change, and they received widespread support among neighbors of the school. Anderson's name was chosen as the result of an online poll of community members.

In addition, plans are in the works for Marian Anderson to become the first Black woman honored with a statue on public land in Philadelphia. The memorial is slated to be placed in front of the Academy of Music, a venue where she performed often.

Sadie Alexander rose to national prominence when she served on President Harry Truman's Civil Rights Committee in 1946. For the most part, though, she is a local figure. Her home in West Mount Airy was given a historical marker in 1993, and in 2022 the house was added to the Philadelphia Register of Historic Places. The Penn Alexander School, a collaboration between the University of Pennsylvania and the School District of Philadelphia, was named in her honor in 2003. Her most significant legacy, however, is the Philadelphia Commission on Human Relations, which continues to fight discrimination more than seventy years after Sadie Alexander wrote it into existence.

Reflection

Jillian Patricia Pirtle is the chief executive officer of the Marian Anderson Museum and Historical Society, as well as a professional stage and opera artist.

Marian Anderson has always been a symbol to me of a woman, an African American, and an artist to aspire to be. She was, and is, a great reflection of beauty, grace, and dignity and someone who, despite the odds and challenges, never gave up and still believed in her dream.

I became a Marian Anderson Scholar-Artist at thirteen under the direction of our beloved late founder, Lady Blanche Burton-Lyles, who was Marian Anderson's protégé. She founded the museum when Marian Anderson passed away in 1993 and purchased the home and sought to start the preservation of that sacred space with historic designations from the City of Philadelphia, the Commonwealth of Pennsylvania, and the U.S. Department of the Interior. Burton-Lyles also reinvigorated the Marian Anderson Scholar-Artist program that Anderson started in 1950, selecting young artists who had the ambition of becoming the next Marian Anderson, Leontyne Price, Todd Duncan, and such.

I am thrilled that one of the long-standing dreams of Lady Blanche Burton Lyles, the creation of a statue honoring Marian Anderson in such a prominent and historic location as the Academy of Music, is becoming a reality. This has been a dream twenty-seven years in the making. It is my sincere hope that this great historical monument will lead people to visit the National Marian Anderson Museum and Historical Society and support our treasured programming.

To Do

▸ Visit the National Marian Anderson Museum at 762 South Martin Street and walk around the area. Check the museum's website (https://mariananandersonhistoricalsociety.weebly.com) or call the museum before you visit.

- ► Find Marian Anderson's plaque on the Philadelphia Musical Alliance Walk of Fame on South Broad Street.

- ► Watch "Awakening (1900–1920)," part of the *Philadelphia: The Great Experiment* series produced by History Making Productions, at https://www.youtube.com/watch?v=15mkmy8weAQ.

- ► Read Sadie Alexander's thesis, "The Standard of Living among One Hundred Negro Migrant Families in Philadelphia." A digital copy is available at https://www.google.com/books/edi tion/The_Standard_of_Living_Among_One_Hundred/35pw AAAAIAAJ?hl=en&gbpv=1&printsec=frontcover.

- ► See the Sadie Alexander home and historical marker at 700 Westview Street.

- ► Learn about the history and efforts to preserve the Henry O. Tanner House, where Sadie Alexander was born and married, by watching *Judith Robinson and Evan Curtis on Preserving the Henry O. Tanner House* at https://www.youtube.com /watch?v=qkqtskZinI0. Follow the ongoing efforts of the Friends of the Tanner House by visiting the organization's website at https://savethetannerhouse.org.

14

⌒

THE ALL WARS MEMORIAL
TO COLORED SOLDIERS AND SAILORS

The Prolonged Battle for a Place on the Parkway

"My dad always flew an American flag in our front yard." So begins Nikole Hannah-Jones's opening essay in the groundbreaking *New York Times* supplement *The 1619 Project*. Hannah-Jones describes her long path to understanding the deep patriotism of her Mississippi-born father, a man who worked hard his whole life but remained poor. He had enlisted in the U.S. Army at seventeen under the mistaken impression that military service would prove to white America that he and other Black people were worthy of civil rights and economic opportunity. Hannah-Jones wonders, "How could this black man, having seen firsthand the way his country abused black Americans, how it refused to treat us as full citizens, proudly fly its banner?"

Philadelphia's Samuel Beecher Hart (1863–1936) understood how a strong feeling of loyalty to the United States could coexist with an awareness of America's deep-seated and ongoing racism. Like Hannah-Jones's father, Hart served in the armed forces and recognized that African Americans have been part of the fabric of this country since its earliest inception. While Hannah-Jones's father flew a flag to symbolize his devotion to the United States, Samuel Beecher Hart created a monument: The All Wars Memorial to Colored Soldiers and Sailors.

A Circuitous Path to a Permanent Home

Today, the All Wars Memorial sits on the Benjamin Franklin Parkway, across Twentieth Street from the Franklin Institute and opposite Logan Circle. Hart had envisioned the Parkway as the appropriate site for a monument honoring the military service of African American men. Unfortunately, it took six decades for Hart's plan to be realized.

Hart served Philadelphia's Seventh Ward in the Pennsylvania House of Representatives. First elected in 1924, he stayed in office until his death in 1936. Born in Philadelphia, Hart had been a captain in the Gray Invincibles, a Black National Guard unit that was disbanded with little warning in 1900. His family belonged to St. Peter Claver Catholic Church on Twelfth and Lombard streets and resided at 2021 Waverly Street. In 1920, Hart's wife Anna was the first woman to vote in Philadelphia after the Nineteenth Amendment gave women the franchise. According to a front-page headline in the *Philadelphia Tribune*, "Colored Woman First of Her Sex to Vote in Phila[delphia]; Honor Conceded to Mrs. Samuel B. Hart, Who, on Tuesday, at 7 A.M., Voted the Entire Republican Ticket." A few years later, she would have the opportunity to vote for her husband in his first of six successful runs for the state legislature.

During his first term as a state representative, Hart proposed a bill to commission a monument honoring 150 years of military service by African Americans. The bill was defeated, but two years later Hart was more familiar with how to maneuver in Harrisburg, and in 1927 his proposal was passed and signed into law. A seven-person Colored Soldiers Statues Commission was formed, which included Hart and four other Black members. As the result of a design competition, J. Otto Schweizer, a Swiss-born sculptor based in the Tioga neighborhood, was selected to create the monument.

The selection of Schweizer and the approval of his design were much smoother than the process of choosing a location for his work once completed. The city's powerful, all-white Art Jury denied the Colored Soldiers Statue Commission's request to place the memorial on the Parkway. The Art Jury claimed it didn't want to turn the city's intended "Champs-Elysees" into an avenue of war memorials, yet it had recently approved the placement of two new Civil War monuments on the Parkway. The Art Jury suggested Fitler Park as an alternative site. Although Fitler Square today is a charming spot in an upscale neighborhood, in the early 1930s it was a neglected parcel of land adjacent to a Black neighborhood to the south and a working-class Irish neighborhood to the west.

Many white residents were opposed to the placement of the memorial in their neighborhood. The landlord of a Pine Street apartment building facing the park feared that the presence of the memorial and the visitors it was likely to attract would cause him to lose tenants. Black Philadelphians were even more resistant to putting the memorial in Fitler Park.

John Marquess, the Exalted Ruler of the Quaker City Lodge of Elks (the Black Elks based on Christian Street), visited the site and described it this way: "To my surprise and utter disgust, I found Fitler Park a miniature wilderness in a God-forsaken section of this metropolitan city. . . . [L]eaves, litter and rags upon the day of my visit were scattered everywhere. The seats were dirty and had apparently exhausted themselves begging for a little paint to hide their nakedness." Marquess returned to the park at dusk and was even more dismayed: "Dirty children, drunken bums, pot hounds of sure mongrel strain—these were the lot which sported on the spot where there was to be erected a monument to heroic Negro soldier dead."

Although not all detractors used such colorful language, opposition to the Fitler Park location appears to have been nearly universal among African Americans. Not only was the site remote and in disrepair, but it was also likely to be unsafe for both the monuments and its visitors, given the longtime antipathy between Philadelphia's Black and Irish communities.

A five-year standoff ensued. To maintain the support of Black voters, Republican members of the City Council passed a resolution endorsing the placement of the monument on the Parkway. Although the resolution was also signed by the mayor, it had no enforcement mechanism, and the Art Jury remained adamantly opposed. Eventually, a compromise was reached. On June 7, 1934, the All Wars Memorial to Colored Soldiers and Sailors was dedicated in an obscure corner of Fairmount Park behind Memorial Hall. According to the art historian Ilene Lieberman, "The protracted battle to situate *The All Wars Memorial* had ended with the monument stranded in the depths of the nation's largest urban park, across the Schuylkill River on the fringes of the city."

Samuel Beecher Hart, though disappointed with the monument's location, did have the satisfaction of participating in its dedication. Fol-

A Memorial Day ceremony in 1969 at the All Wars Memorial to Colored Soldiers monument in Fairmount Park. Note the extensive wear on the statues. (Photograph by Salvatore C. DiMarco, Special Collections Research Center, Temple University Libraries, Philadelphia)

lowing a two-hour parade that began at Sixteenth and Spruce streets, about three thousand people attended the opening ceremonies. The keynote address was given by Reverend Robert Bagnall of the St. Thomas African Episcopal Church (though the *Philadelphia Inquirer* mistakenly called it St. Thomas Protestant Episcopal Church) and a former high-ranking leader of the National Association for the Advancement of Colored People. In referring to World War I, Bagnall stated "black soldiers fought for democracy they did not win, for the world is less democratic since the war than before as far as Negroes are concerned." He continued by calling for "a war on everything that robs men of their rights; that robs black men of opportunity and therefore blocks the progress of our Nation."

The All Wars Memorial to Colored Soldiers and Sailors in its current location in front of the Franklin Institute along the Parkway. (Photograph by Stella James Ragas)

Another speaker, Mayor J. Hampton Moore, defended the controversial placement of the memorial, saying, "This monument needed to be placed on a mountain-top; somewhere in a place, like this, to which people may come without fear of being run down by automobiles." Although annual Memorial Day ceremonies were held at the Fairmount Park site, the remote location continued to rankle, and the monument succumbed to weathering, vandalism, and neglect. Hart's granddaughter, Doris Jones Holliday, participated in the opening ceremonies and later spent many years trying to find support to relocate the memorial.

In 1988, West Philadelphia City Councilman Lucien Blackwell spearheaded an unsuccessful effort to get the monument moved to a more prominent location. In 1993, Michael Roepel, a member of the Philadelphia City Planning Commission, formed the Committee to Restore and Relocate the All Wars Memorial to Colored Soldiers and Sailors. Roepel's group garnered the endorsements of Mayor Ed Rendell, the Fairmount Park Commission, and the Art Commission, which had replaced the Art Jury. The City Council appropriated funds to restore and relocate the monument. The granite and bronze memorial was thoroughly refurbished, and on Veterans Day, November 11, 1994, the monument was at last rededicated at its long-intended location.

Among those participating in the rededication ceremonies on the Parkway was Doris Jones Holliday, the granddaughter of Samuel Beecher Hart. As she had in the earlier dedication, she pulled one of the cords at the unveiling of the monument. She told a reporter that day, "The dream has come full circle." Although Hart had served in the Pennsylvania legislature for more than ten years and was the oldest and longest-serving Black representative at the time of his death, the completion of the All Wars Memorial to Colored Soldiers and Sailors—the monument he had always pictured on the Parkway—remained his proudest accomplishment.

Focus on the Memorial and Its Meaning

Now that the All Wars Memorial is located on a major city thoroughfare, it is visible to large numbers of city residents and visitors. Given that it is a large granite shaft surrounded by bronze figures and bronze plaques, it is, at first glance, like other traditional monuments that dot the Parkway. On the front of the monument, the largest, highest, and central figure is a woman representing justice. She holds two wreaths symbolizing honor and reward. On each side of her are life-size figures of Black men in World War I uniforms. On her left are three soldiers; on her right are two soldiers and a sailor. On the back of the monument are four female figures symbolizing war, peace, liberty, and plenty. Like the figure of justice, each of these women appears to be white.

In the twenty-first century, it seems odd that this monument honoring Black military men has such a large presence of white women. Perhaps Hart and other members of the mostly Black Colored Soldiers Statue Commission recognized that a design using traditional symbols and white imagery would be the most palatable to the Art Jury and other authorities. This may also be why they chose Otto Schweizer to do the work. He had already designed numerous war memorials, including seven for the Gettysburg Battlefield (more than any other sculptor), eight busts of military leaders for Philadelphia's Union League, and a sculpture of General Van Steuben for Valley Forge National Historical Park. In addition, he created the Monument to Confederate Women for the Arkansas State Capitol.

Though the All Wars Memorial may strike us today as dated, it was commissioned during an era in which almost no civic monuments depicted Black people or recognized Black contributions to American society. It was also a time when the American military remained strictly segregated, even though Black people had fought and died in every war in American history. In both the American Revolution and the Civil War, Black people were first barred from fighting and then eagerly recruited when it became clear their manpower was needed. Black men known as "Buffalo Soldiers" fought against native peoples in the American West. Black soldiers helped the Rough Riders win the Battle of San Juan Hill and were instrumental in defeating guerrillas during the Philippine Insurrection. And within the memory of men like Hart, Black men had fought bravely during World War I. In each of these conflicts, Black people served in segregated units and were assigned to the dirtiest and most menial tasks. They were usually under the command of white officers. And even in uniform, they risked discrimination, humiliation, and violence because of their skin color.

The All Wars Memorial honoring the sacrifices of these brave and patriotic Black veterans is now a visible part of the Philadelphia landscape. Next time you find yourself near Twentieth Street and the Parkway, take time to visit this monument and consider how long it took to get it to its rightful place. Like the flag that graces the home of Hannah-Jones's father, the All Wars Memorial is a powerful tribute to Black people who have, throughout American history, worked and sacrificed for a country that is based on, but has never lived up to, the ideals of liberty and equality. Even though the United States has long mistreated its Black citizens, as Hannah-Jones states in her *1619 Project* essay, "For generations, we have believed in this country with a faith it did not deserve. Black people have seen the worst of America, yet, somehow, we still believe in its best."

To Do

▸ Visit the All Wars Memorial to Colored Soldiers and Sailors on Twentieth Street and the Benjamin Franklin Parkway.

▸ Find the historical marker for Samuel B. Hart's family church, St. Peter Claver, at Twelfth and Lombard streets.

▸ Walk by Samuel B. Hart's home at 2021 Waverly Street; the two-story house is still standing. Consider applying for a historical marker honoring Hart.

▸ Take a tour at the ACES Veterans Museum at 5801 Germantown Avenue in Germantown. The museum is housed in Parker Hall, which was used as the USO for Black soldiers during World War II. Exhibits focus on the experiences of African Americans and other racial minorities in the military, particularly during World War II. You can also take a virtual tour at https://acesveteransmuseum.com.

15

⁓

PAUL ROBESON

The Philadelphia Retirement of a Renaissance Man

As a high school junior, I needed a topic for my first major research paper. My mother suggested I write about an incident that took place in Peekskill, New York, in 1949 involving a man named Paul Robeson. She told me a bit about Robeson, and I was intrigued enough to choose to spend the next few months learning about his remarkable talents and his terrible treatment by many fellow Americans. Robeson has been a hero to me ever since. Now, more than forty years later, I am delighted again to be writing about Paul Robeson—and deeply grateful to the staff and supporters of the Paul Robeson House, who have ensured that Robeson's story is remembered and presented as a continual inspiration to Philadelphians.

Robeson's Rise

Paul Robeson's father fled enslavement in North Carolina and eventually became a Presbyterian minister in New Jersey. His mother was a great-granddaughter of Cyrus Bustill, a creator of the Free African Society and baker for Revolutionary War troops. Robeson, born in 1898, grew up in Princeton, excelling as a student, actor, and athlete. Valedictorian of his high school class, he won a full scholarship to Rutgers University, where he continued to shine.

The Blockson Collection at Temple University has a copy of the 1920 Rutgers yearbook, *The Scarlet Letter*. Although Robeson's is the only Black face, he appears quite often because of his many activities and achievements. Robeson was elected to Phi Beta Kappa and was one of four students invited to join Cap and Skull, an honor society for Rutgers students who demonstrate excellence and leadership in academics, athletics, and the arts. He was an All-American football player and a stand-out in track, baseball, and basketball. He wrote the yearbook's description of the basketball season, which begins with a note from the editor: "Paul LeRoy Robeson is one of the best basketball players in the college. At center he has been of inestimable value to the team. His natural physical abilities, combined with his excellent head-work, make him as one of our best players of all time." The winner of fifteen varsity letters, Robeson was also valedictorian of his college graduating class.

The multitalented Robeson studied at Columbia University Law School, the only Black man in his class, while playing for the National Football League and singing and acting professionally. Columbia's proximity to Harlem enabled Robeson to befriend the leading luminaries of the Harlem Renaissance. In 1921, Robeson married Eslanda Goode. Like Robeson's mother, Eslanda was a member of a prominent Philadelphia family. When she and Robeson met, she had a degree in chemistry from Columbia University and was working in the surgical pathology department at New York-Presbyterian Hospital, though she soon resigned to help her husband pursue a career as an entertainer.

Robeson became frustrated by the lack of opportunity for Black lawyers, but he continued to find success as a performer. His baritone voice and charismatic stage presence garnered high praise from critics and the adoration of audiences. Starring theatrical roles in *All God's Chillun Got Wings*, *The Emperor Jones*, and *Show Boat* catapulted Robeson to fame in the United States and abroad. The 1933 film version of *The Emperor Jones* was the first major movie to feature a Black man in a starring role. In the 1936 version of *Show Boat*, Robeson's iconic performance of "Old Man River" enhanced his celebrity. With Robeson playing the lead, *Othello* became the longest-running Shakespeare production on Broadway (1943–1944). In addition, he sang and recorded in genres that included spirituals, folk songs, and show tunes. His voice, whether on the radio, on records, or in live performance, thrilled audiences of all races and nationalities. He is often considered the first Black superstar.

A Turn to Activism

As his fame grew, Robeson took a keen and active interest in political issues. He expressed pride in his African American and African heritage, denounced colonialism, and opposed fascism. After spending time in the Soviet Union, where he was treated with respect, Robeson was convinced that socialism was the best hope for a better future. He became involved in the trade union movement and affiliated himself with progressive forces across the globe, attracting the attention of the Federal Bureau of Investigation (FBI). His world travels exposed him to various forms of oppression but also underscored the particularly iniquitous plight of Black Americans.

As World War II approached, Paul and Eslanda returned to the United States from a prolonged period abroad. Robeson encouraged African Americans to support the fight against fascism by buying war bonds and enlisting in the armed forces. He was bitterly disappointed when the brave service of Black soldiers failed to diminish Jim Crow, pervasive racism, and anti-Black violence. In 1946, Robeson met with President Harry Truman to advocate for anti-lynching legislation.

At the World Peace Conference in 1949, an event that took place in Paris under Soviet sponsorship, Robeson gave a speech in which he spoke out against growing tension between the United States and the Soviet Union and indicated that war was not inevitable. In the post–World War II era, however, his Soviet sympathies were out of step with the emerging Cold War ethos. Robeson was misquoted by the American press as saying that Black people would refuse to fight in a war against the USSR. These controversial remarks made Robeson a pariah to many in the United States. Jackie Robinson, formerly a friend, denounced Robeson before the House Un-American Activities Committee—an action he later regretted.

In August 1949, Robeson was scheduled to perform at a benefit concert for the Civil Rights Congress in Peekskill. Hundreds of locals, convinced that Robeson was a threat to the nation, attacked would-be concertgoers, throwing stones and beating them with baseball bats. Robeson was burned in effigy. The concert was rescheduled for September 4 (Labor Day). Robeson and the other performers, including Pete Seeger and Woody Guthrie, were able to complete the show, but performers and audience members were set on by a mob as they left the concert venue. Cars were stoned and overturned; people were dragged out and beaten. More than 140 people were injured, many as police looked on without

A photograph by John Mosley of Paul Robeson in 1943 standing among Black men in the military. (John W. Mosley Photograph Collection, Charles L. Blockson Afro-American Collection, Temple University Libraries, Philadelphia)

taking action. Soon afterward, some former colleagues in the fight for civil rights distanced themselves from Robeson, fearing that an association with a perceived Soviet sympathizer would jeopardize the movement.

The U.S. State Department revoked Robeson's passport in 1950, and the FBI intensified its surveillance of him. He was blacklisted in Hollywood. Robeson's films were removed from circulation, and his albums were pulled from record stores' shelves and ceased to get radio play. Other than a few Black churches, venues were unwilling to book engagements with this suspected "red." In 1956, Robeson himself was called before the House Un-American Activities Committee, where he refused to disclose his political affiliation or renounce communism. In a heated exchange with Pennsylvania Representative Francis Walter, Robeson—making the most of his professionally trained, bass-baritone voice and inherent dignity—invoked his family history:

> I am not being tried for whether I am a Communist, I am being tried for fighting for the rights of my people, who are still second-class citizens in this United States of America. My mother was born in your state, Mr. Walter, and my mother was a Quaker, and my ancestors in the time of Washington baked bread for George Washington's troops when they crossed the Delaware, and my own father was a slave. I stand here struggling for the rights of my

people to be full citizens in this country. And they are not. They are not in Mississippi. And they are not in Montgomery, Alabama. And they are not in Washington. They are nowhere, and that is why I am here today.

Once his passport was returned in 1958, Robeson performed worldwide, attracting enthusiastic receptions abroad, particularly in Great Britain and the Soviet Union. He never, however, attained his former celebrity status. A variety of physical and mental health challenges hobbled Robeson in the early 1960s, years that he spent primarily in Europe.

Philadelphia Connections

In 1966, Paul Robeson moved to his older sister's twelve-room home at 4915 Walnut Street, where he spent the last decade of his life. These final years were not his only ties to Philadelphia. Both his mother and his wife came from prominent Black Philadelphia families; his parents were married at the First African Presbyterian Church, the church to which Cyrus Bustill had belonged and where Octavius Catto's father, William, had been a pastor. Robeson was a cousin of Sadie Tanner Mossell Alexander and a longtime friend of her husband, Raymond Pace Alexander. Robeson recalled years later: "As a young fellow still in college I was always in and out of Philadelphia, to parties and such. Place was just full of pretty girls."

In 1930, a bronze statue of Robeson, who by then was internationally famous, was to be exhibited at the annual Rittenhouse Square exhibition hosted by the Art Alliance. According to an editorial in the *Journal of Negro Life* titled, "The City of Brotherly Love," the sculptor was told that "the executive committee. . . . expressed their apprehension of the consequences of exhibiting such a figure in a public square, especially the figure of a Negro as the colored problem seems to be unusually great in Philadelphia." In his monthly column in *The Crisis*, W. E. B. Du Bois stated bitterly, "After all, the naked manhood of Paul Robeson would scare Philadelphia."

But Robeson was also honored in Philadelphia. In 1939, he received the Silver Loving Cup from Northeast High School and went to the school to accept the honor in person. In 1940, he performed with the Philadelphia Orchestra at the Robin Hood Dell to a record-breaking audience of 7,500 people. According to the *Philadelphia Inquirer*, "Robeson gave a miniature recital, singing three songs with the orchestra in the first half of the program, then adding four more—plus a generous list of encores." On the heels of this sold-out performance, Robeson signed a lucrative contract for a fifty-one-city tour.

His next concert in Philadelphia, in December 1946, was at the Academy of Music. Even though Robeson had a cold, his performance received a rave review in the *Inquirer*: "The range and content of the program served to underscore two things—that Robeson is an outstanding personality, and that Robeson with a cold is still far better than most singers without a cold. Aside from the cold, the great Negro basso and actor has never appeared to better advantage, not only because of his superlative artistry in acting and singing, but because the warmth of his nature and his genuine love for all peoples came across the footlights." Robeson performed fourteen programmed songs and fourteen encores, many in different languages, including Italian, Russian, Chinese, and Hebrew. Not only did he sing, but he also performed Othello's final speech. Robeson's reception at the Academy of Music underscores the sacrifice he made by putting his dedication to social justice and human rights before his own financial and artistic success.

The summer of 1948 saw Philadelphia host three political conventions. The Republicans nominated New York's Governor Thomas Dewey in June; the Democrats chose President Harry Truman amid a mid-July heatwave and a schism over civil rights. Robeson traveled to the city later that month to speak at Shibe Park during the convention of the new Progressive Party. He had come to support the Progressive Party's candidate, Henry Wallace, and the party platform advocating national health insurance, an end to the military draft and the Cold War, and equal rights for women and racial minorities. Robeson was the opening speaker at a Youths for Wallace convention that followed the main convention. Wallace ended up garnering less than 3 percent of the vote in November, slightly fewer votes than Strom Thurmond, who represented the States' Rights Democratic Party (a.k.a. the Dixiecrats) that same year.

Robeson Remembered

Robeson's last years were quiet ones. This once world-famous performer was known to sit on the porch of his sister Marian Robeson Forsythe's twin row house in the Walnut Hill section of West Philadelphia. Many of the neighbors he greeted had no idea that the old man was once an international superstar whose friends included Lena Horne, Langston

Hughes, Albert Einstein, Marian Anderson, Eleanor Roosevelt, Kwame Nkrumah, Jawaharlal Nehru, Jomo Kenyatta, W. E. B. Du Bois, and countless other celebrated figures. Some of his prominent friends, including Harry Belafonte, Sidney Poitier, Ossie Davis, and Ruby Dee, visited Robeson in Philadelphia.

Always a dapper dresser, Robeson continued to wear a button-down shirt and tie each day. He enjoyed singing, reading (in several languages), watching football on television, going to movies, spending time with friends and family, and keeping up with current events. Although his politically active days were behind him, FBI agents kept watch on the Robeson home from a car parked across Walnut Street.

Robeson's health eventually failed, and he died at Presbyterian Hospital on January 23, 1976, at seventy-seven. Marian Forsythe died one year later. The house at 4951 Walnut Street was left to Forsythe's daughter Paulina, but it fell into disrepair and became home to squatters. Despite the condition of the house, one of Charles Blockson's first group of historical markers was unveiled at the site in 1991. The marker reads, "A Rutgers athlete and Columbia law graduate, Robeson won renown as a singer and actor. He was a noted interpreter of Negro spirituals. His career suffered because of his political activism, and he lived his last years here in retirement."

Fortunately, the West Philadelphia Cultural Alliance (WPCA) purchased the house and its attached twin in 1994. Under the visionary leadership of Frances Aulston, this neighborhood arts organization has refurbished the adjoining buildings and turned them into a house museum and community gathering spot. The home where Robeson spent his final years is now a place to learn Robeson's story and to become inspired to continue his legacy. His former bedroom contains original and period furniture; other rooms are dedicated to different aspects of his varied career. The WPCA also uses the space for art exhibits, musical performances, readings by authors, chess club meetings, and so forth. In March 2023, the City Council approved giving the 4900 block of Walnut Street the honorary street name Paul L. Robeson Way.

In December 2022, the Eslanda Robeson Reading Room was opened at the Paul Robeson House and Museum.[1] Although Eslanda died the year before her husband moved to Philadelphia, Robeson House leaders

---

1. Ten blocks east of the Robeson House, the Du Bois College House on the University of Pennsylvania campus has a Paul Robeson Reading Room.

Christopher Rogers facilitating an event in December 2022 at the Paul Robeson House Museum. (Photograph by Amy Jane Cohen)

thought it was important also to honor her legacy. The reading room features a digital archive of the many Robeson-related sources that were stored in the house.

A few blocks from the Paul Robeson House, the Paul Robeson High School for Human Services is located at 4125 Ludlow Street, the former site of the O. V. Catto Disciplinary School. At the urging of Paul Robeson House staff, Robeson students, nearly all of whom are Black, learn about the man in whose honor their school was named. Ninth-graders from the Robeson School visit the Robeson House each year to foster the connection.

Appropriate for a larger-than-life figure, a four-story mural depicting Paul Robeson graces a wall at Forty-fifth and Chestnut streets across from Paul Robeson High School. Robeson is shown in a suit and tie. A chain attached to his vest holds his Phi Beta Kappa key, an item he wore with pride throughout his long and complicated life. The mural was originally painted in 1999 and restored in 2013, on the 115th anniversary of Robeson's birth.

The mural rededication ceremony was also a celebration for the students and staff of Paul Robeson High School. The 2012–2013 academic year was supposed to be the school's last, but emulating the institution's namesake, students and teachers fought back, and the shutdown order was rescinded. Just four years later, Paul Robeson High School was named the most improved high school in the city. Between 2017 and 2022, the school won forty-five separate awards, and Principal Richard Gordon IV was thrice named national principal of the year. In one of his final speeches as the governor of Pennsylvania, Tom Wolf, while visiting the school in December 2022, declared: "I believe that Paul Robeson [High School] is a model for Pennsylvania." As a man who treasured education, Paul Robeson, one can assume, would be pleased to hear this praise.

To Do

- ▶ Visit the Paul Robeson House and Museum, the Eslanda Robeson Reading Room, and the Robeson historical marker at 4915 Walnut Street (a.k.a. Paul Robeson Way).

- ▶ View the Robeson mural at Forty-fifth and Chestnut streets.

- ▶ Listen to Robeson's remarkable testimony before the House Un-American Activities Committee, available on YouTube. Numerous recordings of Robeson singing and interviews with Robeson are also available on YouTube.

- ▶ Watch *Paul Robeson: Here I Stand*, a two-hour documentary available at https://www/youtube.com/watch?v=BUki-v-NvoE.

16

THE BRIEF LIFE OF
MALCOLM X HIGH SCHOOL

What's in a Name?

[With a Reflection by Kenneth Hamilton]

Malcolm Little was born on May 19, 1925, in Omaha, Nebraska. His parents, Earl Little and Louise Norton Little, had lived in Philadelphia from 1918 to 1921 before moving to Omaha. By the time Earl and Louise Little's son had arrived in Philadelphia in the winter of 1954, he had experienced the burning down of his family home in Lansing, Michigan; the loss of his father, a Baptist minister and active member of Marcus Garvey's Universal Negro Improvement Association; his mother being sent to a mental hospital; separation from his siblings as the Little children went into foster care; a stint as a hipster and hustler in Boston, New York, and Detroit; and six years in prison, beginning at twenty, for grand larceny, breaking and entering, and firearms possession. He had also gotten rid of his "slave name" and was known as Malcolm X.

It was while in prison that Malcolm was introduced to the Nation of Islam (NOI), a religious and political movement founded in Detroit in 1930 that combines elements of traditional Islam with Black nationalism. Through four of his siblings who had become members, Malcolm corresponded with the NOI's leader, Elijah Muhammad. Upon his release from prison in 1952, Malcolm X quickly became known as a persuasive orator and a charismatic recruiter for the NOI. After tripling membership at the first NOI temple in Detroit, Malcolm X was sent by Elijah Muhammad to Boston and Hartford, Connecticut, to attract NOI members in those cities. His next assignment: Philadelphia.

Malcolm X did not live in Philadelphia for long, but his impact was significant. And as such an important national figure, his name and likeness are present in the city's landscape. Although an effort in the late 1960s to rename a school in his honor failed, in the twenty-first century the idea of school name changes in general, and the viewpoints of Malcolm X in particular, have become more widely accepted.

Malcolm X in Philadelphia

According to Muhammad Abdul Baasit, Malcolm X arrived in Philadelphia in March 1954 with a small bag, a newspaper, a briefcase, and orders to invigorate the NOI's Temple Number 12, which at that point lacked a home.[1] Malcolm stayed at various locations, including a hotel on Broad Street between York and Cumberland avenues that was convenient to the North Philadelphia train station. He often resided at 2503 Oxford Street, a Unity House or Fruit of Islam House where single male members of the NOI frequently gathered.

When Malcolm X first came to Philadelphia, a small number of NOI members convened regularly at the Universal Negro Improvement Association's Marcus Garvey Hall at 1609 Columbia Avenue (now Cecil B. Moore Avenue). Many of them had been influenced by Charlie Sims, a barber who, like Malcolm X, learned the teachings of Elijah Muhammad while in prison. Malcolm X found a building to house Temple Number 12 at 1643 North Bailey Street in North Philadelphia. The temple later moved to 4218 Lancaster Avenue in West Philadelphia.

Tall and immaculately dressed, Malcolm was a compelling speaker who attracted attention wherever he went. As Baasit recalled, "They came by the thousands to hear him deliver the 'message' of his mission." In his autobiography, Malcolm X recalled that in "the City of Brotherly Love black people reacted even faster to the truth about the white man than the Bostonians had."

Despite his rising fame in and beyond the NOI, Malcolm X needed paying work. He found employment as a longshoreman on the Delaware River. Baasit describes the respect Malcolm X gained from his fellow dockworkers, who "listened to his every pronouncement on the so-called

---

1. Baasit wrote an article describing Malcolm X's time in Philadelphia for an undated publication entitled *Showcase: The Progressive Magazine* that is in the Blockson Collection at Temple University. I was unable to determine Baasit's identity or relation to Malcolm X.

'negro' problem." When there was neither work nor NOI responsibilities, Malcolm explored the city by foot. He would walk from Strawberry Mansion to the Parkway, where he became a frequent visitor to the Philadelphia Museum of Art; the Central Branch of the Free Library; the Franklin Institute; and his favorite Parkway institution, the Academy of Natural Sciences. In West Philadelphia, he went to the Commercial Museum (in the since demolished Civic Center), the Wistar Institute, and the University of Pennsylvania's Museum of Archaeology. Another preferred spot was Fairmount Park at Thirty-third and Diamond streets, where Malcolm X would exercise, read, and relax. "He had many friends throughout the city in all walks of life, in every area that you could imagine," Baasit fondly recollected.

During Malcolm X's months in Philadelphia, he succeeded in bringing many new members to the NOI. Malcolm X continued to teach regularly at Temple Number 12, even after he was told to move to Harlem by Elijah Muhammad in May 1954. Malcolm X visited Philadelphia frequently for the next ten years and had encounters with many of the leading figures of the local civil rights movement, including Reverend Leon Sullivan and the attorney Cecil B. Moore.

Malcolm X was a frequent guest on *The Listening Post*, a radio show on WDAS, a station popular with Black Philadelphians. For an appearance on the program on December 29, 1964, he was accompanied by dozens of police officers because there had been credible threats against him by a hostile Muslim faction. By this point, Malcolm X had broken with Elijah Muhammad and had founded the Organization of Afro-American Unity, which was perceived as a rival to the NOI.[2] Although Malcolm X's WDAS visit went smoothly, four of his bodyguards were attacked by a group of ten men as they exited the Sheraton Hotel at Eighteenth Street and John F. Kennedy Boulevard.

Malcolm X's final appearance in Philadelphia was for a speech at the Blue Horizon Auditorium in January 1965. He told the crowd, "You'll go all the way to Mississippi to freedom ride and protest, while right here in Philadelphia, your children can't go to Girard College, which is in the middle of the Black Belt. Well brother, you should hang

---

2. Malcolm X was disciplined by Elijah Muhammad for referring to the assassination of President John F. Kennedy as a case of "chickens coming home to roost." Following a pilgrimage to Mecca, Malcolm X's views differed from those of Elijah Muhammad and the NOI. He softened his antiwhite stance and began advocating for solidarity with Muslims across the globe, particularly in Africa.

your head in shame."[3] One month later, Malcolm X was assassinated at the Audubon Ballroom in Harlem.

Name Change Denied

Malcolm X's message of Black pride and self-reliance continued to resonate in the years following his death, particularly among African American youth. Students at Benjamin Franklin High School attempted to memorialize their fallen hero by renaming their school in his honor. Ben Franklin, located at Broad and Green streets, was an all-male and overwhelmingly Black, poor, and underachieving school when the name change was initiated in the 1968–1969 school year. It was a particularly divisive moment in Philadelphia public schools.

Bok Vocational High School in South Philadelphia had been taken over by two thousand white residents of the blocks surrounding Bok, who were demanding a reduction in the number of Black students enrolled at the school. Tensions between the largely Black student body and the overwhelmingly white neighborhood residents had been a long-standing problem that resulted in frequent skirmishes and exchanges of racial epithets. A group of about two hundred Ben Franklin students planned to go to Bok to help the Black students, whom they had heard were being beaten at Bok. Benjamin Franklin High School's new Black principal, Leon Bass, persuaded the Franklin students that their presence would exacerbate the situation at Bok and that they were better off staying put to collectively choose a productive course of action.[4]

Instead of going to Bok, the Franklin students staged an overnight sit-in in the auditorium. The students asked white teachers to leave the building, and about twenty-five Black teachers and parents, along with Principal Bass, spent the night with the students. During the sit-in, the students came up with a list of demands. They wanted an African American teacher appointed athletic director, at least one Black department head, and a Swahili class and a Black history course added to the high school curriculum. In addition, they asked that the name of the school

---

3. As described in Chapter 18, Cecil B. Moore took on Girard College by launching a major protest in May 1965.

4. Philadelphia-born Leon Bass (1925–2015) volunteered to serve in the segregated U.S. Army during World War II. His unit fought in the Battle of Bulge and helped to assist survivors of Buchenwald concentration camp. He lectured frequently about the Holocaust and its connection to racism.

be changed to Malcolm X High School. The sit-in ended peacefully the next morning, and classes resumed without incident. Other than the name change, all the demands were agreed to by the Board of Education.

Prominent figures such as the president of the Philadelphia Federation of Teachers, Frank Sullivan, and Police Commissioner Frank Rizzo decried the school board for allowing the sit-in to take place and eschewing disciplinary action. The *Philadelphia Daily News* editorial board wrote: "Some 200 students at Ben Franklin, supported by their principal, ousted white teachers, camped in the school overnight and then presented a list of 'demands.' Both the school principal and School Superintendent Mark R. Shedd described the students' actions as 'constructive.' The era of permissiveness has reached a new low with this response to educational anarchy. . . . For the life of us, we can't understand what is 'constructive' about a bunch of rambunctious schoolboys demanding that the name of their school be changed from Benjamin Franklin High to Malcolm X High School."

Shortly after the sit-in, the student body voted by a two-to-one margin to change the name of their school to Malcolm X High School. Three members of the student council made a formal request to the Board of Education on November 25, 1968. Although Benjamin Franklin became the head of the Pennsylvania Abolition Society late in his life, as the student representatives explained, he had previously owned enslaved people and published a newspaper full of advertisements related to the slave trade. The students were applauded, and the only Black member of the board, Reverend Henry Nichols, praised the trio for their powerful and well-reasoned presentation. In contrast, School Board President Richardson Dilworth said the name change would be a "derogation" of Benjamin Franklin. Nonetheless, the Board of Education agreed to consider the students' request.

Although the official name change had not yet been granted, students, teachers, and administrators began calling the school Malcolm X High School during the 1968–1969 school year. Principal Leon Bass was in his first year as the school's leader and initially embraced the new name. In May 1969, Reverend Nichols announced that the school board had decided against the name change explaining that "there's no magic in a name." The official decision, however, had little immediate impact.

Malcolm X's widow, Betty Shabazz, spoke at graduation that year, and she was on hand when a sign saying "Malcolm X High School" was hung outside of the school. When school reopened in September 1969,

Photograph of students hanging a Malcolm X High School sign, ca. 1969. (Photograph courtesy of Kenneth Hamilton)

a large bust of Malcolm X made by an art teacher at the school sat in the entryway. The auditorium was labeled "Malcolm X Hall," teams were called the "Xers," notebooks and banners bore the Malcolm X High School imprint, and intraschool communication was done on Malcolm X High School letterhead.

Among the students who led the campaign for the name change was Wesley Cook. While taking an African studies class at Franklin, Cook adopted a Swahili first name, Mumia. Cook was suspended by Leon Bass for distributing revolutionary literature and eventually dropped out of high school. Later, after the birth of this son, he added Abu-Jamal as his surname. Mumia Abu-Jamal was convicted of first-degree murder in the 1981 shooting of Philadelphia police officer, Daniel Faulkner. Initially sentenced to death, and currently serving life in prison, Abu-Jamal has garnered international attention due to controversy surrounding his case and his continuing activism and political writing. Another student leader was Ron White, who became a prominent and politically connected attorney in Philadelphia.

Kenneth Hamilton, a faculty ally to the activist students, recalls that many students and teachers continued to call the school Malcolm X High School for several years. The moniker faded, however, once the students who had been at the school in 1968 graduated or left. Hamilton keeps memorabilia from the period, including an "Xers" basketball schedule; a poster from Wes "Mumia" Cook's campaign for student body president; and a photograph of Leon Bass, Betty Shabazz, Ron White, and himself, as well as the large bust of Malcolm X that once graced the entrance to the school.

A New Era in Name Changes

Malcolm X High School did not become an official name, and, in retrospect, it is not surprising that even a school board that was considered progressive was not ready to replace Benjamin Franklin with Malcolm X in the late 1960s. As a concession to the Franklin students, the school board agreed to name a school under construction on Stenton Avenue for a Black person. Martin Luther King High School opened in 1970.

In recent years, however, much of mainstream American society has become more open to replacing place names honoring enslavers, Confederates, and other oppressors with those that reflect more enlightened values. In 2018, activists collected more than eight hundred names on a petition in an initial effort to change the name of Andrew Jackson School, an elementary school at Twelfth and Federal streets in South Philadelphia. Jackson, the seventh president of the United States, was an enslaver and forcefully removed indigenous people and sent them west on what became known as the Trail of Tears. Following the police murder of George Floyd in 2020, another name change petition circulated in the Jackson community. This time, the school district acceded to the request and sponsored a town hall for community members to weigh in on options for a new name.

Although the Andrew Jackson School is not majority–African American, the School District of Philadelphia is more than two-thirds Black. And of 339 schools, only twenty-seven (roughly 5 percent) are named for people of color. Thus, all the top choices for a new name belonged to African Americans. An online poll allowed stakeholders to vote, choosing among options, including "Father of the Underground Railroad" William Still; Barbara Rose Jones Powell, who fought school segregation in her native Virginia and had a long career as a public school librarian in Philadelphia; and the Black journalist Acel Moore, who grew up in the neighborhood.

The number one vote getter, however, was Fanny Jackson Coppin. She was born enslaved in Washington, DC, in 1837, Andrew Jackson's final year in office. When she was twelve, her aunt purchased her freedom. After working as a domestic in Rhode Island, Coppin graduated from Oberlin College at a time when few women and few African Americans achieved this level of education. She came to Philadelphia in 1865 to teach at the Institute for Colored Youth (ICY), the rigorous school where Octavius Catto was a student, teacher, and administrator. Coppin was promoted to principal, the first woman, Black or white, to hold such a position in a coeducational school. She led the ICY until 1902 and then traveled as a missionary to South Africa and later returned to Philadelphia to write her autobiography. It is hard to think of a more worthy person for whom to name a school. At the official name-change ceremony in March 2022, the president of Coppin University, a university in Baltimore named in her honor, announced a scholarship program to allow any graduate of the Fanny Jackson Coppin School to attend the university tuition-free.

The effort to rename Andrew Jackson School was initiated by members of the school community. Once the effort was underway, they received additional support from a coalition called the Committee to Rename Philadelphia Streets and Schools. The committee formed as a direct response to the police murder of George Floyd. The educator Dana Carter launched a Facebook group on June 7, 2020, called PROGRESS in the Spirit of George Floyd. On June 9, she posted, "It sure would be a great time to research and rename some School District of Philadelphia schools," and many agreed with her. The Facebook thread led to the formation of a committee that met numerous times. Although the committee's activities have subsided, one of its suggestions was to rename Ben Franklin for Malcolm X, and the group created a logo that features an imagined façade of Malcolm X High School.

Memorializing Malcolm X

As the years have passed, Malcolm X has retained a strong hold on the imaginations and aspirations of Black Americans, especially Black youth. Furthermore, Malcolm X's reputation has been burnished with time. Moore reflected on the change when the U.S. Postal Service issued a stamp honoring Malcolm X in 1999: "Thirty years ago, I would have said that Malcolm X would be among the last persons the Postal Service would honor with a stamp. . . . But more and more, Malcolm X is being viewed in a better light by historians and others who look back at his time. Instead of an intellectual bomb-thrower, he is seen as an intensely engaged intellect whose thought was evolving rapidly at the time of his death." This changed understanding of Malcolm X is reflected in the Philadelphia landscape.

Most notably, there is Malcolm X Park situated from Larchwood Avenue to Pine Street between Fifty-first and Fifty-second streets in West Philadelphia. It was formerly known as Black Oak Park; the city changed the name in 1993 in accordance with the wishes of community activists who sought a name to inspire African American youth to take an interest in caring for the park and the surrounding neighborhood. The six-acre parcel has become a gathering place for events such as Juneteenth, and a gazebo accommodates jazz shows and other performances.

Across from Malcolm X Park, the mural *Breaking Chains* depicts Malcolm X among other notable Black historical figures who exemplify the importance of education in the ongoing struggle for justice and equality. Dedicated in May 2018, it is one of several Philadelphia murals featuring Malcolm X. Since 2005, a large mural of Malcolm X at Thirty-third and Diamond streets has included a portrait and the quotation: "Education is our passport to the future. For tomorrow belongs to the people who prepare for it today." Nearby, at 3032 Girard Avenue, is a mural depicting Malcolm X, Martin Luther King Jr., Ella Baker, and Frederick Douglass as "Four American Patriots Who Dedicated Their Lives to Civil Rights and a Better America." Both murals are located close to the Oxford Street house where Malcolm X resided in 1954. Unfortunately, an application to add this house to the city's historical register was unsuccessful, and the house appears dilapidated.

A 2016 historical marker in front of Muhammad's Temple of Islam Number 12 mentions Malcolm X's role as an administrator and teacher at the site. A half-block west of the historical marker is the New Africa Center and Muslim American Museum led by Abdul-Rahim Muhammad. Muhammad, who was raised in the NOI, remembers when Malcolm X still made regular visits to Temple Number 12. He views his passion for Black and Muslim history as a "continuation of the spirit of my ancestors." Currently, the museum is housed in one large room, but Muhammad envisions expanding its footprint to adjoining buildings.

The former Fruit of Islam House at 2503 Oxford Street in December 2022. The house is in significant disrepair, but a new home was for sale next door. The asking price was $445,000 in this rapidly gentrifying neighborhood. The cross street has the honorary name of Rev. Robert J. Lovett Sr. Way. Lovett (1936–2017) had been the pastor at nearby Wayland Baptist Temple Church. (Photograph by Amy Jane Cohen)

The New Africa Center also owns a grassy lot across the street that it has dubbed New Africa Freedom Square and furnished with picnic benches for neighborhood use. A wall on one side of the lot has a mural entitled *Local Heroes* that was painted in 2008. The opposite wall holds a large sign that says, "Welcome to the New Freedom District," and shows photographs of fourteen sites in West Philadelphia related to Black history. As he observes rampant gentrification, Muhammad hopes that the sites will be preserved if the neighborhood is rebranded and becomes a popular tourist destination for people interested in Black history. "We need to put our footprint in this community," he explains, "so that we know Black people struggled and survived." If the New Freedom District is indeed established, the story of Malcolm X's time in Philadelphia will certainly be central to the story that it tells.

Reflection

Kenneth Hamilton *worked at Benjamin Franklin High School from 1966 to 1999. He was a history teacher and renowned basketball coach, and he served in a variety of positions, including acting assistant principal, department chair, and faculty sponsor of the Black Student Union.*

never met Malcolm X, but I was his follower and disciple. I had all his records and books. He really turned my head around. I was a history teacher, and he gave me a totally different perspective on history and life in America. He spoke in the language of the grassroots, and he was very intelligent—maybe too intelligent for his own good.

Looking back on the period when Ben Franklin was called Malcolm X, there was an energy and a pride among those students that I'd never seen before. They were really proud to be part of that movement. Some of them went on to do fantastic things. Given the type of students that we had, for them to all of a sudden be proud of themselves and proud of who they are, it was just very rewarding. That was Malcolm X. That is what he did for us.

To Do

▶ Attend an event at Malcolm X Park and look at the murals within the park and on Fifty-second Street and Larchwood Avenue.

▶ See the historical marker at Muhammad's Temple Number 12, and visit the New Africa Center and New Africa Freedom Square, all on the 4200 block of Lancaster Avenue.

▶ Find the two Malcolm X murals in the Strawberry Mansion neighborhood, at Thirty-third and Diamond streets and Thirtieth Street and Girard Avenue.

▶ See the historical marker at the Universal Negro Improvement Association Marcus Garvey Hall, at 1609 Cecil B. Moore Avenue, that was home to the earliest NOI congregation in Philadelphia.

▶ Visit the former site of Temple Number 12, at 1643 North Bailey Street, now the Holy Ghost Crusade Church.

▶ Watch *Seeds of Islam: The Early Nation of Islam in Philadelphia*, available at https://www.youtube.com/watch?v=rK0LdroU9E0.

17

REVEREND LEON SULLIVAN

North Philadelphia's Lion of Zion

[With a Reflection by Mable Ellis Welborn]

Leon Sullivan was born in Charleston, West Virginia, in 1922. His family lived in a small clapboard house along a dirt alley. After attending West Virginia State College on a basketball scholarship, Sullivan chose a career in the clergy. The powerful preacher and politician Adam Clayton Powell took Sullivan under his wing and brought him to Harlem, where he studied at the Union Theological Seminary and assisted Powell at the Abyssinian Baptist Church. In 1950, Sullivan moved to Philadelphia to become the pastor at Zion Baptist Church at Broad and Venango streets.

Neither the dirt alleyways of West Virginia nor the tough streets of Harlem had prepared Sullivan for the poverty and despair he found in North Philadelphia. His determination to improve the lives of residents and congregants led him to develop a series of economic empowerment programs. North Philadelphia today bears the stamp of Sullivan's groundbreaking efforts.

The Challenge of North Philadelphia

In the early 1900s, North Philadelphia was the site of factories and modest workforce housing. Wealthy industrialists built mansions along the Broad Street corridor, and several shopping areas served the racially integrated and economically mixed neighborhood. A variety of factors, however, led to North Philadelphia becoming overwhelmingly Black and poor by the mid-twentieth century. In 1900, there were about 63,000 Black residents of Philadelphia; by 1950, there were more than 375,000. Most of these new Philadelphians had come north in search of job opportunities and a less overtly racist society. As southern Blacks migrated to Philadelphia in large numbers, discriminatory policies limited where they were able to find housing. Formerly single-family residences in North Philadelphia were divided into smaller units, often managed by absentee landlords who did little to maintain the properties. Redlining precluded investment in improving the existing housing stock, and city services neglected the increasingly overcrowded neighborhood.

As African Americans moved into North Philadelphia, many white residents left the area. White flight to Northeast Philadelphia and the suburbs accelerated during the post–World War II building boom. Exclusionary policies prevented Black families from purchasing homes in these new areas, the regions to which industry and jobs were moving, as well. In 1930, North Philadelphia was 22 percent Black; by 1960, it was 69 percent Black.

In his memoir *Build Brother Build*, Sullivan recalls his first impressions of North Philadelphia:

> A few days after I had arrived in town a member of the church took me on an automobile tour of the community. . . . He showed me areas where the whites used to live, that had turned all black, and we passed through areas in transition, where the "For Sale" signs everywhere pointed up the white mass exodus into a newly developing all white Northeast section and other outlying white-inhabited older parts of the city. I was flabbergasted at what I saw. I had heard a great deal about Philadelphia's black society and the good life of the Philadelphia colored man, but I had never seen so many dilapidated houses, row upon row, in my life. Harlem was bad enough, but North Philadelphia, where I rode that day, beat Harlem in housing decay. Buildings were deteriorating everywhere, and trash and garbage littered the streets. Wherever my eyes fell, I saw little black boys and little black girls in clusters playing on sidewalks, on stoops, and in hallways, trying to find childish joy and fun in the midst of dirt, roaches and garbage. I knew then that my work was cut out for me.

Although Sullivan's training focused on spiritual uplift, he took a more practical approach to improving life in North Philadelphia. He often stated, "Some people look for milk and honey in heaven, while I look for ham and eggs on earth, as well as for heaven eventually."

Economic Empowerment

Soon after his arrival, Reverend Sullivan began organizing efforts to reduce crime, particularly among young residents of North Philadelphia. He founded the Youth Employment Service to place young people in jobs. He soon realized, however, that discriminatory hiring practices severely limited opportunities for employment, even for Black graduates of high school and college.

Sullivan, along with a network of four hundred Black ministers, organized a series of carefully planned Selective Patronage campaigns to convince local employers to hire Black workers for non-menial and public-facing jobs. First, the top executives of a targeted company were presented with a list of specific hiring demands and a deadline by which those demands needed to be met. If the ministers' demands were not met in full, the following Sunday the ministers would inform their congregations not to make any purchases from that company. "Don't buy where you can't work" was the movement's rallying cry.

The first company targeted was the Tasty Baking Company, the producers of Tastykakes, a favorite regional treat. The campaign lasted three months, until the company finally agreed to hire Black salesman-drivers, office workers, and production-line personnel. Eventually, there were twenty-nine successful campaigns between 1959 and 1963 against companies that included A&P supermarkets, Sun Oil, and the *Evening Bulletin* newspaper. Some companies, including PepsiCo and Coca-Cola, gave in to the ministers' demands rather than face boycotts. The movement spread to other cities and gained national attention.

Although the Selective Patronage campaigns were considered a huge success, Sullivan recognized that more needed to be done to provide Black people with the job skills employers were looking for. Coining the slogan, "Integration without Preparation Is Frustration," Sullivan's next major initiative was to launch training sites called Opportunities Industrialization Centers (OICs). The first OIC was housed in a former police station and prison at Nineteenth and Oxford streets. Although the city leased the dilapidated building to Sullivan for $1 a year, significant

Leon Sullivan examining an oscilloscope (an instrument used to display and analyze the waveform of electronic signals) with an Opportunities Industrialization Center student, January 1965. (Jack Tinney, Special Collections Research Center, Temple University Libraries, Philadelphia)

money was needed to refurbish the property and set up the training programs. Much of the funding was raised through a grassroots effort within the Black community.

When it opened in May 1964, the OIC had three hundred participants—and a waiting list of five thousand. Enrollees were trained in fields such as drafting, sheet metal work, and power machine operation. Sullivan quickly realized that many trainees lacked basic literacy and numeracy skills. He asked OIC staff to develop a program to address these shortcomings. Known as the Feeder Program, the curriculum also included African American history to instill pride and build the self-esteem of OIC students. The OIC expanded quickly to meet overwhelming demand. Centers were set up in Germantown, West Philadelphia, and South Philadelphia and on North Broad Street.

The OIC was the product of self-help from within the Black community, but its success in both job training and job placement attracted the support of corporate and government entities. Senator Robert Kennedy, who hoped to open a similar center in Brooklyn, toured the North Philadelphia OIC in 1966. The following year, President Lyndon Johnson visited and remarked, "What Reverend Sullivan has shown me this morning opens my eyes and I hope will open the eyes of all of the Nation to the opportunity that lies here." President Johnson saw the OIC as a successful weapon in his "War on Poverty." Johnson's successor, Richard Nixon, viewed the OIC as an example of "Black Capitalism." With bipartisan support, the OIC received significant federal funding. By the early 1970s, centers had been opened across the United States and internationally. The OIC, although smaller than during its peak, continues to change lives in North Philadelphia, in fifteen states, and in Africa.

Build Brother Build

Another Sullivan innovation was the 10–36 Plan, in which he asked that fifty members of his congregation give $10 a month for thirty-six months for community development projects. Within a few weeks, hundreds of members were participating in the program. Thousands joined over the next several years. The funds were directed toward both charitable and for-profit enterprises. In 1965, a 10–36 Plan affiliate began constructing Zion Gardens, a complex of garden apartments in North Philadelphia that was the city's first major Black-owned housing development.

Two years later, the group began building Progress Plaza, a shopping center along Broad Street. This was the nation's first Black-owned shopping mall, and it was built largely by graduates of OIC training programs. Many of the tenant businesses were also controlled by African Americans. Chain stores based at the mall had to agree to hire Black people in managerial positions. The Progress Haddington Plaza was built at Fifty-sixth and Vine streets in 1970 and continues to operate today. Nixon visited Progress Plaza as a presidential candidate in 1968, and Sullivan's national profile continued to rise.

In 1971, Sullivan became the first African American to serve on the board of General Motors. In that position he developed the Global Sullivan Principles, guidelines for American companies doing business in apartheid-era South Africa. By signing onto the Sullivan Principles,

Leon Sullivan in front of the Progress Plaza sign on Broad Street in October 1969.
(Richard Rosenberg, Special Collections Research Center, Temple University Libraries, Philadelphia)

companies agreed to desegregate their facilities and to promote qualified Black workers. He later urged businesses to divest completely from operating in South Africa. Sullivan's efforts helped hasten the end of the apartheid regime and to enable Nelson Mandela to transition from political prisoner to president of South Africa.

A Powerful Legacy

Reverend Leon Sullivan died in 2001 at seventy-eight, but his presence continues to loom large in North Philadelphia, particularly along Broad Street. The Philadelphia chapter of the OIC is currently located on a stretch of Broad Street between Oxford Street and Girard Avenue that in 2019 was given the honorary name Leon Sullivan Way. The OIC continues to provide job training, though today's trainees learn skills for the twenty-first-century economy such as banking, culinary arts, hospitality, and smart energy technology.

One block north of the OIC is the Leon H. Sullivan Human Services Center, which houses the Leon Sullivan Charitable Trust, the national headquarters of the OIC, and other social service organizations. The building was constructed in 1966 by a group affiliated with Sullivan that grew out of his 10–36 Plan, and it was the first office building in Philadelphia owned and operated by African Americans.

To the north of this office building sits the continuously operating Progress Plaza. Barack Obama campaigned at Progress Plaza in 2008, and in 2010 First Lady Michelle Obama visited the Fresh Grocer there to promote her "Let's Move" campaign. In 2016, Progress Plaza was refurbished and renamed Sullivan Progress Plaza, and a historical marker was unveiled at the site.

Continuing north, Zion Baptist Church still sits at Broad and Venango, and directly across the street is the Leon H. Sullivan Community Impact Center, also owned by Zion Baptist Church. In 2004, a mural was painted nearby with a portrait of Sullivan, an outline of the United States and the African continent, and the caption "Envision a Bridge from America to Africa." The church, where Sullivan spent nearly four decades as pastor, had to be rebuilt after a fire in the early 1970s. A historical marker honoring the "Lion of Zion" was dedicated in 2017. Even farther north, at Broad and Stenton, a post office was renamed for Sullivan in 2002.

Echoes of Reverend Sullivan's impact on North Philadelphia are found beyond Broad Street, as well. In 1990, a state historical marker was installed in front of the original OIC building at Nineteenth and Oxford streets. Currently home to the Sultan Jihad Ahmad Community Center, the building was placed on the Philadelphia Register of Historic Places in 2022 due to its connection to Sullivan and the OIC.

Zion Gardens, the first major project to use 10–36 Plan funding, is still a housing complex in the Yorktown neighborhood of North Philadelphia, stretching over two city blocks on the 1100 and 1200 blocks of Girard Avenue. The Opportunities Towers 1 and 2, located on Hunting Park Avenue in the Nicetown/Tioga neighborhood, were built by Progress Construction, another Sullivan-affiliated company, and remain in the portfolio of yet another Sullivan entity. The Opportunity Towers 3 stands at the 5500 block of Haverford Avenue in West Philadelphia. Indeed, the 10–36 Plan led to the purchase of more than four hundred properties in the city; thus, there are buildings in many parts of Philadelphia that have a Sullivan connection.

Greenbelt Knoll

Perhaps surprisingly, Sullivan's legacy is also reflected in the landscape of Northeast Philadelphia, a region that was nearly all white until the late twentieth century. In 1956, Reverend Sullivan and his family were among the original residents of Greenbelt Knoll, Philadelphia's first intentionally integrated housing development. Set in bucolic Pennypack Park, Greenbelt Knoll became a national model of integration. Morris Milgram, who built Greenbelt Knoll, was a leader in the "open housing movement," a civil rights activist, and an original resident. During a time when integrated communities were rare, Milgram made sure that at least 45 percent of Greenbelt Knoll's residents were nonwhite. Today, Greenbelt Knoll is still an integrated community of mid-century modern homes in a peaceful, leafy setting. A historical marker erected in 2007 mentions both Reverend Sullivan and Robert N. C. Nix Sr. by name.[1]

A Centenary Honor

In the week that Sullivan would have turned one hundred, the city honored him by naming the international arrivals hall at Philadelphia International Airport in his honor. A permanent exhibit about Sullivan's life was installed in the hall, the gateway to Philadelphia for people arriving from around the globe.

As an awardee of the Presidential Medal of Freedom and an internationally admired advocate for economic empowerment, social justice, and human dignity, Reverend Leon Sullivan is a world-famous figure. He met every president from Lyndon Johnson through Bill Clinton and had interactions with Kofi Annan, Nelson Mandela, Mikhail Gorbachev, and countless other global leaders. Nowhere on the planet, however, is Sullivan's influence as significant and well marked as in North Philadelphia.

---

1. Robert N. C. Nix Sr. (1898–1987) was the first African American elected to represent Pennsylvania in the U.S. House of Representatives, where he served from 1958 to 1979. The federal building and U.S. Post Office on the corner of Ninth and Chestnut streets is named in his honor. His son, Robert N. C. Nix Jr. (1928–2003), was the first Black person to win statewide office in Pennsylvania when he was elected to the Pennsylvania Supreme Court in 1972. He served as chief justice for twelve years.

Reflection

Mable Ellis Welborn *chairs the board of the Leon H. Sullivan Charitable Trust (formerly the Zion Non-profit Charitable Trust). She was an employee of the trust from 1966 through 1976 and was appointed to the board by Reverend Sullivan in 1981.*

I believe markers, buildings, and street names are important because of the work Reverend Dr. Leon H. Sullivan did in the 1950s, 1960s, and 1970s that changed life in Philadelphia and went worldwide. It is not the man who is being revered but the work the man did. I believe that Dr. Sullivan's name, like anybody's name, on a building has significance. It is eyebrow-raising, and it invokes questions so that people who see it will want to know why.

What Dr. Sullivan did was groundbreaking at the time, but as somebody once said, "The more things change, the more they stay the same." If you stop and look at the news, read the paper, look out your window, or walk on the street, you will find that most everything that is happening in society today, right here in the city of Philadelphia, is comparable to what he was trying to change.

It says in the Book of Jeremiah: "Set thee up waymarks, make thee high heaps: set thine heart toward the highway, even the way which thou wentest." That's the reason we need these markers—so that people will say, "Oh, they did this? We may need to go back and try that again." The blueprint is there; that's why these markers, these buildings, these street names are significant.

To Do

- ▶ Visit the stretch of Broad Street described earlier in the chapter or, even better, take the "Lion of Zion 10–36: Power of the Multitude Tour." Contact the Society to Preserve Philadelphia African American Assets at preserveus@sppaaa.org and visit the website at https://sppaaa.org.

- ▶ Watch *Leon Sullivan: A Principled Man*, a one-hour documentary available at https://whyy.pbslearningmedia.org/resource/a-principled-man/a-principled-man-reverend-leon-sullivan-motion-masters.

- ▶ Check out the Leon Sullivan exhibition in the international arrivals hall in Terminal A at the Philadelphia International Airport.

- ▶ See the historical marker at Greenbelt Knoll.

18

~

CECIL B. MOORE

Civil Rights Boss

[With a Reflection by Karen Asper Jordan]

As described in the previous chapter, visitors to North Philadelphia would be unlikely to miss the name Leon Sullivan on street signs, buildings, historical markers, and murals. It would be nearly impossible for such visitors to miss the name of another larger-than-life, West Virginia–born activist: Cecil B. Moore. While Sullivan was an even-tempered pastor who gained worldwide renown, Moore was a confrontational and charismatic attorney who spent his entire career fighting for the rights of poor and working-class Black residents of North Philadelphia.

Civil Rights Warrior

Cecil Bassett Moore was born in Dry Fork Hollow, West Virginia, in 1915. After graduating from Bluefield College, a historically Black institution in his home state, he joined the Montford Point Marines, a segregated unit based at Camp Lejeune, North Carolina. Moore was stationed in the South Pacific during World War II and commanded Black and white soldiers in combat. He achieved the rank of master sergeant and was discharged from Philadelphia's Fort Mifflin in 1951. Known for his fiery, colorful remarks, Moore is quoted as saying, "I was determined when I got back that what rights I didn't have I was going to take, using every weapon in the arsenal of democracy. After nine years in the Marine Corps, I don't intend to take another order from any son of a bitch that walks."

Moore used the GI Bill to earn his law degree by attending Temple University Law School at night. During the day, he worked as a wholesaler of liquor, a job that enabled him to forge connections with North Philadelphia's poor and working-class residents, the people who would become his clients and greatest supporters. Once Moore became a criminal defense attorney, he had so many clients that at one point he was assigned his own courtroom with the same judge and prosecutor to try to clear up his substantial backlog of cases. District Attorney Arlen Spector convinced the court to prohibit Moore from taking on new cases until his many outstanding cases had been completed. Moore objected to this ban, asserting, "I'm not concerned about getting rid of the backlog; I'm concerned about getting justice." The Pennsylvania Supreme Court ruled that limiting Moore's caseload was unconstitutional.

Moore also took on cases involving police brutality, workplace discrimination, and other civil rights-related issues. His offices were often crowded with people waiting to ask him to represent them, many having heard that he would work with clients who were too poor to pay for his services. Former Chief Justice Robert C. Nix of the Pennsylvania Supreme Court recalled Moore's legal acumen: "He was a skilled advocate. His persuasiveness before a jury, his effectiveness on cross examination and his precise, logical compelling presentation to an appellate tribunal are important aspects of this great man which should not be forgotten."

Impatient with the gradualist, moderate approach of most Philadelphia civil rights leaders, Moore launched a successful run for the presidency of the Philadelphia branch of the National Association for the Advancement of Colored People (NAACP) in 1962. With his sharp outfits, ever present cigar, spicy language, and fondness for strong drink, Moore became the self-described "goddamn boss" of North Philadelphia. Under his leadership, membership in the Philadelphia NAACP increased from seven thousand in 1962 to fifty thousand by the mid-1960s, making it the largest branch in the country. The NAACP had long been a staid, middle-class organization, but most of these new members were poor and working class and open to more aggressive tactics.

Like Sullivan, Moore recognized that exclusionary hiring practices were preventing African Americans from advancing economically. While Sullivan and the four hundred ministers engaged in the relatively quiet Selective Patronage campaigns, Moore organized pickets of construction projects and other workplaces that had no or few Black employees. Protests at the building site of Strawberry Mansion Junior High School were occasionally violent but led to agreements by unions and contractors to meet specific goals for employing skilled Black workers. Demonstrations at the Greyhound and Trailways bus terminals and the main branch of the U.S. Post Office (in collaboration with the Congress on Racial Equality) yielded similar results. His efforts led to the "Philadelphia Plan," a policy that required federal contractors to practice non-discrimination in hiring and employment. Moore also led the effort to force a ban on the practice of wearing blackface at the annual New Year's Day Mummers Parade.

The Will to Break a Will

Moore's best-known campaign took place at Girard College, an all-white residential school situated in an all-Black neighborhood of North Philadelphia. The school was created by the City of Philadelphia in 1848 using funds provided by the estate of the wealthy financier (and enslaver) Stephen Girard. In his 1831 will, Girard stipulated that the money should be used to support a boarding school for "poor white male orphans." After the U.S. Supreme Court's *Brown v. Board of Education* decision in 1954 banned segregation in public schools, City Councilman Raymond Pace Alexander filed suit to desegregate Girard College. The U.S. Supreme Court ruled that as a city-run institution, Girard College had to admit Black students. School leaders turned control over to a group of private trustees to maintain its whites-only policy.

The segregated school in the middle of a Black neighborhood was a daily affront to many North Philadelphia residents. Moore thought direct action would be the most effective means of putting pressure on Girard College's board of trustees to end its exclusionary practices. Beginning on May 1, 1965, and continuing for seven months and seventeen days, Moore and his followers marched around the ten-foot walls of Girard College day and night. Many of the protestors were young people in their teens and twenties who called themselves the Young Militants. Some were members of neighborhood street gangs who were persuaded to drop their beefs with rival gangs to fight a powerful common enemy.

The marchers faced harassment from police officers that sometimes escalated into physical confrontations and arrests, but they continued

Photograph by John Mosley of Dr. Martin Luther King Jr., Cecil B. Moore, and DJ Georgie Woods at the Bellevue Stratford Hotel in 1965. (John W. Mosley Photograph Collection, Charles L. Blockson Afro-American Collection, Temple University Libraries, Philadelphia)

to show up. Deputy Commissioner (and future Mayor) Frank Rizzo was the officer in charge of the police monitoring the Girard College protests. Moore and Rizzo, two outsize personalities, had frequent confrontations that cemented each of their reputations. Moore was the embodiment of aggressive civil rights activism, while Rizzo was the symbol of iron-fisted "law-and-order" policing.

When Martin Luther King Jr. visited Philadelphia in the summer of 1965, Moore initially discouraged him from going to Girard College. According to Moore, "The imported Gandhi philosophy of nonviolence still existent in the South will not be accepted in Philadelphia where we believe in self-help and self-defense." Moore eventually concluded that Black unity was more important than his ideological differences with King. When King addressed a crowd of ten thousand at Fortieth Street and Lancaster Avenue, Moore was by his side.[1] They traveled together

1. A historical marker, sculpture of King, and mural of the event showing both Moore and King were unveiled in 2010. The mural was threatened with destruction in 2022 when a developer purchased the host building, but an effort by local groups to save it resulted in a compromise that will leave the mural intact.

to Girard College, where they both spoke about the importance of desegregating the school.

Local and national attention put increasing pressure on city and state officials to find a resolution to the Girard College conflict. The board of trustees refused to budge, so in September 1965, Governor William Scranton asked two well-known attorneys, William Biddle and William T. Coleman Jr., to file suit in federal court.[2] Once the lawsuit was filed on December 16, 1965, the daily Girard College protests, the longest sustained protest in Philadelphia history, were called off. Sporadic demonstrations continued until May 1968, when the Supreme Court ruled that the trustees were required to break Girard's will and desegregate the school. On September 11, 1968, the first Black students were enrolled at Girard College.

Although Moore's combative style earned him the adoration of many, he was a thorn in the side of moderate civil rights leaders. Moore was quoted in a *Time* magazine profile saying, "I run a grassroots group, not a cocktail party, tea-sipping, fashion show-attending group of exhibitionists," a clear affront to his more bourgeois counterparts. In spring 1967, the national NAACP broke the Philadelphia branch into five parts, leaving Moore as the president of the North Philadelphia chapter rather than of the whole organization. That summer, he was suspended from office for alleged mishandling of funds, but he remained a popular figure for many poor and working-class African Americans.

After an unsuccessful run as a third-party candidate for mayor, Moore was elected to the City Council in 1976 as a representative of North Philadelphia's Fifth District. In 1979, another brash resident of North Philadelphia, John Street, challenged Moore for his City Council seat. As Moore's health began to fade, so did his prospects for retaining his seat. Moore died of cardiac arrest on February 13, 1979, at sixty-three. At his funeral, Reverend Leon Sullivan told the two thousand

---

2. William T. Coleman Jr. (1920–2017) grew up in Germantown. He was suspended twice from Germantown High School—once for cursing at a teacher who told him he would grow up to be a "wonderful chauffeur," and once for trying to join the all-white swim team. He graduated summa cum laude and Phi Beta Kappa from the University of Pennsylvania and was first in his class at Harvard Law School. When hired in 1948 by Felix Frankfurter, he became the first African American to clerk for a Supreme Court justice. Coleman went on to work with Thurgood Marshall on the *Brown v. Board of Education* case and to become secretary of transportation under President Gerald Ford.

Cecil B. Moore and other NAACP leaders marching around the walls of Girard College in 1966. (Russell Hamilton, Special Collections Research Center, Temple University Libraries, Philadelphia)

mourners not to worry about Cecil; he was probably organizing a picket line around the gates of heaven.

Columbia Avenue Renamed

Cecil B. Moore's name continues to loom large in the neighborhood that loved him. In 1985, a grassroots campaign was launched to rename Columbia Avenue to honor Moore. The Cecil B. Moore Ad Hoc Committee organized high school students to collect signatures on petitions calling for the City Council to approve the name change. Frustrated by a lack of progress, they took a page from Moore's playbook and blocked traffic at the intersection of Broad Street and Columbia Avenue. Two weeks later, Moore's successor in the City Council, John Street, helped to pass legislation to rename Columbia Avenue from Front Street to Thirty-third Street for Cecil B. Moore. Mayor Wilson Goode, the city's first Black chief executive, signed the bill into law. On Saturday, April 11, 1985, Mayor Goode proclaimed Cecil B. Moore Day in Philadelphia and presided over a joyous ceremony in which the new street signs were unveiled.

The new Cecil B. Moore Avenue was a shadow of the vibrant street that had been part of Moore's stomping grounds. It had been damaged in riots that Moore and other leaders were unable to control. On the night of Friday, August 28, 1964, an African American couple were having an argument in a stalled car at Twenty-second Street and Columbia Avenue. Police approached the car to clear the intersection, and the woman turned her anger on them. Within a short time, the woman was arrested, as was a bystander who had tried to intervene on her behalf. The police called for backup, and onlookers threw rocks and bottles at both the departing and arriving police cars. Rumors spread that cops had beaten a pregnant Black woman. Pent-up frustration with harassment by police, dilapidated housing, substandard schools, unemployment, and poverty bubbled over, and rioting broke out across a large swath of North Philadelphia. Along Columbia Avenue, store windows were smashed, and looting wrecked nearly all the shops not owned by African Americans.

Local Black leaders such as Reverend Leon Sullivan and Judge Raymond Pace Alexander tried to calm the situation, to no avail. Moore, who had been attending the Democratic National Convention in Atlantic City, returned to North Philadelphia and made calls for calm on the streets, at one point driving through the neighborhood speaking from a sound truck. His pleas were ignored, and rioters threw stones at the vehicle. That evening, Moore spoke at a concert at the Uptown Theater organized by the civil rights activist and DJ Georgie Woods. Moore implored the young crowd not to repeat the activities of the previous evening, but the rioting continued the next two nights.

Eventually, two thousand police officers and more than seven hundred arrests were needed to bring the area back under control. Two people were killed, and hundreds, both residents and police officers, were injured. Scores of businesses were destroyed, never to reopen. In the aftermath of the riot, most of the few remaining white families left the neighborhood permanently, as did many middle-class Black families. The affected stretch of Columbia Avenue never recovered from the riots, and by the time of the renaming ceremony in 1987, the street was home to dive bars, pawn shops, decrepit houses, vacant storefronts, and empty lots. Today, Cecil B. Moore Avenue cuts through the vibrant campus of Temple University, and new homes and businesses have been built, with more planned.

While many Philadelphians have had portions of streets named for them with an honorary addition to a longtime official name (e.g., the block of Broad Street in front of the Uptown Theater, which was given the supplemental name Georgie Woods Boulevard in 2009), very few have had a street name fully replaced in their honor. Such a change is never undertaken lightly, since it requires residents and business owners to change addresses on mortgages, drivers' licenses, bank loans, and other official documents. Given Moore's stature in the North Philadelphia community, it is not surprising that his name is among the very few for whom the city has undertaken the effort and expense of fully changing the name of a major artery. John F. Kennedy Boulevard, Martin Luther King Jr. Drive, and Cecil B. Moore Avenue are among the few that have met the test.

Fighting for a Legacy

Even such a major change as a renamed street, however, does not guarantee that a legacy will be preserved. The effort to keep Moore's achievements in the public eye has been led by his three daughters and by the Cecil B. Moore Philadelphia Freedom Fighters, a group made up of the young people who became active in the Civil Rights Movement under Moore's leadership and continued their activism after his death. The Freedom Fighters have spoken widely at schools and community events, and they have advocated to maintain Moore's profile in the neighborhood he served.

In late 2011, the Southeastern Pennsylvania Transportation Authority (SEPTA) changed the route signs on the buses that run along Cecil B. Moore Avenue to say "C. B. Moore," an affront to the Freedom Fighters, who wanted the buses to continue displaying Moore's full name. They let their discontent be known, and following a meeting between the activists and SEPTA officials, the full name was restored.

Cecil B. Moore's name was added to the Temple University subway stop at Broad Street and Cecil B. Moore Avenue in 1995, making him the first person to have a SEPTA stop named in their honor. In 2013, the station was rededicated, and at the request of the Freedom Fighters, a mosaic depicting key scenes from Moore's career and an explanatory plaque were unveiled. In 2015, however, large red decals saying Temple University were plastered on the subway station as part of an advertising campaign. The Freedom Fighters demanded a meeting with SEPTA, and the decals were hastily removed. In 2019, explanatory plaques were installed at the street level, another move pushed by the Freedom Fighters to inform people about Moore's historical importance.

The Columbia Branch of the Free Library was renamed for Cecil B. Moore, and there is a Cecil B. Moore Playground and Recreation Center on Twenty-second Street in Strawberry Mansion.

In 2000, a mural of Moore was dedicated on the side of his longtime residence on the corner of Jefferson and Bouvier streets. Cecil B. Moore frequently vented his wrath on moderate, middle-class Black leaders who moved out of Black population centers. While Reverend Sullivan lived in Northeast Philadelphia, and many Black professionals moved to the verdant, integrated neighborhoods of Northwest Philadelphia, Moore was committed to living among the people he led. Fittingly, he bought his home at 1708 Jefferson Street from Raymond and Sadie Alexander Pace when they decamped to Westview Street in Mount Airy in 1959. When a racial slur was painted on the mural in February 2020, the Freedom Fighters quickly organized a demonstration, and the mural was restored. Another North Philadelphia mural honoring Moore was torn down in 2013, underscoring the challenge of keeping even recent history visible in the landscape.

Looking Forward

Today, the youngest of the Cecil B. Moore Freedom Fighters is in her seventies; Moore's three daughters are senior citizens, as well. Their hope is that Moore's historical contributions will remain familiar to future generations of Philadelphians. One of the institutions where Moore's legacy is most vibrant is Girard College. The school is a coeducational residential school for first grade through high school. The president of Girard College and most of its senior leadership are Black, as are about 90 percent of the students. When the Freedom Fighters visit, which they have done often, they are treated like royalty. Members of the Freedom Fighters speak each year at the annual Greater Philadelphia Martin Luther King Jr. Day of Service, which is hosted at Girard College. The Founder's Hall Museum on the Girard College campus tells the story of the desegregation of Girard College. And recently, a large, colorful mural was dedicated on school grounds. (See book cover.)

The new mural, installed well above the ten-foot wall and thus easily visible from outside of the campus, depicts Cecil B. Moore and Georgie Woods. Significantly, however, it also features the young protestors who made Moore's actions effective. Moore's name and likeness are stamped on North Philadelphia, and now the Freedom Fighters who have spent decades ensuring his continued prominence have also been recognized in the landscape. The Freedom Fighters have done their part to keep civil rights-era history alive. Now it is our turn.

Reflection

A retired nurse and the president of the Cecil B. Moore Philadelphia Freedom Fighters, **Karen Asper Jordan** *was a sixteen-year-old student at Gratz High School when the demonstrations began at Girard College. Her father's family lived on College Avenue across from Girard, and like everyone in the neighborhood, she knew that the school was only for white orphan boys. She eagerly took part in the demonstrations and today remains close to many of the young people she met while walking around the Girard College walls. Asper Jordan fondly recalls Cecil B. Moore saying, "They're not going to mess with any of my damn people," when she told him about harassment by police on the first day of the demonstrations. Moore, whom she describes as "the best lawyer in the world," represented Asper Jordan in court when she was arrested at other civil rights demonstrations. He was widely known for representing the poor expertly and for free. Asper Jordan remembers Moore as a person who "galvanized the masses to stand together to defeat injustice." She reflects on the importance of his visibility in the landscape.*

It's a symbol of resistance, triumph, and bravery. It's about realizing that where you are today is from someone fighting for you. In those days, we couldn't be salespeople in a store; we could only clean up. Cecil, to us, was the man in the proverbial white hat; he was our Lone Ranger. With him, it was instant gratification.

You didn't have to wait years and years to see change happen. To me, it's a symbol of triumph against all odds, and it's a symbol of the people who followed him. It's also a symbol of sacrifice. You sacrifice yourself, your family, your job, but through it all there's triumph. It's a symbol of the struggle for equal rights in this country.

To Do

▸ Watch *Cecil's People: The Freedom Fighters*, an Emmy Award–winning twenty-three-minute documentary available at https://www.historymakingproductions.com/cecils-people.

▸ See the Freedom Fighters mural from outside Girard College; it is on Twenty-second Street just north of Cecil B. Moore Avenue. Virtual and in-person tours of Founders Hall Museum at Girard College are also available through the museum's website (https://www.girardcollege.edu/visitors/founders-hall-museum).

▸ Visit the Temple–Cecil B. Moore subway stop on the northeastern corner of Broad Street and Cecil B. Moore Avenue, on the Broad Street Line, to view the mosaic inside the station and the informational panels at street level.

▸ Walk north from the subway stop on Cecil B. Moore Avenue for six blocks to Bouvier Street. Take a left and walk two blocks to 1708 Jefferson Street, Moore's home, which has a mural on the Bouvier Street side.

▸ Go to the *Civil Rights in a Northern City: Philadelphia* website (http://northerncity.library.temple.edu/exhibits/show/civil-rights-in-a-northern-cit), presented by Temple University, to access information and a plethora of primary sources related to the Columbia Avenue riots and the Girard College protests.

19

~

PHILADELPHIA'S BLACK POWER MOVEMENT

Coming Full Circle

[With a Reflection by Aden Gonzales]

We been saying freedom for six years and we ain't got
nothin. What we got to start saying now is Black Power!
We want Black Power.

—STOKELY CARMICHAEL

B y the time Stokely Carmichael, then president of the Student Non-
violent Coordinating Committee (SNCC), made this famous call
for "Black Power" in June 1966, Black activists in Philadelphia had
been practicing the major tenets of the Black Power philosophy for many
years. Black Power encompasses the ideals of self-determination, indigenous leadership, economic self-help, community control of institutions,
and cultural pride. In contrast to their counterparts in the southern
Civil Rights Movement, Philadelphia leaders such as Reverend Leon
Sullivan and Cecil B. Moore led organizations that did not rely on the
support or participation of liberal white people. When Black Power
emerged as the dominant civil rights philosophy in the late 1960s and
early 1970s, Philadelphia became a national center of activism. Though
some of the landmarks of the Black Power era are long gone, the Black
Power philosophy is reflected in Philadelphia's current politics and, if
one knows where to look, in its landscape, as well.

The Birth of the Black People's Unity Movement

The Freedom Library was a community center founded in 1964 by John
Churchville, a civil rights activist who had recently returned to Philadelphia after working for SNCC in Georgia and Mississippi. Churchville had met Malcolm X and spent time at the Nation of Islam head-

quarters in Harlem, which inspired him to become a Black nationalist, a supporter of unity and political and economic autonomy for Black people. Housed in a storefront on Ridge Avenue in North Philadelphia, the Freedom Library offered classes on African and African American history to children during the day and hosted lectures and discussions for teens and adults in the evenings.

The Freedom Library became a gathering place for people seeking Black empowerment, many of whom were disillusioned with the integrationist goals of the mainstream Civil Rights Movement. A group of these people, including Churchville, launched the Black People's Unity Movement (BPUM) in 1965. The BPUM set out to bring African Americans together across class and ideological lines in a quest for Black self-determination. Among the founders of the BPUM were Walter Palmer, a medical technician at Children's Hospital and the creator of the Black People's University, a Black history and self-esteem-building program for youth in West Philadelphia; Mattie Humphrey, a Germantown-based nurse, hospital administrator, and community activist; and Edward Robinson, a successful insurance salesman from Mount Airy with a passion for African history.

In February 1966, the BPUM held a Black Unity Rally at the Church of the Advocate at Eighteenth and Diamond streets in North Philadelphia. The pastor of the Church of the Advocate, Father Paul Washington, surprised many members of his congregation and participants in the mainstream Civil Rights Movement by aligning himself with the separatist BPUM. Churchville had been hired as an anti-gang worker at the Church of the Advocate and become friendly with Father Washington. In his autobiography, *Other Sheep I Have*, Washington explains his transition to a Black nationalist mindset: "John sat down with me one day and said that he felt that gang activity was not the problem in itself. It was only a symptom of a much deeper problem: the feeling of powerlessness among black people. He suggested the solution was to work for black unity, to the end of achieving black power and ultimately self-love and respect. Only when we gained power through unity would our problem be solved." Father Washington came to embrace a philosophy that he dubbed the Theology of Black Power.

Despite considerable pushback from the hierarchy of the Episcopal Church, the Church of the Advocate emerged as an important meeting place and event venue for the burgeoning Black Power movement. Stokely Carmichael, then the president of SNCC, spoke to a large crowd in the church sanctuary in July 1966; the following month, two thousand people gathered to hear Carmichael give an address from the church steps. Carmichael had returned to Philadelphia in response to police raids on four homes where SNCC members resided. Acting Police Commissioner Frank Rizzo had ordered the raids, falsely claiming that SNCC planned to blow up Independence Hall. The case fell apart due to lack of evidence, but Rizzo continued to broadcast his intention to target Black militants.

Nonetheless, Black Power and the BPUM continued to attract adherents in Philadelphia. During the summer of 1967, the BPUM organized weekly street-corner rallies in Black neighborhoods. Cecil B. Moore, then a third-party candidate for mayor, joined the BPUM's call for intraracial solidarity. Moore and the Black Power activists visited numerous predominantly Black high schools during the fall of 1967 to hold rallies and lead workshops on Black history and culture. On Election Day, November 15, 1967, Moore placed third behind the Republican candidate, Thacher Longstreth, and the winner, incumbent Mayor James Tate, a Democrat and a Rizzo supporter.

Student Walkout

The most remarkable Black Power–era event in Philadelphia history took place on Friday, November 17, 1967, when several thousand high school students walked out of their schools at around 10 A.M. Arriving by foot and by public transit, they converged on the Board of Education headquarters at Twenty-first Street and the Benjamin Franklin Parkway. Many chanted "Black Power!" along the way. Participants came from schools throughout the city, including Germantown High School, Benjamin Franklin High School, William Penn High School, Bok Vocational High School, South Philadelphia High School, Gratz High School, Kensington High School, Bartram High School, West Philadelphia High School, Overbook High School, and West Catholic High School.

The students and their adult leaders, including Walter Palmer, Mattie Humphrey, and Ed Robinson's nephew David Richardson, had spent many hours planning the protest, the largest of its kind in American history. The young people compiled a list of twenty-five demands that reflected the Black Power ethos that had sparked their activism. Students wanted to see more Black teachers, Black administrators, and Black history classes, especially since most of them attended schools

A peaceful gathering of students outside the Board of Education building at Twenty-first and Parkway before the arrival of police on November 17, 1967. (Special Collections Research Center, Temple University Libraries, Philadelphia)

that were majority–African American. They wanted to be allowed to wear African garb and Afro hairstyles. Asserting that "liberty and justice for all" did not yet exist, they wanted the right to sit silently through the Pledge of Allegiance. Other demands were about improving conditions: they wanted working water fountains and an end to police presence in the schools. They also wanted an end to academic tracking policies that kept Black students in low-level courses.

The school district was led by Superintendent Mark Shedd and School Board President Richardson Dilworth, both of whom held progressive views on race and education. As the students gathered on the courtyard and street outside, Shedd and Dilworth met with student representatives and adult organizers in a conference room. School district officials had asked the nonuniformed Civil Disobedience Unit of the Police Department, led by Lieutenant George Fencl, to keep an eye on the student demonstrators. Father Paul Washington had also shown up to monitor the event, but it seemed so peaceful—even joyful—that Washington had left the scene by midday. One of the students attending the meeting inside called from a second-floor window to announce that Shedd and Dilworth had accepted all of the students' demands.

As the number of students swelled, however, Lieutenant Fencl called for backup. Rizzo, who was at a swearing-in ceremony for newly promoted police officers at City Hall, decided to bring busloads of police to the demonstration. Several hundred helmeted cops arrived at the Board of Education. Reports are contradictory about what happened next, but it seems that a few of the students grew boisterous and climbed atop parked cars, including police cars. Numerous eyewitnesses recall hearing Rizzo declare, "Get their asses!" or "Get their Black asses!" The police began attacking students and adult organizers using nightsticks and blackjacks. Dozens of people were injured, some seriously enough to be hospitalized. Some of the students fleeing the scene ran through Center City, vandalizing property and assaulting pedestrians. Eventually, fifty-seven people were arrested—thirty-nine juveniles and eighteen adults.

In the immediate aftermath of the bloody attack on the peaceful demonstrators, Black Philadelphians were horrified, as were many of their liberal white supporters. In a press conference, Shedd and Dilworth blamed the police rather than the demonstrators for causing mayhem. Eight hundred Black people attended a mass meeting that weekend, and protest rallies were held at several high schools and at the Police Administration Building. On Wednesday, November 22, about five hundred predominantly white protestors demonstrated at City Hall in support of the Black students and against police brutality. They carried signs with messages such as, "Rizzo Must Go," "Control Your Police, Mayor Tate," and "We Support Black Student Rights."[1]

Many white working-class city residents, however, supported Rizzo's actions. As days passed, the description of events shifted in the press. The "student demonstrators" of early coverage in the *Philadelphia Inquirer* and *Philadelphia Daily News* became "black radicals" and "black

---

1. One of the organizers was David Hornbeck, who had witnessed the events of November 17 and became superintendent of Philadelphia schools from 1994 to 2000. Another organizer was Temple University Professor John Raines. In 2014, Raines admitted to driving the getaway car in March 1971 for a cadre of coconspirators who had raided the FBI office in Media, Pennsylvania. Thousands of purloined documents revealed the agency's misdeeds, including its COINTELPRO program, which infiltrated and disrupted political groups, including civil rights and Black Power organizations. The break-in took place on the night of a hyped boxing match between Muhammad Ali and the Philadelphia-based fighter Joe Frazier.

power activists." Policemen circulated petitions in support of Rizzo and demanding the ouster of both Shedd and Dilworth. John Harrington, president of the Philadelphia Fraternal Order of Police, declared, "We need new members on the Board of Education because if Dick Dilworth wants to be the Pied Piper of anarchy and permit students—thousands of them—to take off from school whenever they want and demonstrate in the streets, then it's plain the board is surrendering." Mayor James Tate stood by Rizzo, making him the official police commissioner just a month after the walkout.

An Ecclesiastical Home Base for Black Power

Following the student demonstrations, Superintendent Shedd continued to meet with Black student leaders, and in the short run, several of their demands were implemented or partially implemented. Nevertheless, some Black parents, including Father Paul Washington and his wife, Christine, chose not to send their children back to public schools. Working with Ed Robinson and other BPUM leaders, a Black history-centered school was established at the Church of the Advocate and a few other sites.

As the Church of the Advocate became increasingly known as the center of the Black Power movement in Philadelphia, Father Washington agreed to host a national Black Power conference that would bring thousands of activists from around the country to Philadelphia in the late summer of 1968. The multiday conference, for which the Black Panthers provided security, went smoothly. One of the tangible results of the conference was the launch of the *Voice of Umoja* newspaper by Falaka Fattah, who would later create the House of Umoja as a refuge for Black boys, particularly those caught up in gang activity.

The Rise and Fall of the Black Panther Party

Founded in Oakland, California, in 1966, the Black Panther Party for Self-Defense formed to protect Black communities from police brutality. The Panthers advocated a Ten-Point Program that called for full economic and political rights for Black citizens, an end to police brutality, and the release of all Black prisoners, as well as "Land, Bread, Housing, Education, Clothing, Justice and Peace." Through mainstream media, the Panthers became known primarily for wearing militaristic garb, marching in formation, and openly carrying weapons. The Black Panther Party, like other Black nationalist groups, attracted the attention of local law enforcement, as well as of COINTELPRO, the secret counterintelligence program the Federal Bureau of Investigation (FBI) used to infiltrate and undermine political organizations deemed radical. Indeed, Father Paul Washington quotes extensively from his own FBI file obtained through the Freedom of Information Act in the sections of his autobiography that describe his involvement with the Black Power movement.

The Philadelphia chapter of the Black Panther Party had headquarters at 1928 Columbia Avenue in North Philadelphia. Other sites opened at 428 West Queen Lane in Germantown, 3625 Wallace Street in Mantua, 523 South Seventeenth Street in South Center City, and 6600 Germantown Avenue in Mount Airy. Under the leadership of Defense Minister Reggie Schell, Panthers took classes in ideology and weaponry. The party offered community political education classes, hosted a revolutionary film festival, and described police officers as "pigs." A Philadelphia Black Panther Party flyer states, "THE RACIST DOG POLICEMEN MUST WITHDRAW IMMEDIATELY FROM OUR COMMUNITIES, CEASE THEIR WANTON MURDER AND BRUTALITY AND TORTURE OF BLACK PEOPLE . . . OR . . . FACE THE WRATH OF THE ARMED PEOPLE!!!" Like other Black Panther Party chapters, the Philadelphia affiliate sold Panther newspapers to raise funds and organized demonstrations against police brutality. It also organized free breakfast programs for children, free clothing giveaways, and a free medical clinic at 1609 Susquehanna Avenue in North Philadelphia.

When the Chicago Panther leaders Fred Hampton and Mark Clark were killed by police in a surprise attack on their home, a huge memorial service was held at the Church of the Advocate in December 1969. Soon afterward, Father Washington agreed that the church could be used as a venue for registration and large gatherings during the Black Panther Party's Revolutionary People's Constitutional Convention, to be held over the Labor Day weekend in September 1970. Temple University agreed to make McGonigle Hall, a large athletic facility, available for the gathering, as well.

On the Saturday prior to the convention, however, Philadelphia Police Officer Frank Von Colln was fatally shot in a Cobbs Creek Park guardhouse. (Von Colln Field on the Parkway was later named in his honor.) The gunman was reported to be a Black revolutionary, though not a member of the Black Panther Party. The next night, two more officers were shot in West Philadelphia. Police Commissioner Rizzo, who had openly declared his hatred of Black nationalists, used these attacks on police as a pretense for ordering early morning raids on three Black Panther sites. The Panthers, most of whom were asleep when the raids began, were taken outside by heavily armed police officers, held at gunpoint, and stripped of their clothing. Photographs of the nearly nude Black Panthers circulated throughout the world. Fourteen Panther leaders were jailed and held on $100,000 bail each, an amount many viewed as excessive. Philadelphia-area Quakers and other church groups posted the bail.

Despite the raids and subsequent arrests, the Black Panther convention went on as planned. Thousands of Black nationalists and antiwar activists came to North Philadelphia, including the Panthers' founder, Huey Newton, who had recently been released from prison in California. A federal injunction required Philadelphia police to keep their distance, and the three-day convention was an overwhelmingly orderly and peaceful gathering. Nonetheless, factional division and ideological disputes within both the local and the national organization—along with ongoing harassment by police and the FBI—led to the group's decline. By the early 1970s, the Philadelphia chapter of the Black Panther Party had ceased to exist.

Rizzo in Charge; Black Power Evolves

Frank Rizzo's violence during the Girard College protests, the student walkout, and the raids on the Black Panther Party made him anathema to most Black and liberal nonwhite Philadelphians. He was, however, a hero in the eyes of many working-class whites. By promising to bring "law and order," Rizzo was elected mayor on the Democratic ticket in 1971 and reelected by a landslide in 1975. He managed to evade charges of promoting police brutality brought by the Pennsylvania Crime Commission, the federal Civil Rights Commission, and the U.S. Justice Department. He also survived a massive recall campaign. Rizzo's effort to change the city charter to enable him to run for a third consecutive term failed, and a run for mayor as a Republican fell short in 1987. Rizzo died in the summer of 1991 while campaigning yet again to become Philadelphia's mayor.

The coalition of Blacks and liberal white Philadelphians who worked together to fight police brutality and to defeat Rizzo became an important component of Philadelphia politics. In 1975, Charles Bowser ran as an independent, the first Black candidate to run a viable, albeit unsuccessful, citywide mayoral campaign. To defeat the charter-change referendum, the interracial anti-Rizzo alliance organized massive voter registration drives in Black communities. As the activist James Lester told a *Philadelphia Bulletin* reporter in 1978, "[Rizzo's] the best organizer of black folks in this city. He's pulling us together by his polarization." A *Bulletin* columnist concurred: "Frank Rizzo was a tremendous help . . . He may have unwittingly triggered the eve of a new era among blacks in American politics."

Black Power in Philadelphia had become Black electoral power, a major and ongoing force in Philadelphia politics. David Richardson, for example, went directly from working with youth during the Black Power era to serving a Germantown district in the Pennsylvania House of Representatives, from his election in 1972 at twenty-four until his death from a heart attack in 1995 at forty-seven. Black electoral power led to the election in 1983 of Wilson Goode, the city's first Black mayor, and paved the way for the many Black politicians who currently serve Philadelphia in city, state, and national office.

The Visible Legacy of the Black Power Era

David Richardson appears in a mural on an exterior wall of the Pastorious-Richardson School, a charter school in his former district renamed in his honor. Part of Chelten Avenue and a post office in Germantown also bear his name. Many Black Power sites, though, are no longer visible. The Freedom Library and the several Black Panther headquarters have either been demolished or are unmarked.

The most salient feature in the landscape that evokes the Black Power era is the Church of the Advocate. The late nineteenth-century Gothic Revival edifice still stands at Eighteenth and Diamond streets. A historical marker outside, installed in 1999, refers to the church as "host to major Black Power events in the 1960s and 1970s." In the early 1970s, Father Paul Washington commissioned the artists Walter Edmonds and Richard Watson (a demonstrator at Girard College) to paint a series of fourteen murals in the church sanctuary. The murals are based on biblical stories, arranged as "Stations of the Civil Rights Movement," and feature heroes of Black history such as Harriet Tubman, W. E. B. Du Bois, Paul Robeson, Malcolm X, and Dr. Martin Luther King Jr. The blocks of Diamond Street from Sixteenth to Nineteenth were given the honorary name of Father Paul Washington Avenue in 2007.[2]

Father Washington is also the subject of a mural along Ridge Avenue in Strawberry Mansion. It was originally painted by Walter Edmonds in 1991 for the Anti-Graffiti Network, which became the Philadelphia Mural Arts Program. A row of identically dressed men with their fists raised is a visual reference to Father Washington's connection to the Black Power movement. The mural also depicts Barbara Harris, the first woman to become an Episcopal bishop, who was ordained, quite controversially, by Father Washington in 1974.

Coming Full Circle

Although the Church of the Advocate may be the largest structure connected to the Black Power era, the most significant legacy came from an idea launched at the Freedom Library and furthered by the BPUM and the participants in the 1967 student walkout: the notion that learning Black history should be a priority for the young people of Philadelphia. Following the student walkout, Superintendent Mark Shedd worked toward meeting the demands of the protestors, but in 1971 he resigned before his inevitable firing by incoming Mayor Frank Rizzo. Efforts to infuse Black history into the curriculum continued with varying degrees of success, taking hold more strongly in schools with Black teachers and Black students.

Finally, in 2005 the School District of Philadelphia became the first in the nation to mandate a year of African American history as a requirement for high school graduation. Under the leadership of School Reform Commissioner Sandra Dungee Glenn, the African American history mandate received unanimous approval from her fellow commissioners. Ed Robinson, who had shared his passion for African and African American history at the Freedom Library, was still alive when this came to pass.

---

2. I read about the street renaming in the *Inquirer*. Through the journalist who had written the story, I reached out to Father Washington's widow, Christine, and his son, Kemah. They graciously agreed to speak to my students, and it was through Kemah that I met the Cecil B. Moore Philadelphia Freedom Fighters.

With a year of African American history required at Philadelphia public high schools, students today learn many of the stories contained in this book and gain a perspective on American history for which the student protestors were fighting in the late 1960s. According to John Phillips, a former student and now a high school journalism teacher near Chicago, "The biggest benefit of having African American History in tenth grade was how it normalized viewing history from lenses other than white Americans. . . . While so many teachers have scrambled in the wake of 2020 to ensure their curriculum and their classrooms were antiracist in practice and pedagogy, I had been doing that work since my first day as a student teacher, and that is in large part because of how African American history shaped my world view."

Madeline Elwell, a Class of 2014 Philadelphia high school graduate, shares this perspective: "Learning about Black history, and especially the connections that we could make to Philadelphia while learning, was a vital part of my education. I ended up studying Africana studies in college, which I would have likely not had an interest in (or even really known existed) without the mandate."

A powerful and tangible result of the African American history mandate occurred when a diverse group of five Masterman High School students—Tatiana Bennet, Taryn Flaherty, Alison Fortenberry, Aden Gonzalez, and Nia Weeks—successfully applied to the Pennsylvania Historical and Museum Commission for a historical marker at the former Board of Education building commemorating the 1967 walkout. In a ceremony in March 2022, the marker was installed. Among the speakers that day were Walter Palmer, one of the adult leaders of the walkout, and Karen Asper Jordan and Mary Seymour, two of the participants. In a true full-circle moment, the beneficiaries of the determination and sacrifice on the part of the student protestors had taken the initiative to officially mark the space where the protest-turned-police-riot took place.

The text of the marker reads: "Thousands of middle and high school students organized a city-wide demonstration here to demand a culturally inclusive education program such as electives in black history, only to be met with unwarranted police violence. This was one of the largest and earliest youth-led demonstrations for ethnic studies and broader educational equality, presaging the national ethnic studies movement. In 2005, Philadelphia became the first school district in the nation to establish an African American studies mandate."

The state historical marker commemorating the 1967 walkout was dedicated on March 19, 2022. *From left to right*: Yaasiyn Muhammad, Amy Cohen, Ismael Jimenez, Keziah Ridgeway, Taryn Flaherty (*in front*), Alison Fortenberry, Tatiana Bennet, Nia Weeks, Karen Asper Jordan. (Photograph by Jessica Waber)

An Overdue Removal

In 1999, a larger-than-life bronze statue of Frank Rizzo was installed in the plaza in front of the Municipal Services Building. For more than twenty years, this prominent memorial to a symbol of police brutality and white supremacy rankled many city residents, particularly Black Philadelphians. In the wake of the "Unite the Right" demonstration in 2017 in Charlottesville, Virginia, there has been increased focus on the meaning of historical monuments. In 2017, a petition to remove the statue garnered twenty thousand signatures. Rizzo's likeness was frequently vandalized, such as when an activist spray-painted the statue with the words "Black Power." During the Black Lives Matter protests that followed the police murder of George Floyd, the Rizzo statue became the focus of outrage. Protestors covered it in paint, tried to pull it down using ropes, and attempted to set it on fire. On the early morning of June 3, 2020, the statue was removed. Mayor Jim Kenney stated: "The battle for equal rights and justice is still being fought decades later, and our city is still working to erase that legacy. We now need to work for true equity for all Philadelphia residents, and toward healing our communities. The removal of this statue today is but a small step in that process."

Black Power may be a phrase that sounds like a relic of the late 1960s and early 1970s, but the ongoing spirit of the Black Power movement has made Philadelphia a city in which the actions of student protestors are visibly commemorated, and the legacy of a brutal cop and mayor has been eradicated from a prominent civic space. This is a fitting place to conclude this book. The thread that connects the removal of the Rizzo statue and the installation of the walkout marker is the idea that we, as residents and as citizens, have the power to shape how history is depicted in public space. We have a role in determining whose stories get told and which people and events are celebrated. These choices reflect and express our collective values and our common aspirations. Historical markers, murals, monuments, street names, and so forth are more than just symbols. They are the stories we tell about where we have been and where, together, we hope to arrive. As the young poet Amanda Gorman said at the 2021 presidential inauguration:

> It's because being American is more than a pride we inherit.
> It's the past we step into and how we repair it.

Reflection

Aden Gonzales is one of the students who applied for the historical marker commemorating the 1967 student walkout. She is majoring in history and education studies at Yale University and plans to become a high school social studies teacher.

History is our blueprint and our roadmap. It can show us that a greater future is possible and can provide us the steps to get there. However, it's not as accessible as it should be. Before learning about the walkouts in my African American history class, I knew nothing of them. Such a display of youthful drive and determination deserves to be recognized and celebrated. That's why I started working on this project.

It's so important to make the history of the walkouts accessible to all. Everyone who walks down Winter Street should know the fight that Philly students have been engaged in. For decades, students have been devoted to their schools and have been fighting for access to high-quality education. The fight in schools today is an extension of the fight in 1967—that a good education means classrooms where students feel comfortable and loved rather than policed and where the curriculum is relevant to them and their communities.

To Do

▶ Visit the Church of the Advocate to take a tour of the sanctuary and murals. Check the website (http://www.churchoftheadvo cate.org) for availability.

▶ See the historical marker in front of the former Board of Education building at Twenty-first and Winter streets.

▶ Watch "The Fight (1965–1978)," part of the *Philadelphia: The Great Experiment* series produced by History Making Productions, at https://www.youtube.com/watch?v=1h_iuuLaw5Y.

▶ See the mural of Father Paul Washington on the 3300 Ridge Avenue and the David Richardson mural at Pastorious-Richardson Elementary Mastery Charter School at 5650 Sprague Street.

ACKNOWLEDGMENTS

My seventh-grade English teacher, Gaynelle Lewis-Fleming, taught me how to write; my high school social studies teacher Gene Kerrick inspired my love of history; and thirteen years of Quaker education at Friends Select School inculcated me with a commitment to pursuing social justice.

The late Michael Katz and Steve Conn steered my path toward Philadelphia history; Sandra Dungee Glenn led the charge that enabled me to teach African American history as a full-year course; and Sam Katz gave me the opportunity to continue learning about and finding new ways to educate others about Philadelphia's Black history.

Michael Bixler invited me to become a monthly contributor to *Hidden City Philadelphia*, and my longtime friends John Featherman and Chris Bartlett encouraged me to move from articles to a book.

Once the book was underway, I received help from so many! For the first section of the book, I am indebted to Aslaku Berhanu, Leslie Willis-Lowry, and Diane Turner at the Blockson Collection; Karie Diethorn, Doris Fanelli, Tyler Love, and Coxey Toogood, current and former members of the National Park Service; Laura Keim at Stenton; Margaret Jerrido at Mother Bethel Church; Edward Lawler, who was so generous with his expertise on the President's House; and Michael Coard for his passionate activism, depth of knowledge, and willingness to help out in spite of his daunting list of responsibilities and commitments.

For the second section of the book, I am grateful to the author and scholar Beverly Tomek; Dan Biddle and Murray Dubin for our many years of Catto-related collaboration; Amy Hillier, my longtime Du Bois mentor and friend; and Valerie Abitbol for showing me around the Deacon.

The final section of the book introduced me to new people and places and furthered my connection to longtime friends and acquaintances. I thank David Brownlee and Paul Steinke, lovers of Abele and heroes of preservation; Cicely Peterson-Mangum and Dwayne Wharton for insights into the Marian Anderson statue and for connecting me to Jillian Patricia Pirtle, who graciously hosted me at the Marian Anderson Museum; Vernoca Michael, Joyce Moseley, and Janice Sykes-Ross for spending an afternoon with me at the Robeson house and Christopher Rogers for connecting me to this formidable trio; Coach Kenneth Hamilton for sharing his experiences and memorabilia from the Malcolm X High School era; Abdul-Rahim Muhammad for welcoming me to the Islamic Center and providing further resources about Malcolm X in Philadelphia; Dana Carter and Angela Crawford for telling me about recent efforts to change school names; Aisha Dennis for showing me around the Opportunities Industrialization Center; Deborah Gary for leading a fantastic tour of Sullivan-related sites; Mable Welborn for sharing her personal memories of Reverend Sullivan; Karen Asper Jordan for talking to me (yet again) about her time at Girard College and her ongoing work as a Freedom Fighter; Joe Certaine for reaching out and for sharing his story; and Aden Gonzales and Alison Fortenberry for embodying the promise of the future.

Thanks, too, to Brenda Galloway at the Urban Archives at Temple University's Special Collections Research Center for the help she has given to my students and me over the years and with this project.

A remarkable constellation of people is involved in preserving, researching, writing about, and educating about local Black history. The ones not yet mentioned, but whose words and actions have influenced this book, include Faye Anderson, Erica Armstrong Dunbar, Justina Barrett, Joe Becton, Oscar Beisert, Greg Carr, V. Chapman-Smith, Matthew Countryman, Karen Falcon, Ismael Jimenez, Cindy Little, Yaasiyn Muhammad, Larry Robin, Judith Robinson, Lenwood Sloan, Shaquita Smith, Elizabeth Taylor, Dianne Thomas, Keshler Thibert, Adrienne Whaley, and Jacqueline Wiggins.

At Temple University Press, I thank Aaron Javsicas for being such a supportive editor; William Forrest for answering my many questions; Gary Kramer for dealing with my overeagerness; and Ann-Marie Anderson for encouraging me to take on this challenge. I also thank Susan Deeks for copyediting this first-time author's manuscript.

Nikki Hagedorn made beautiful maps and was a pleasure to work with as we both learned how to depict our hometown in a new way.

I have been in the same book group for more than three decades. Two members of the group, Janet Ginzberg and Anne Kringle, were extremely helpful in reading each chapter and giving me incisive feedback. I also thank Margy Klaw for author advice and encouragement. Rob Goldberg is responsible for several small but notable improvements and corrections. Nell Strachan's eagle eye caught several crucial typos and misspellings, and I'm truly grateful.

My mother, Nancy Nance, has been my rock, cheerleader, friend, favorite lunch date, and sharer of humor for my whole life. Thanks to my stepdad, Dean, for his consistent interest in the endeavors of his five grandchildren, as well as those of Linda and me, including the writing of this book. Eliza and Chloe, my amazing daughters and fellow members of the "chicas" group chat, I am so proud of both of you and love you with all my heart. And, yes, you are expected to read this book. All of it.

And, of course, thank you to Michael. Although I had to move out of our shared office to find the quiet needed to write a book, you have been with me every step of the way. Not many people get to meet their soulmate in nursery school. You are a wonderful husband, dad, and life partner, as well as an outstanding TV concierge, a cogent explainer of politics, a strategic master of logistics, a fastidious proofreader, and an uncomplaining caretaker of the practical side of life. Most important, you are an endless source of laughter. In more ways than I can possibly list here, I could never have written this without you.

BIBLIOGRAPHY

CHAPTER 1

Blockson, Charles L. *Philadelphia Guide: African American Historical Markers*. Philadelphia: Charles L. Blockson Afro-American Collection, 1992.

———. *Philadelphia, 1639–2000*. Charleston, SC: Arcadia, 2000.

Gigantino, James. "Slavery and the Slave Trade." *The Encyclopedia of Greater Philadelphia*, December 31, 2012. https://philadelphiaencyclopedia.org/archive/slavery -and-the-slave-trade.

Nash, Gary. *First City: Philadelphia and the Forging of Historical Memory*. Philadelphia: University of Pennsylvania Press, 2002.

Tasca, Ed. "The Philadelphia Slave Traders." *Philly Talk*, September 1971, 68–78.

Turner, Edward R. *The Negro in Pennsylvania: Slavery, Servitude, and Freedom, 1639–1861*. Washington, DC: American Historical Association, 1911.

Wax, Darold D. "The Demand for Slave Labor in Colonial Pennsylvania." *Pennsylvania History* 34, no. 4 (1967): 331–45.

CHAPTER 2

Blockson, Charles L. *Philadelphia, 1639–2000*. Charleston, SC: Arcadia, 2000.

Brouwer, Merle G. "Marriage and Family Life among Blacks in Colonial Pennsylvania." *Pennsylvania Magazine of History and Biography* 99, no. 3 (1975): 368–372.

DHM Design, Pressley Associates, and RK&K Engineering. *Cultural Landscape Report for Washington Square: Independence National Historical Park*. Report prepared for the National Park Service, September 2010.

Du Bois, W. E. B. *The Philadelphia Negro: A Social Study*. Rev. ed. Philadelphia: University of Pennsylvania Press, 1996.

Marshall, Jubilee. "Race, Death, and Public Health in Early Philadelphia, 1750–1793." *Pennsylvania History* 87, no. 2 (Spring 2020): 364–89.

Nash, Gary. *First City: Philadelphia and the Forging of Historical Memory*. Philadelphia: University of Pennsylvania Press, 2002.

———. *Forging Freedom: The Formation of Philadelphia's Black Community, 1720–1840*. Cambridge, MA: Harvard University Press, 1988.

Soderlund, Jean R. "Black Women in Colonial Pennsylvania." *Pennsylvania Magazine of History and Biography* 107, no. 1 (1983): 49–68.

Tomek, Beverly. *Slavery and Abolition in Pennsylvania*. Philadelphia: Temple University Press, 2021.

Watson, John Fanning. *Annals of Philadelphia, and Pennsylvania, in the Olden Time*. Philadelphia: E. L. Carey and A. Hart, 1830.

Winberg, Michaela. "William Penn Kept Enslaved People: These Are Some of Their Names." *Billy Penn*, March 6, 2021. https://billypenn.com/2020/08/17/william-penn-owned-enslaved-people-these-are-some-of-their-names-e.

Wright, Richard. *The Negro in Pennsylvania: A Study in Economic History*. Philadelphia: A.M.E. Book Concern Press, 1912.

CHAPTER 3

Soderlund, Jean. "Black Women in Colonial Pennsylvania." *Pennsylvania Magazine of History and Biography* 107, no. 1 (1983): 49–68.

Uzwiak, Beth A. "Memorializing Dinah and Reckoning with Enslavement." *Public Historian* 43, no. 3 (2021): 55–86.

CHAPTER 4

Bacon, Jacqueline. "Rhetoric and Identity in Absalom Jones and Richard Allen's 'Narrative of the Proceedings of the Black People, during the Late Awful Calamity in Philadelphia.'" *Pennsylvania Magazine of History and Biography* 125, nos. 1–2 (2001): 61–90.

Coard, Michael. "How 3,000 Desecrated Black Graves Were Found and Saved in South Philly." *Avenging the Ancestors*, July 29, 2013. http://www.avengingtheancestors.com/how-3000-desecrated-black-graves-were-found-and-saved-in-south-philly.

De Groot, Kristen. "Historic Black Burial Site under Playground to Get Memorial." *Philadelphia Tribune*, July 6, 2018.

Diemer, Andrew. "Free Black Communities." *The Encyclopedia of Greater Philadelphia*, 2017. https://philadelphiaencyclopedia.org/essays/free-black-communities.

Flores, Sarai. "Local Church Joins Fight for African-American Graveyard." *Temple News*, April 22, 2014.

Mitchell, John N. "Historical Marker Unveiled for Bethel Burying Ground." *Philadelphia Tribune*, October 2, 2019.

Muhammad, Jehron. "Coalition Fights for Historic Burial Ground." *Final Call*, March 13, 2014.

Nash, Gary. *Forging Freedom: The Formation of Philadelphia's Black Community, 1720–1840*. Cambridge, MA: Harvard University Press, 1988.

Newman, Richard. *Freedom's Prophet: Bishop Richard Allen, the AME Church, and the Black Founding Fathers*. New York: New York University Press, 2008.

Persinger, Ryanne. "Richard Allen Statue to Stand Tall, Honor Church's Founder." *Philadelphia Tribune*, June 2, 2018.

Russ, Valerie. "Winning Design for the Bethel Burying Ground Is Called 'Spiritually and Culturally Ingenious.'" *Philadelphia Inquirer*, March 13, 2021.

Salisbury, Stephen. "Archaeological Survey Set for Unmarked Mother Bethel Cemetery." *Philadelphia Inquirer*, May 20, 2013.

Sudler, Arthur K. "Revised Absalom Jones Biographical Information." *House of Deputies of the Episcopal Church*, January 30, 2018. https://houseofdeputies.org/2018/01/30/new-biography-absalom-jones.

CHAPTER 5

Bruggeman, Seth C. "The President's House: Freedom and Slavery in the Making of a New Nation." *Journal of American History* 100, no. 1 (June 2013): 155–158.

Coard, Michael. "The 'Black' Eye on George Washington's 'White' House.'" *Pennsylvania Magazine of History and Biography* 129, no. 4 (2005): 461–471.

Conn, Steven. "Our House? The President's House at Independence National Historical Park." *Pennsylvania Magazine of History and Biography* 135, no. 2 (2011): 191–197.

Fanelli, Doris Devine. "History, Commemoration, and an Interdisciplinary Approach to Interpreting the President's House Site." *Pennsylvania Magazine of History and Biography* 129, no. 4 (2005): 445–460.

Holt, Sharon Ann. "Questioning the Answers: Modernizing Public History to Serve the Citizens." *Pennsylvania Magazine of History and Biography* 129, no. 4 (2005): 473–481.

Lawler, Edward. "The President's House in Philadelphia: The Rediscovery of a Lost Landmark." *Pennsylvania Magazine of History and Biography* 126, no. 1 (2002): 5–95.

———. "The President's House Revisited." *Pennsylvania Magazine of History and Biography* 129, no. 4 (2005): 371–410.

Lewis, Michael. "Trashing the President's House: How a Great American Discovery Was Turned into a Disgrace." *Commentary Magazine*, April 2011, https://www.commentary.org/issues/2011-april.

Nash, Gary B. "For Whom Will the Liberty Bell Toll? From Controversy to Collaboration." *George Wright Forum* 21, no. 1 (March 2004): 39–52.

Rothstein, Edward. "Reopening a House That's Still Divided." *New York Times*, December 14, 2010.

Saffron, Inga. "Brick Pile's Colliding Rales." *Philadelphia Inquirer*, December 17, 2010.

CHAPTER 6

Anti-Slavery Convention of American Women. *Proceedings of the Anti-slavery Convention of American Women, Held in Philadelphia. May 15–18, 1838*. Philadelphia: Merrihew and Quinn, 1838. https://archive.org/details/proceedingsofant00anti/page/n5/mode/2up.

Biddle, Dan, and Murray Dubin. *Tasting Freedom: Octavius Catto and the Battle for Equality in Civil War America*. Philadelphia: Temple University Press, 2010.

Nash, Gary. *Forging Freedom: The Formation of Philadelphia's Black Community, 1720–1840*. Cambridge, MA: Harvard University Press, 1988.

Stanton, Elizabeth Cady, Susan B. Anthony, and Matilda Joslyn Gage, eds. *History of Woman Suffrage*. 3 vols. Rochester, NY: Charles Mann, 1887.

Tomek, Beverly C. "Pennsylvania Hall." *The Encyclopedia of Greater Philadelphia*, 2015. https://philadelphiaencyclopedia.org/archive/pennsylvania-hall.

———. *Pennsylvania Hall: A "Legal Lynching" in the Shadow of the Liberty Bell.* Oxford: Oxford University Press, 2013.

Webb, Samuel. *History of Pennsylvania Hall Which Was Destroyed by a Mob on the 17th of May, 1838.* Philadelphia: Merrihew and Quinn, 1838. https://archive.org /details/historyofpennsyl00penn.

CHAPTER 7

Bacon, Margaret Hope. *But One Race: The Life of Robert Purvis.* New York: State University of New York Press, 2021.

———. "The Double Curse of Sex and Color: Robert Purvis and Human Rights." *Pennsylvania Magazine History and Biography* 121, nos. 1–2 (January–April 1997): 53–76.

Beisert, Oscar, J. M. Duffin, Rachel Hildebrandt, and Donna Rilling. "625 South Delhi Street." Nomination of Historic Building, Structure, Site or Object to the Philadelphia Register of Historic Places, December 11, 2017. https://www.phila.gov /media/20190401092648/625-S-Delhi-St-nomination.pdf.

Blockson, Charles. *The Underground Railroad.* Hoboken, NJ: Prentice Hall, 1987.

Clemmons, Michael, and Donna Rilling. "919–921 Lombard Street." Nomination of Historic Building, Structure, Site or Object to the Philadelphia Register of Historic Places, December 14, 2021. https://www.phila.gov/media/20220324130114/919 -21-Lombard-St-nomination.pdf

Haas, Kimberly. "Finding Freedom in the Footsteps of William Still." *Hidden City Philadelphia*, November 1, 2022. https://hiddencityphila.org/2022/11/finding -freedom-in-the-footsteps-of-william-still.

Kashatus, William. *William Still: The Underground Railroad and the Angel at Philadelphia.* Notre Dame, IN: University of Notre Dame Press, 2021.

Okur, Nilgun Andalou. "Underground Railroad in Philadelphia, 1830–1860." *Journal of Black Studies* 25, no. 5 (May 1995): 537–557.

Thorton, Audrey R. J. *The Crown Jewel of Fairmount Park: Belmont Mansion.* Glenside, PA: American Women's Heritage Society, 2001.

Tomek, Beverly C. "Underground Railroad." *The Encyclopedia of Greater Philadelphia*, 2018. https://philadelphiaencyclopedia.org/archive/pennsylvania-hall.

CHAPTER 8

Biddle, Dan, and Murray Dubin. *Tasting Freedom: Octavius Catto and the Battle for Equality in Civil War America.* Philadelphia: Temple University Press, 2010.

Cohen, Amy, prod. *Octavius V. Catto: A Legacy for the 21st Century.* Film, History Making Productions, Philadelphia, 2017. The full text is available at catto.ushistory.org.

Smith, Aaron X. "The Murder of Octavius Catto." *The Encyclopedia of Greater Philadelphia*, 2015. https://philadelphiaencyclopedia.org/essays/murder-of-octavius-catto.

CHAPTER 9

Blumgart, Jake, and Jim Saksa. "From Slums to Sleek Towers: How Philly Became Cleaner, Safer, and More Unequal." WHYY.org, March 12, 2018. https://whyy.org /segments/slums-sleek-towers-philly-became-cleaner-safer-unequal.

Du Bois, W. E. B. *Dusk of Dawn: An Essay toward an Autobiography of a Race Concept.* New York: Schocken, 1971.

———. *The Philadelphia Negro: A Social Study*. Rev. ed. Philadelphia: University of Pennsylvania Press, 1996.

Hunter, Marcus. *Black Citymakers: How the Philadelphia Negro Changed Urban America*. Oxford: Oxford University Press, 2013.

Katz, Michael B., and Thomas J. Sugrue, eds. *W. E. B. Du Bois, Race, and the City: The Philadelphia Negro and Its Legacy*. Philadelphia: University of Pennsylvania Press, 1998.

Lewis, David Levering. *W. E. B. Du Bois: Biography of a Race, 1868–1919*. New York: Henry Holt, 1993.

McGrail, Steven. "Philadelphia Negro (The)." *The Encyclopedia of Greater Philadelphia*, 2013. https://philadelphiaencyclopedia.org/essays/philadelphia-negro-the.

Peinado, Nicole. "W. E. B. Du Bois Receives Honorary Emeritus Professorship." *Daily Pennsylvanian*, February 19, 2012.

Russ, Valerie. "What Does the Future Hold for the Tanner House? Historic Preservation Grad Students Have Ideas." *Philadelphia Inquirer*, December 21, 2022.

Zeitlin, Dave. "House of Resiliency." *Pennsylvania Gazette*, November–December 2022, 42–48.

CHAPTER 10

Beisert, Oscar. "The First African Baptist Church, 1600–06 Christian Street." Nomination of Historic Building, Structure, Site or Object to the Philadelphia Register of Historic Places, April 7, 2015. https://keepingphiladelphia.org/wp-content/uploads/2019/06/1600.06.Christian.FirstAfricanBaptist.Final-with-form.pdf.

Block, Kevin, and Adrian Trevisan. "Christian Street/Black Doctors Row Historic District." Nomination of Historic Building, Structure, Site or Object to the Philadelphia Register of Historic Places, February 1, 2022. https://www.phila.gov/media/20220708152420/Historic-District-Christian-St-Black-Doctors-Row.pdf.

Brey, Jared. "Over Pastor's Objections, First African Baptist Added to City's Historic Register." *Philadelphia Inquirer*, October 9, 2015, https://www.inquirer.com/philly/news/breaking/Over_pastors_objections_First_African_Baptist_added_to_citys_historic_register.html#loaded

Brooks, Charles H. *Official History of the First African Baptist Church*. Philadelphia: Charles H. Brooks, 1922.

"Colored Citizens Own Much Property: Don't Have to Live in Slum Dives and Dilapidated Shacks." *Philadelphia Tribune*, December 20, 1919, 1, 9.

Harris, Linda. "Congregation Praying for Historic Church." *Baltimore Sun*, May 17, 2001.

Nelson, H. Viscount. "Philadelphia's Thirtieth Ward, 1940–1960." *Pennsylvania Heritage*, Spring 1979. http://paheritage.wpengine.com/article/philadelphia-thirtieth-ward-1940-1960.

Pew Charitable Trusts. "Philadelphia's Changing Neighborhoods: Gentrification and Other Shifts since 2000." Report, May 2016. https://www.pewtrusts.org/en/research-and-analysis/reports/2016/05/philadelphias-changing-neighborhoods.

Robinson, Richard E., dir. *Ground Truth: Archeology in the City*. Documentary film, Silverwood Films, 1988. https://archive.org/details/groundtrutharcheologyinthecity.

CHAPTER 11

Block, Kevin, and Adrian Trevisan. "Christian Street/Black Doctors Row Historic District." Nomination of Historic Building, Structure, Site or Object to the Philadelphia Register of Historic Places, February 1, 2022. https://www.phila.gov/media/20220708152420/Historic-District-Christian-St-Black-Doctors-Row.pdf.

Brownlee, David. *Building the City Beautiful*. Philadelphia: Philadelphia Museum of Art, 2017.

Cohen, Amy. "Loyal Classmen." *Pennsylvania Gazette*, February 24, 2020.

———. "Unraveling Myths about Philly's Pioneering African American Architect." *Hidden City Philadelphia*, May 23, 2019. https://hiddencityphila.org/2019/05/unraveling-myths-about-phillys-pioneering-african-american-architect.

"Colored Citizens Own Much Property: Don't Have to Live in Slum Dives and Dilapidated Shacks." *Philadelphia Tribune*, December 20, 1919, 1, 9.

Harbeson, John. *The Study of Architectural Design with a Special Reference to the Program of Beaux-Arts Institute of Design*. New York: Pencil Points, 1926.

King, William. *Julian Abele and the Design of Duke University*. Durham, NC: Duke University Press, 2017.

"Owner and Public Comment Received Regarding the Christian Street Historic District." Email communication from Deborah Gary, Society to Preserve Philadelphia African American Assets, to Philadelphia Historical Commission, April 28, 2022. https://www.phila.gov/media/20220706100452/Christian-St-Historic-District comment.pdf.

Rogers, Jocelyn. "Julian Abele: Honoring a Legacy No Longer in 'the Shadows.'" *American Institute of Architects*, June 2020. https://www.aia.org/articles/6306869-julian-abele-honoring-a-legacy-no-longer-i.

Russ, Valerie. "Will Demolition Moratorium Help Historic Preservation for Christian Street's Doctors' Row? City Council Takes a Look." *Philadelphia Inquirer*, June 14, 2021.

Saffron, Inga. "Racing against Time to Save South Philadelphia's 'Black Main Street.'" *Philadelphia Inquirer*, May 30, 2021.

Tifft, Susan E. "Out of the Shadows." *Smithsonian Magazine*, February 2005. https://www.smithsonianmag.com/history/out-of-the-shadows-85569503.

Wilson, Dreck Spurlock. *Julian Abele: Architect and the Beaux Arts*. New York: Routledge, 2019.

CHAPTER 12

Stewart, Jeffrey. *The New Negro: The Life of Alain Locke*. Oxford: Oxford University Press, 2019.

Young, David W. *The Battles of Germantown*. Philadelphia: Temple University Press, 2019.

———. "When the Harlem Renaissance Came to Germantown." *Germantown Crier*, vol. 59, no. 1, 2009.

CHAPTER 13

Anderson, Marian. *My Lord What a Morning: An Autobiography*. Champaign: University of Illinois Press, 1956.

Countryman, Matthew. *Up South: Civil Rights and Black Power in Philadelphia*. Philadelphia: University of Pennsylvania Press, 2006.

Finkel, Ken. "100 Years Ago, South Philadelphia Saw Violent Race Riots." *Philadelphia Inquirer*, July 27, 2018.

Graham, Kristen. "Philly Elementary School Gets a New Name: Goodbye, Chester A. Arthur. Hello, Marian Anderson." *Philadelphia Inquirer*, July 11, 2023.

Hildebrandt, Rachel. "Demolition in the Works for Marian Anderson Church." *Hidden City Philadelphia*, August 18, 2015. https://hiddencityphila.org/2015/08/demolition-in-the-works-for-marian-anderson-church.

"Lone Woman Holds a Mob of 500 White Brutes at Bay." *Philadelphia Tribune*, August 3, 1918.

Mossell, Sadie Alexander. "The Standard of Living among One Hundred Negro Migrant Families in Philadelphia." *Annals of the American Academy of Political and Social Science* 98 (November 1921): 173–218.

Scribe Video Center. "Historical Overview." *The Great Migration: A City Transformed (1916–1930)*, 2021. https://greatmigrationphl.org/node/24.

Wolfinger, James. *Philadelphia Divided: Race and Politics in the City of Brotherly Love*. Chapel Hill: University of North Carolina Press, 2007.

Wolfman-Arent, Ari. "A 1918 Race War and its Ties to Philadelphia's Present." WHYY.org, July 26, 2018. https://whyy.org/segments/a-1918-race-war-and-its-ties-to-philadelphias-present.

CHAPTER 14

"All Wars Memorial to Colored Soldiers and Sailors." Online exhibition, *Controversial Public Art*. Accessed June 6, 2022. https://hst4080.omeka.net/exhibits/show/controversial-public-art/allwarsmemorial.

Clark, Joe. "Final Battle? 50G Will Care for Monument Forever." *Philadelphia Inquirer*, September 10, 1998.

"Colored Woman First of Her Sex to Vote in Phila[delphia]." *Philadelphia Tribune*, November 6, 1920.

Davis, Samuel. "Black Vets Receive Overdue Recognition." *Philadelphia Tribune*, November 11, 1994.

"The Disturbing and Inspiring Story of the All Wars Memorial." Association for Public Art, June 30, 2020. https://www.associationforpublicart.org/apa-now/story/the-all-wars-memorial.

Duffy, Edward W. "A Victory for Heroes: The Battle behind the All Wars Memorial to Colored Soldiers and Sailors." *Hidden City Philadelphia*, August 12, 2020. https://hiddencityphila.org/2020/08/a-victory-for-heros-the-battle-behind-the-all-wars-memorial-to-colored-soldiers-and-sailors.

Hannah-Jones, Nikole. "Our Democracy's Founding Ideals Were False When They Were Written: Black Americans Have Fought to Make Them True." *New York Times Magazine*, August 14, 2019. https://www.nytimes.com/interactive/2019/08/14/magazine/1619-america-slavery.html.

Landry, Peter. "Belated but Monumental Move: Sixty Years Later, a Memorial to Black Soldiers Will Go on the Parkway." *Philadelphia Inquirer*, March 29, 1994.

"Last Rites for Samuel B. Hart, Vet Legislator." *Chicago Tribune*, April 4, 1936.

Lieberman, Ilene D. "Race and Remembrance: Philadelphia's 'All Wars Memorial to Colored Soldiers and Sailors' and the Politics of Place." *American Art Journal* 29, nos. 1–2 (1998): 19–51.

Rubin, Daniel. "In Heart of City, Basking in Glory Veteran's Day Marchers Greet a Long-Slighted African American Monument." *Philadelphia Inquirer*, November 12, 1994.

CHAPTER 15

Bell, Charlotte Turner. *Paul Robeson's Last Days in Philadelphia*. Bryn Mawr, PA: Dorrance, 1986.

Brin, Joseph. "West Philly Home Still Sings the Praises of Paul Robeson." *Hidden City Philadelphia*, March 25, 2016. https://hiddencityphila.org/2016/03/west-philly-home-still-sings-the-praises-of-paul-robeson.

Brown, Lloyd. *The Young Paul Robeson: On My Journey Now*. New York: Basic, 1998.

"The City of Brotherly Love." *Journal of Negro Life* 8, no. 6 (June 1930): 168–169.

Du Bois, W. E. B. "As the Crow Flies." *The Crisis* 37, no. 7 (July 1930): 221.

Graham, Kristen. "Philly's Robeson High, a School on the Rise, Now in National Spotlight." *Philadelphia Inquirer*, December 12, 2017.

———. "What Makes This High School Philly's Most Improved?" *Philadelphia Inquirer*, June 19, 2017.

———. "Wolf Touts Philly School as a Positive Role Model." *Philadelphia Inquirer*, December 21, 2022.

Horne, Gerald. *Paul Robeson: The Artist as Revolutionary*. London: Pluto, 2016.

Russ, Valerie. "A Newly Opened Reading Room at West Philly's Paul Robeson House Honors Paul's Wife, Eslanda Cardoza Goode Robeson." *Philadelphia Inquirer*, December 28, 2023.

"7,500 Hear Paul Robeson Sing at Dell." *Philadelphia Inquirer*, July 10, 1941.

Singer, Samuel L. "Robeson Gives Concert at Academy Despite Cold." *Philadelphia Inquirer*, December 12, 1946.

Stories from the Paul Robeson House: Lives Touched by a Renaissance Man. Philadelphia: West Philadelphia Cultural Alliance, 2009.

CHAPTER 16

Baasit, Muhammad Abdul, "The Malcolm X They Didn't Know." *Showcase: The Progressive Magazine*, vol. 17, no. 1, n.d. A copy is available at the Charles L. Blockson Afro-American Collection at Temple University.

Bixler, Michael. "Breaking through Historic Preservation's Color Line." *Hidden City Philadelphia*, February 4, 2016. https://hiddencityphila.org/2018/06/a-brief-history-of-race-contested-space-in-west-philly.

Corr, John P. "2000 Whites Sit-in at Bok, Reject She'd Concession; Only Beset by Disorder." *Philadelphia Inquirer*, October 16, 1968.

File, Nate. "Afromation Avenue Aims to Help W[est] Philly Feel Seen." *Philadelphia Inquirer*, November 4, 2022.

"Franklin Principal Resents 'Tough' Label." *Philadelphia Tribune*, September 22, 1969.

Gillespie, John T. "Board to Study Demand to Rename Franklin High." *Philadelphia Bulletin*, October 17, 1968.

Haley, Alex, and Malcolm X. *The Autobiography of Malcolm X*. New York: Random House, 1964.

Kannik, Hannah. "South Philly's Andrew Jackson School to Be Renamed for Fanny Jackson Coppin." *PhillyVoice*, June 25, 2021. https://www.phillyvoice.com/andrew-jackson-school-renamed-fanny-jackson-coppin-school-south-philadelphia-history.

Lewis, Claude. "Franklin vs. Malcolm X: A School Board Travesty." *Philadelphia Bulletin*, June 4, 1969.

———. "Name of the Game Is Malcolm X at Benjamin Franklin High School." *Philadelphia Bulletin*, February 24, 1970.

"Malcolm X Guarded after Death Threat." *Philadelphia Daily News*, December 30, 1964.

Marable, Manning. *Malcolm X: A Life of Reinvention*. New York: Penguin, 2011.

McDonough, Donald A. "Benjamin Franklin." *Philadelphia Inquirer*, October 15, 1968.

———. "School Board Laxity Assailed by Rizzo as Reason for Violence." *Philadelphia Inquirer*, October 16, 1968.

Mezzacappa, Dale. "Andrew Jackson School Becomes Fanny Jackson Coppin School." *Chalkbeat Philadelphia*, March 29, 2022. https://philadelphia.chalkbeat.org/2022/3/29/23002337/andrew-jackson-philadelphia-school-fannie-jackson-coppin-slaves.

Moore, Acel. "Stamp Honoring Malcolm Shows How Times Change." *Philadelphia Inquirer*, February 23, 1999.

"No Anarchy in Streets, Plenty in Our Schools." *Philadelphia Daily News*, October 16, 1968.

"Teachers Union Head Blasts School Board for Allowing Sit-in." *Philadelphia Inquirer*, October 15, 1968.

"Want Franklin High Renamed 'Malcolm X.'" *Philadelphia Tribune*, November 26, 1968.

Wilder, John Brantley. "Refuse to Name 'Ben' Franklin Malcolm X High." *Philadelphia Tribune*, May 31, 1969.

Wiley, Lauren. "Advocates Seek to Change School Names with Racist Histories." *The Notebook*, August 5, 2020.

Williams, Mariam. "A Brief History of Race and Contested Space in West Philly." *Hidden City Philadelphia*, June 11, 2018. https://hiddencityphila.org/2018/06/a-brief-history-of-race-contested-space-in-west-philly.

CHAPTER 17

Countryman, Matthew J. *Up South: Civil Rights and Black Power in Philadelphia*. Philadelphia: University of Pennsylvania Press, 2006.

Fuller, Charles. "Greenbelt Knoll Historic District." Nomination of Historic Building, Structure, Site or Object to the Philadelphia Register of Historic Places, June 9, 2006. https://www.phila.gov/media/20190213125234/Historic-District-Greenbelt-Knoll.pdf.

Gary, Deborah. *Philadelphia's North African American History Tour—One: Exploring North Broad Street and Historic Germantown Avenue*. Philadelphia: DHEx Enterprises, 2020.

"Greenbelt Knoll—Philadelphia's Newest Historic District." *Preservation Matters*, newsletter of the Preservation Alliance for Greater Philadelphia, Fall 2006.

Jones, Ayana. "Nation's First Shopping Center Owned, Operated by Blacks Turns 50." *Philadelphia Tribune*, October 21, 2018.

Mitchell, John N. "Stretch of Broad Street to Be Renamed after Rev. Leon Sullivan." *Philadelphia Tribune*, November 15, 2019.

"Our Founder: Reverend Dr. Leon Sullivan." Sullivan Progress Plaza, 2020. Accessed September 15, 2022. https://progressplaza.com/about-us/our-founder.

Russ, Valerie. "Celebrating the Late Rev. Leon H. Sullivan's 100th Birthday." *Philadelphia Inquirer*, October 15, 2022.

———. "P[hiladelphia International Airport] Arrivals Hall Renamed to Honor Philly's Rev. Leon Sullivan." *Philadelphia Inquirer*, October 19, 2022.

Sullivan, Leon H. *Build Brother Build*. Philadelphia: Macrae Smith, 1969.

———. *Moving Mountains*. Valley Forge, PA: Judson, 1998.

CHAPTER 18

Borden, Sara A. "Cecil B. Moore." *Civil Rights in a Northern City: Philadelphia*, digital archive. Accessed September 29, 2022. http://northerncity.library.temple.edu/exhibits/show/civil-rights-in-a-northern-cit/people-and-places/moore--cecil-b-.

Clark, Vernon. "Activists Protest Cecil B. Moore Bus Route Name Change." *Philadelphia Inquirer*, April 25, 2012.

Coard, Michael. "Cecil B. Moore: Anger, Intellect and Black Pride Personified." *Philadelphia Tribune*, April 2, 2016.

Countryman, Matthew J. *Up South: Civil Rights and Black Power in Philadelphia*. Philadelphia: University of Pennsylvania Press, 2006.

Crimmins, Peter. "Teenagers Who Desegregated Girard College to Be Honored with a Mural." WHYY.org, February 26, 2021. https://whyy.org/articles/teenagers-who-desegregated-girard-college-to-be-honored-with-a-mural.

Danz, Jack. "The Freedom Fighters Respond to Racial Slur Painted on a Mural Honoring Cecil B. Moore." *Temple News*, February 20, 2020.

Daugen, Joseph R. "Dr. King Asked to Stay Out of Girard College Dispute." *Philadelphia Bulletin*, July 30, 1965.

Dirienzo, Rob. "SEPTA on Temple–Cecil B. Moore Station Flap: 'We Made a Mistake.'" *Philadelphia Magazine*, November 11, 2015.

Odom, Maida. "Crowd Recalls Moore's Battle for Civil Rights." *Philadelphia Inquirer*, April 12, 1987.

Oputu, Edirin, and Nick Eiser. "Perseverance and Grit: The Life and Legacy of Cecil B. Moore." Temple University Shorthand Stories, n.d. Accessed September 28, 2022. https://templeuniv.shorthandstories.com/--perseverance--and-grit--the-life-and-legacy-of--cecil-b--moore-/index.html.

"Pennsylvania: The Goddam Boss." *Time*, September 11, 1964. https://content.time.com/time/subscriber/article/0,33009,830637-1,00.html.

Perry, Jamyra. "Upcoming Mural Will Honor Philadelphia Freedom Fighters." *Philadelphia Tribune*, February 26, 2021.

Poindexter, Malcolm. "Dr. King Ends Visit Here, Attacks Girard Policy." *Philadelphia Bulletin*, August 4, 1965.

Potts, Carolyn. "Cecil B. Moore Station Will Teach History of Namesake." *Temple News*, October 22, 2018.

Russ, Valerie. "New Mural Honors Cecil B. Moore and Teenage Protestors Who Helped at Philly's Girard College." *Philadelphia Inquirer*, November 13, 2021.

Sauer, Scott. "SEPTA, Freedom Fighters Install Honorary Plaques at Cecil B. Moore Station." *Temple News*, April 3, 2019.

Sutton, William W., Jr. "Effort to Honor Cecil B. Moore Finally Pays Off." *Philadelphia Inquirer*, April 12, 1987.

Wallace, Ethan. "Ruminating on Lost Columbia Avenue." *Hidden City Philadelphia*, August 29, 2014. https://hiddencityphila.org/2014/08/ruminating-on-lost-columbia-avenue.

Willis, Arthur C. *Cecil's City*. New York: Carlton, 1990.

CHAPTER 19

Birger, Jon S. "Race, Reaction, and Reform: The Three Rs of Philadelphia School Politics, 1965–1971." *Pennsylvania Magazine of History and Biography*, July 1996: 164–216.

Bixler, Michael. "Remembering the 1967 Student Walkout and the Attack on Teen Activism." *Hidden City Philadelphia*, March 13, 2018. https://hiddencityphila .org/2018/03/remembering-phillys-1967-school-walkout-the-attack-on-teenage-ac tivism.

Chappel, Bill. "Frank Rizzo Statue Is Removed in Philadelphia: It Is Finally Gone, Mayor Says." National Public Radio, June 3, 2020. https://www.npr.org/2020/06/03/86884 8550/frank-rizzo-statue-is-removed-in-philadelphia-it-is-finally-gone-mayor-says.

Cohen, Amy. "Exploring the Rizzo Boycott of 1967." *Hidden City Philadelphia*, December 6, 2019. https://hiddencityphila.org/2019/12/exploring-the-rizzo-boycott -of-1967.

———. "More than a Month: The Importance of Teaching Black History Year-round." *Hidden City Philadelphia*, February 16, 2022. https://hiddencityphila.org/2021/02 /more-than-a-month-the-importance-of-teaching-black-history-year-round.

Countryman, Matthew J. *Up South: Civil Rights and Black Power in Philadelphia.* Philadelphia: University of Pennsylvania Press, 2006.

Genovese, Holly. "Black Power." *The Encyclopedia of Philadelphia*, 2017. https://phila delphiaencyclopedia.org/essays/black-power.

Gorman, Amanda. "The Hill We Climb." January 20, 2021. https://www.cnbc.com /2021/01/20/amanda-gormans-inaugural-poem-the-hill-we-climb-full-text.html.

Edmonds, Arlene. "The Late State Rep. David R. Richardson Jr. Is Immortalized Renaming Pastorious Elementary, Pastorious-Richardson Elementary." *Philadelphia Sun*, November 15, 2018.

Hamilton, Fred. "Racial Tension Bad, Getting Worse." *Philadelphia Bulletin*, September 14, 1978.

Janofsky, Michael. "Philadelphia Mandates Black History for Graduation." *New York Times*, June 22, 2005.

Kabungo, Elijah Joy. "Student Leaps from Window to Join Melee." *Philadelphia Inquirer*, November 18, 1967.

Kashatus, William. "Frank Rizzo: Philadelphia's Tough Cop Turned Mayor." *Pennsylvania Heritage*, Spring 2007. https://hsp.org/blogs/fondly-pennsylvania/civil-rights -and-rise-frank-rizzo-1960s-philadelphia.

Lewis, Claude. "For Rizzo: Black Tuesday." *Philadelphia Bulletin*, November 10, 1978.

Lombardo, Timothy J. "Civil Rights and Rise of Rizzo in 1960s Philadelphia." *Pennsylvania Legacies*, Fall 2008. https://hsp.org/blogs/fondly-pennsylvania/civil-rights -and-rise-frank-rizzo-1960s-philadelphia.

Manzo, Kathleen Kennedy. "Course in African, African-American History Debuts in Philadelphia." *Education Week*, November 2, 2005. https://www.edweek.org /teaching-learning/course-in-african-african-american-history-debuts-in-philadel phia/2005/11.

Rossman, Sean. "'Black Power' Painted on Philly Mayor Statue." *USA Today*, August 18, 2017.

Taubman, Philip. "U.S. Files Its Rights Suit Charging Philadelphia Police with Brutality." *New York Times*, August 14, 1979.

Washington, Paul M. *Other Sheep I Have: The Autobiography of Father Paul M. Washington.* Philadelphia: Temple University Press, 1994.

INDEX

Page numbers in italics refer to illustrations.

Amy Jane Cohen is an educator, historian, and writer. After twenty years of teaching social studies, she became Director of Education for History Making Productions and is a contributing writer for *Hidden City Philadelphia*. Visit her online at amyjanecohen.com.